A Dictionary of the First or Oldest Words in the English Language / From the Semi-Saxon Period of A.D. 1250 to 1300

Herbert Coleridge

PREFACE.

The present publication may be considered as the foundation-stone of the Historical and Literary portion of the Philological Society's proposed English Dictionary. Its appearance in a separate form has been necessitated by the nature of the scheme, on which that work is being constructed. Without entering into details, which will be found in the Society's published Prospectus,[1] it will be sufficient for the present purpose to mention, that the raw material of the Dictionary, the words and authorities, are being brought together by a number of independent collectors, for whom it is consequently necessary to provide some common standard of comparison, whereby each may ascertain what he is to extract, and what to reject, from the author, or work, he has undertaken. This standard for works of earlier date than 1526 is furnished by the following pages, which contain an alphabetical inventory of every word found in the printed English literature of the 13th century. As, however, a mere index verborum would but inadequately fulfil its object, a certain amount of explanatory and etymological matter has been added, which it is hoped may render the work more generally interesting and useful than could otherwise have been the case. It is only proper to add that English literature, as distinguished from Semi-Saxon, is assumed to commence about the middle of the 13th century.

[1] London, Trübner and Co., Paternoster Row, price 6d.

All words are arranged under their modern forms, where such exist, but the older forms, except where utterly unimportant, are always noticed. The more remarkable of these older forms are also entered in the Glossary in their alphabetical order, with cross references to that under which the word is discussed. Thus under 'Hymn' and 'Isle' will be found the forms 'ympne' and 'ydle;' but 'ympne' and 'ydle' appear also in their proper places in the Glossary. Obsolete words are of course entered as they are spelt in the passage whence they are taken, a rule which applies as much to different forms of the same word, as to different words. As to the etymological matter, nothing further as a general rule has been attempted than to indicate the

3

nearest cognate, or cognates, of the particular word; but it has not been thought necessary, or desirable, to load the Glossary with illustrations of this nature in very simple cases. I have to thank Hensleigh Wedgwood, Esq., for many kind and valuable suggestions in this part of my work.

My best thanks are also due to the Rev. J. Eastwood, the Rev. W. H. Herford, to my colleague Mr F. J. Furnivall, and to Messrs M'Ewan and Harrison, for their valuable assistance in the formation of separate indexes to several of the works comprised in this Glossary. Their respective shares in the work are pointed out in the List of Books and Editions, which will be found in page v.

And I cannot terminate this brief preface without expressing my deep sense of the obligations I am under to Sir F. Madden, not merely for the help of his invaluable editions of Laȝamon and Havelok, without which this work would have been far less complete than it now is, but also for much kind personal advice and assistance, which probably few, if any, living philologists beside himself would have been competent to bestow. It only remains for me to add that, although no pains have been spared to render the book as complete as possible, I cannot but expect that some omissions and errors will be discovered, more especially as the largest and most laborious portion of the work was carried on during a long period of ill health. I shall feel very grateful to those who discover any addenda, if they will kindly communicate them to me for insertion hereafter in the Dictionary itself.

HERBERT COLERIDGE.

10, Chester Place, Regent's Park,

June 13th, 1859

LIST OF BOOKS AND EDITIONS REFERRED TO.

⁑ All the following pieces are cited by the number of the verse, except where the contrary is expressly mentioned.

Havelok the Dane. Edited by Sir F. Madden, for the Roxburgh Club. (By Mr H. Coleridge.)

Geste of Kyng Horn. Edited by M. Michel, for the Bannatyne Club. (By Mr H. Coleridge.)

(N.B. The text of this poem in the second vol. of Ritson's Metrical Romances is taken from a later MS., and differs considerably from the Bannatyne text.)

Kyng Alysaunder. In Weber's Metrical Romances, vol. I. (By Mr H. Coleridge.)

The Land of Cokaygne. In Hickes's Thesaurus, vol. I. p. 231. (By Mr Furnivall.)

The Life of St Margaret (cited by stanzas), } in Hickes's Thesaurus, vol. I. pp. 224, 233. (By Mr Furnivall.) *Metrical Version of the Athanasian Creed,* *The Owl and Nightingale.* Edited by Mr Wright for the Percy Society. (By Mr Furnivall and Mr H. Coleridge.)

Fragment on Popular Science, from the Early English Metrical Lives of Saints, in Mr Wright's 'Popular Treatises on Science.' (By Mr H. Coleridge.)

Specimens of Lyric Poetry, temp. Edw. I. Edited by Mr Wright, for the Percy Society. (By Mr M'Ewan.)

Various Pieces in the Reliquiæ Antiquæ (cited by volume and page). (By Mr H. Coleridge.)

Political Songs, temp. Hen. III. and Edw. I. Edited by Mr Wright, for the Camden Society. (By the Rev. W. H. Herford.)

Ritson's Ancient Songs, Class I. Most of these songs, however, are contained in the Specimens of Lyric Poetry, temp. Ed. I., and are quoted from that collection. (By Mr Harrison.)

Religious Songs, printed at the end of the Percy Society's edition of the Owl and Nightingale. (By Mr H. Coleridge.)

Dialogue between the Soul and Body. In the Appendix to Mapes's Poems, edited by Mr Wright, for the Camden Society, p. 334. (By the Rev. J. Eastwood.)

The Early English Psalter. Edited by the Rev. J. Stevenson, for the Surtees' Society. Cited by the psalm and verse. (By Mr H. Coleridge.)

Robert of Gloucester's Chronicle. Ed. Hearne (2nd ed., 1810). Cited by the page. (By Mr. H. Coleridge.)

The Legend of St Brandan. Edited by Mr Wright, for the Percy Society. (By the Rev. J. Eastwood.)

The Life and Martyrdom of Thomas Beket. Edited by Mr Black, for the Percy Society. (By the Rev. J. Eastwood.)

(Owing to the gross inaccuracy of the marginal numbering in the printed edition of this poem, it has been found necessary to go over the whole afresh, and to cite according to the amended reckoning. The following data will assist the reader:—The first error occurs in page 64, where the line numbered 1280 should be 1282. The second occurs in page 100, where ten lines are dropped, and 1961 is printed for 1973, the true number. The third will be found in page 110, where 2049 is made to succeed 2139, and after this, of course, the confusion is hopeless. The exact number of lines in the poem is 2515, while the printed numbers give only 2398. Readers are therefore requested to renumber their copies from page 64 onwards, before attempting to verify the references in the Glossary.)

The following pieces will be printed in the second part of the Philological Society's Transactions for 1858, and are therefore included in the Glossary. I am indebted to the kindness of my friend and colleague, Mr Furnivall, for the loan of his transcripts.

A Moral Ode. MS. Egerton, 613. Cited by stanzas.

(Hickes printed Extracts from this Ode, in his Thesaurus, vol. I. p. 222, from one of the Digby MSS.; but his text is somewhat different from that of the Egerton MS., and omits nine stanzas contained in the latter.)

A Sermon (cited by stanzas), } MS. Harl. 913. *Signa Ante Judicium, A Fragment on the Seven Sins, The Ten Commandments, Christ on the Cross, A Poem on Miracles,* containing a Tale of an Oxford Student, *The Fall and Passion, The Legends of St Dunstan,* } from MS. Harl. 2277. *St Katherine, St Andrew, St Lucy, St Swithin, St Edward, Pilate, Judas Iscariot,*   A few references will also be found to the

Manuel des Pecches of Robert Brunne, now being edited by Mr Furnivall, for the Roxburgh Club, but the proof-sheets came into my hands too late to allow of anything like a complete analysis of the language of the poem.

OTHER WORKS REFERRED TO IN THE GLOSSARY.

Burguy's Grammaire de la Langue d'Oïl. 3 vols. 8vo. Berlin, 1856. The third volume contains an excellent Glossary.

Cotgrave's French and English Dictionary, by Howell. 1650.

Egilsson's Lexicon Poeticum Antiquæ Linguæ Septemtrionalis. Hafniæ, 1854-1859. One part is still wanting to complete the work.

Halliwell's Provincial and Archaic Dictionary. 2 vols. 8vo. 1855.

Kilian's Lexicon Teutonicum. Ed. Hasselt. 2 vols. 4to. 1777.

Laȝamon's Brut. Ed. Sir F. Madden. 3 vols. 8vo. 1847. (Cited by volume and page.)

The Ormulum. Ed. White. 2 vols. 8vo. 1852.

The Philological Society's Transactions, from 1842-1856. 9 vols. 8vo.

Roquefort's Glossaire de la Langue Romane. 2 vols. 8vo. 1808.

A Volume of Vocabularies, forming vol. I. of a Library of National Antiquities. Edited by Wright. 1857. (Privately printed.)

Warton's History of English Poetry. 3 vols. 8vo. Ed. 1840.

LIST OF ABBREVIATIONS MADE USE OF IN THE GLOSSARY.

Alys. Kyng Alysaunder. AS. Anglo-Saxon. B. The Life of Beket. β The Legend of St Brandan. comp. comparative. Cok. The Land of Cokaygne. Cotgr. Cotgrave. Dut. Dutch. Fall and P. The Poem on the Fall and Passion. Fr. Sci. The Fragment on Popular Science in the Lives of Saints. Fr. French. Hall. Halliwell. HD. Havelok the Dane. Kil. Kilian. Laȝ. Laȝamon. L. P. Specimens of Lyric Poetry, ed. Wright. lit. literally. Marg. The Life of St Margaret. M. G. Mæso-Gothic. M. Ode. The Moral Ode. N. and Q. Notes and Queries. O. and N. Owl and Nightingale. ON. Old Norse. O. H. G. Old High German. Orm. Ormulum. part. participle. Pol. S. Political Songs. pret. præterite. Ps. Psalm. Rel. S. Religious Songs. RG. Robert of Gloucester. Ritson's AS. Ritson's Ancient Songs. Roq. Roquefort. S. S. Semi-Saxon. sb. substantive. sup. superlative. v. a. verb active. v. n. verb neuter. W. Welsh. Warton, H. E. P. Warton's History of English Poetry.

GLOSSARIAL INDEX.

A

A, *indef. art.* RG. 367
—— == on. O. and N. 20
—— == he. Alys. 7809
—— == and. HD. 359
—— == one. Ps. liv. 14
Aback, *adv.* RG. 131
Abash, *v. a.* Alys. 224
Abate, *v. a.* == put an end to, make to cease. RG. 54. Fr. abattre
—— *v. n.* == cease from doing a thing. RG. 447
Abay, *v. a.* == drive to bay. Alys. 3882
Abbess, *sb.* RG. 370
Abbey, *sb.* RG. 369
Abbot, *sb.* RG. 376, 447
Abece, == ABC. RG. 266
Abed, *adv.* RG. 547
Abelde, *v. n.* == become bold. Alys. 2442
Abenche, == on a bench. St. Kath. 91
Abide, *v. n.* == remain, tarry. RG. 382. AS. bidan
—— *v. a.* == wait for, hence receive. RG. 265, and 302, pret. 'abade.' Ps. xxxix. 2
Abie, *v. a.* == pay for, pay the penalty for. [abigge] 1624. B. pret. 'abouȝte.' 58 B. 'abid.' O. and N. 1775. AS. a-bicgan. See Phil. Soc. Proc. vol. v. p. 33
Abite, *v. a.* == bite. Alys. 7096
Ablende, *v. a.* == make blind. RG. 208
Aboht, *part.* == bought. Wright's L. P. p. 103

9

About, *adv.* == round about (of locality). RG. 369; '3eode aboute' 76 B.

—— 'about to,' with a verb, as a future part. 1593 B.

—— == nearly. RG. 247

—— *prep.* == around, circum. RG. 467; [obout]. Ps. lxxvii. 28

—— == near (of time), 'aboute noon.' Wright's L. P. p. 34

Above, *adv.* 266 B.

—— *prep.* O. and N. 1492

Abow, *v. a.* == make to bend. RG. 46. pret. 'abuyde.' RG. 476

—— *v. n.* == bow, 3s pres. 'abueth.' RG. 193. part. 'abouynde.' RG. 302

Abowes, *sb.* == patron saints. RG. 475. Fr. avoués

Abraid, *v. a.* == open. O. and N. 1042. AS. abredan

Abroad, *adv.* RG. 542

Abrode, *adv.* == breeding, lit. 'on brood.' O. and N. 518. Fragm. on Seven Sins, v. 34

Abusse, *v. a.* == ambush, conceal. 1382 B.

Abuten, *prep.* == without (sine). M. Ode, st. 43

Ac, *conj.* == and, but. RG. 367

Acast, *part.* == disappointed. Pol. S. 149

Accord, *v. a.* == reconcile. RG. 388

—— *v. n.* == agree. RG. 388

—— *sb.* == agreement. RG. 388, 447

Account, *v. n.* == render an account or reckoning. Pilate 86

—— *sb.* == reckoning. 164 B. Sermon, st. 24

Accurse, *v. a.* RG. 296, 474

Accuse, *v. a.* RG. 523. part. 'acoysing,' == accusing or accusation. Alys. 3973

Acele, *v. a.* == seal. RG. 510. See Asele

Ache, *sb.* == smallage or water-parsley. Wright's L. P. p. 26. Fr. ache

Ache, *v. n.* RG. 240 pret. 'ok.' RG. 208

Acoled, == cooled. O. and N. 215

Acomber, *v. a.* == encumber. Alys. 8025

Acopede, == accused. See Aculp

Acore, *v. a.* == make sorry, grieve. RG. 75. part. 'acorye,' ==

chastened, punished. RG. 390

Acost, *adv.* == at the side. Alys. 2443, 3547

Acquaint, *v. a.* RG. 15, 465

Acquit, *v. a.* RG. 565

Acton, *sb.* == a leathern jacket worn under the armour. Alys. 2153. Fr. acoton. See Burguy s. v.

Acue, *adv.* == on his rump. Fr. au cul. Marg. 67

Aculp, *v. a.* == accuse. RG. 544. pret. 'acopede.' 773 B.

Adaunt, *v. a.* RG. 61, 372

Aday, *adv.* == by day. O. and N. 219

—— == of the day, 'aȝen eve aday,' 'on the evening of the day.' RG. 289

Adder, *sb.* Alys. 5262

Addle, *adj.* == rotten. O. and N. 133

Adiȝte, *v. a.* == adapt, prepare. O. and N. 326

Admiral, *sb.* [amyrayl.] RG. 409. [admirald.] K. Horn 95

Admonishment, *sb.* [amonestement]. Alys. 6974

Adown, *prep.* [adun]. O. and N. 1452

—— *adv.* RG. 376.

Adownward, *adv.* RG. 362. Fragm. Sci. 321

Adraw, *v. a.* == draw (as a sword). RG. 361, pret. 'adrou.' == drew. RG. 400

Adread, *v. n.* == fear, be in dread. O. and N. 1264

—— *adj.* == in fear. Rel. S. iv. 2. part. 'adrad.' 44 B.

Adrench, *v. a.* == to drown, pret. 'adrentte.' RG. 384

—— *v. n.* == be drowned, pret. 'adrent.' RG. 401. part. 'adrencte.' RG. 437. 'adronke.' RG. 430

Adriȝe, *v. a.* == endure. K. Horn, 1068. AS. a-dreogan

Adun, *v. a.* == stun. O. and N. 337

Adun, *adv.* == adown, *q. v.*

Advance, *v. a.* == set forward, promote. RG. 503; to *advance* a girl in marriage. RG. 431

Advancement, *sb.* Alys. 2570

Advent, *sb.* == the season of Advent. 1849 B.

Advice, *sb.* 101 B.

Advowson, *sb.* [vowson]. RG. 471

Adwole, *adv.* == in error. O. and N. 177. AS. dwelian, dwola

Ae, *adv.* for 'aʒe,' == against. 1456 B.

Afaitment, *sb.* == address, skill. Alys. 661

Afare, *part.* == gone away. St Kath. 176

Afaytye, *v. a.* == manage, reduce to subjection. RG. 177

—— 3 s pret. 'afighteth.' Alys. 6583. Fr. afaiter

Afar, *adv.* 1226 B.

Afaunce, == affiance? Weber. Gl. ad Alys. 732

Afear, *v. a.* == frighten. RG. 504, 22

Afeard, *adj.* RG. 388

Afell, *v. a.* == fell, cut down. Alys. 5240

Afeng, *v. a.* == take up, receive, pret. afong. RG. 368

Aferd, *part.* == affaired, i.e. charged with an affair to be executed. Alys. 1813

Affair, *sb.* Alys. 410

Affie, *v. a.* == give confidence to a person. Alys. 4753

Affirm, *v. a.* Alys. 7356

Afighteth. See Afaytye

Afiled, == defiled. Alys. 1064

Afind, *v. a.* == find. O. and N. 527

Afingred, *part.* == hungered. 416 β. Cf. 'fyrst' for 'thirst,' 'frefownd' for 'greyhound;' and see Wright's Vocab. pp. 250, 259, note

Afire, *adv.* RG. 380, 541, 546

Afoled, *part.* == befooled, made a fool of. O. and N. 206

Afoot, *adv.* RG. 378

Aforce, *v. a.* == force, compel. RG. 121. Alys. 789

Aforeward, *adv.* == foremost, foreward. 492 B.; first of all. RG. 567

Aforth, *adv.* == forwards. O. and N. 822

Afretie, *v. a.* == devour. Pol. S. 237, 240. AS. fretan

Afte, *sb.* == folly? Pol. S. 210

After, *prep.* == in expectation of, 'after betere wynde hii moste þere at stonde.' RG. 367

—— == of time, 'after Mydsomer.' RG. 407

—— == like. Alys. 5418

—— == in; 'after eche strete.' M. Ode, st. 117

—— == 'behind,' of place. RG. 398

Afterblismed, == pregnant. Ps. lxxvii. 70. AS. blósma == a bud

Afterward, *adv.* == in the after part (of a book). RG. 6

—— == next in order, afterwards. Wright's L. P. p. 24

Aftertale, *sb.* == postscript. 627 B.

Afterwending, *sb.* == following. Alys. 7280

Again, *adv.* == iterum, a second time. RG. 36

—— == back again [aȝé]. 147 B.

Againbuy, *v. a.* == redeem, pret. 'agaynboghte.' Ps. lxxiii. 2

Againbuying, *sb.* == redemption. Ps. xlviii. 9

Againcall, *v. a.* Ps. ci. 25

Againlook, *v. a.* == look back upon. Ps. xxxiv. 3

Againres, *sb.* == meeting. Ps. lviii. 6. [ogain raas]. Ps. xviii. 7

Againsaw, *sb.* == contradiction. Ps. lxxx. 8

Againsaying, *sb.* == contradiction. Ps. cv. 32

Against, *prep.* == contra, [aȝe]. 54 B. [aȝen]. RG. 367. [ogaines] Ps. lxxxii. 4

—— == opposite to, of place, [aȝeyn]. RG. 6

—— == by the time that. Wright's L. P. p. 23

—— == in comparison with, [aȝeynes]. Wright's L. P. p. 68

Againstand, *v. n.* Ps. lxxv. 8

Againturn, *v. n.* == return. Ps. lxxvii. 39

Againward, *adv.* Ps. lxxvii. 57

Againwend, *v. n.* == retreat, part, 'aȝenwendand.' Ps. lxxvii. 9

Agast, *v. a.* == frighten. RG. 387

—— *adj.* == frightened. RG. 402. Alys. 3912. MG. us-gaisjan.

Age, *sb.* == sæculum. RG. 9

Agesse, *vb.* == calculate on, expect. K. Horn, 1219

Agin, *v. n.* == begin. O. and N. 1287

Ago, *v. n.* == go. O. and N. 1451. part. 'agonne.' == proceeded. RG.

Ago, == gone, neglected. Pol. S. 197

Agrame, *v. a.* == make angry. Alys. 3309

Agrief, *v. a.* Alys. 3785

Agrill, *v. a.* == annoy. [a-grulle]. O. and N. 1108. AS. grillan

Agrise, *v. a.* == terrify. RG. 463. pret. 'agros.' RG. 549. part. 'agrise,' == frightened. RG. 539. 'To agrise him,' == become furious. K. Horn, 895. AS. agrýsan

Aground, or 'alaground,' == on the ground. RG. 378

Ahen, *adj.* == own. O. and N. 1284. AS. ágen

Aheve, *v. a.* == lit. lift up; hence, bring up, educate. Marg. 5. AS. a-hefan

Ahte, *sb.* == property, goods. Wright's L. P. p. 46. AS. æht

Ahwene, *v. a.* == vex, trouble. O. and N. 1562. AS. a-hwænan

Aino3e, *adj.* == anew. RG. 397

Air, *sb.* 697 β

—— == airs, pride, vaunting. RG. 51, 397

Aither, == either. 434 β

Aiware—Aihwar, == everywhere. O. and N. 216. Moral Ode, st. 42, ed. Hickes, but the Egerton MS. reads the verse "eiðer he mai him finde"

Akelde, *vb. a.* pret. == cooled. The other reading is 'acoled,' q. v. RG. 442

Aken, *v. a.* == reconnoitre. Alys. 3468

Aknee, *adv.* == on the knee's. 993 B. [aknawe]. Alys. 3540

Alaboute, *adv.* 2258 B. Many other compounds of 'all' are thus written as one word, where they are now generally disjoined, thus—'alaground.' RG. 378

Alamed, *part.* == lamed. O. and N. 1602

Alas! *interj.* RG. 443

Alast, *adv.* == at last. Pol. S. 216

Alb, *sb.* == clothing, lit. a white robe. RG. 347. AS. albe

Albidene, *adv.* == by and by. HD. 730. Wright's L. P. p. 61

Albysi, *adv.* == about, scarcely. RG. 81. The V. L. gives 'unnethe'

Alday, *adv.* == all the day. RG. 197

—— == continually. RG. 92

Aldeman, *sb.* == elder. Ps. civ. 22

Aldest, == oldest. RG. 232

Alderelde, *sb.* == extreme old age. Ps. lxx. 18

Ale, *sb.* HD. 14

Alegge, *v. a.* == to lay down, put down. 1928 B. part, 'aleyd.' == quelled, subdued. Wright's L. P. p. 105

—— (of laws) == to annul. RG. 422. part. 'aleyd.' RG. 144 == 'to confute.' O. and N. 394. AS. a-lecgan

Alesen, *v. a.* == loose. Marg. 24

Alight, *v. a.* == descend, alight. 1897 B. RG. 468. part, 'alight.' RG. 433. AS. a-lihtan

Alighting, *sb.* RG. 430

Alisaundre, *sb.* == the herb alexander, or horse-parsley. Wright's L. P. p. 26. See the Prompt. Parv. s. v.

Alive, *adv.* 67 B. See Gloss. Rem. to Laȝamon, p. 442

Alike, *adj.* [iliche]. 1894 B.

—— *adv.* 714 β

Alinlaz. See Anlace

All, *adj.* RG. 373, == the whole

—— RG. 371, == every one of a number gen. s. 'alles,' used adverbially, == very, entirely. RG. 17; 73 B. gen. pl. 'alre,' 1332 B. 'aller,' RG. 135

All, *adv.* RG. 367, et passim

Allerfurst, == first of all. Alys. 1569

Allermost, *adv.* RG. 44

Alliance, *sb.* RG. 89, 295; [enlyance]. RG. 12

Allong, == during the whole of; 'al longe day.' 403 B. 'allonge niȝt.' 595 β

Allout, *adv.* == entirely. 1940 B.

Ally, *v. a.* RG. 65

Allyng, *adv.* == entirely. RG. 48. AS. eallunga

Almatour, *sb.* == almoner. Alys. 3042

Almesse, *sb.* == alms. RG. 330

Almightand, == almighty. Creed. 33

Almighty, *adj.* 1041 B.

Almost, *adv.* RG. 389. Ps. cxviii. 87

Almsdeed, *sb.* Rel. S. iv. 39

Almsful, *adj.* 1676. B.

Almshede, *sb.* RG. 498

Alnil, == and only? Pol. S. 201

Alond, *adv.* == on the land. RG. 389

Alone, *adj.* 59 B.

Along, *adv.* == straight on, 'to go along.' Alys. 3410

—— == lengthwise [o lonke]. Pol. S. 156

Alothe, *v. n.* == become loathsome. O. and N. 1275

Alour, *sb.* == corridor. Alys. 7210. *pl.* 'alurs.' RG. 192. Fr. aller

Alout, *v. n.* == bow. RG. 476

Alre, *gen. pl.* of 'all,' forms numerous compounds with adjj. in the superlative degree,—thus 'alre-hecst,' == highest of all. O. and N. 687; 'alre-mest,' ib. 684; 'alre-necst,' ib. 685; 'alre-wrste,' ib. 121; &c. &c.

Als, == as. HD. 306, == as if. HD. 508

Alsauf, *adv.* == without fail. RG. 391

Also, == besides. RG. 369

—— == as. RG. 561. HD. 1872

—— == as if. HD. 468

Alswa, *adv.* == also, in like manner. O. and N. 237

—— == as if. O. and N. 146

Altar, *sb.* 2215 B.

Altherbest, == best of all. HD. 182

Alto, *adv.* 99 B.

Alumere, *adj.* == bright. Wright's L. P. p. 68

Alȝare, *adv.* == already. 917 B.

Am, == them. Ps. v. 12

Am, *vb.* == 1s pret. of 'be.' 337 RG.

Amad, *part.* == amaied or dismayed. Alys. 1749. K. Horn. 586

—— == mad. Pol. S. 156

Amaistre, *v. a.* == reduce to subjection. Pilate 60

Amanse, *v. a.* == curse. RG. 474. AS. amánsumian, lit. to disjoin, hence to excommunicate

Amar, *v. a.* Rel. Ant. ii. p. 211

Amarstle, *v. a.* == to stuff full? Wright's L. P. p. 111. AS. amæstan

Ambesas, *sb.* == two aces, the lowest throw on the dice. Hence 'to caste an ambesas,' == to have bad luck, to fail in a thing. 492 β. 450 B. See Roq. *s. v.* Ambezas

Amblant, *part.* == ambling, Alys. 3462

Ambush, *sb.* RG. 51

—— *v. a.* [abusse] 1382 B.

Amen, *interj.* Wright's L. P. p. 51

Amend, *v. a.* RG. 449, 391

Amending, *sb.* == amendment. Alys. 7502

Amendment, *sb.* RG. 404, 472

Amere, *adv.* == bitterly, wrathfully. Alys. 4427. Fr. ameir, Lat. amarus

Amet, *sb.* == emmet, ant. RG. 296; 'amete hulle' == an anthill. RG. 296

Amethyst, *sb.* Cok. 91

Ameye, *sb.* == a mistress. Alys. 520. Fr. amie

Amid, *prep.* == in the midst of. 1139 B.

—— == with, 90 B. for 'mid.'

Amidward, *adv.* Alys. 690

Amiral. See Admiral.

Amiss, *adj.* == wrong. RG. 451

Amiture, *sb.* == friendship. Alys. 3975

Amone, *v. a.* == remember. Sign. 147. AS. gemunan

Among, *prep.* == inter. 6 B.

—— *adv.* == at intervals, O. and N. 6

Amorrow, [amorwe] *adv.* == on the morrow. 49 B.

Amount, *v. n.* RG. 497 == 'vor it ne ssolde *amounti* noȝt,' == because it would amount to or avail nought. So the prep. is omitted in Alys. 6020

'That *amounted* fyve hundred thousand
Knyghtis to armes, so Y fynde'

Amour, *sb.* == lover. Alys. 951

—— == love. Alys. 4573

Amty, == empty, RG. 17

Amye, *sb.* == friend. Alys. 1834. Fr. ami.

An, *indef. art.* == before a cons. RG. 537, 'an stounde.' So also RG. 261

——— == and. *q. v.*

——— == on, 'an urthe' 174 B. 'an honde' == on hand. 71 B. This last phrase seems to have dropped the meaning of 'soon,' 'now,' which it bears in Semi-Saxon. See Gloss. Rem. to Laȝamon, vol. iii. p. 474. 'an hei' == on high. RG. 537. 'an hoker' == with scorn. 710 B. 'an aunter' == on adventure, i. e. in peril. RG. 311, an oniwar == at unawares

——— == one, in acc. 'anne.' RG. 223.

An, *v. a.* == grant, allow, consent. O. and N. 1738. AS. unnan

Analing, == annihilating? Alys. 2166. Sic. Weber in Gloss. Hall *s. v.* suggests 'avaling' as the true reading == pulling down from their horses, which is probably correct

Anarrow, *v. a.* == confine, cramp up; hence, dishearten? Alys. 3346

Ancestor, *sb.* 428 B.

Anchor, *sb.* HD. 521

Ancre, *sb.* == nun. RG. 380

And, *conj.* RG. 368; [an]. O. and N. 31. RG. 264

Aneli, *adj.* == lonely. Ps. xxiv. 16

Anente, *prep.* == opposite to, over against. Fragm. Sci. 241

Anethered, *part.* == lowered, conquered. RG. 217

Angel, *sb.* RG. 254, 255, 441

Angrom, *sb.* == anguish. Ps. cxviii. 143. AS. ange

Anguish, *sb.* RG. 172, 442

Anguishous, *adj.* == full of anguish, RG. 157, 222

Anhang, *v. a.* == hang up, 3 s. pres. 'an-hoð,' O. and N. 1644. pret. 'an-hung.' RG. 509. AS. an-hòn

Anhit, *v. a.* == hit, strike. RG. 185

Anight, *adv.* == during the night. 681 B.

Anilepi, *adj.* == one, single. HD. 2107. AS. 'æn-lipig'. Cf. 'lepi ane.' Ps. xiii. 1; lii. 2, 4

Anise, *sb.* Wright's L. P. p. 26

Annoy, *v. a.* RG. 420, 487; part. annuid. RG. 550

——— *sb.* [anuy]. 1618 B.

Anness, *sb.* == solitude. Ps. ci. 7; [anes]. Ps. liv. 8

Anlace, [alinlaz] == a long knife worn at the girdle. HD. 2554

Anleth, *sb.* == countenance. Ps. xxvi. 9. AS. andwlita

Anon, *adv.* RG 373.

Anoniwar, *adv.* == at unawares. RG. 511

Anonrightes, *adv.* == immediately. Alys. 824

Another, *adj.* RG. 379, 444

Anoven, *adv.* == above. K. Horn, 638

Anoward, *adv.* upon. RG. 419

Anstond, *v. a.* == stand. RG. 267

Answer, *vb. a.* RG. 431

——— *sb.* RG. 500

Anthem, [anteyn] *sb.* St Dunstan, 185

Antre, *sb.* == adventure. RG. 35

——— *v. a.* == risk. Alys. 4265

Any, *adj.* == 'any thing.' 410 B.

——— == any one [eny]. RG. 376

Apair, *v. a.* == impair. St. Kath. 152

Apayed, == pleased. RG. 117, 1642 B. Fr. apaier, paier

Ape, *sb.* Alys. 4344

Apertly, *adv.* == openly. RG. 375

Apeyre, *v. a.* == impair. RG. 279

Apliȝt, *adv.* == immediately, at once. RG. 511

——— == faithfully? Pol. S. 218

Apoison, *v. a.* == to poison. RG. 122

Apostle, *sb.* RG. 70

Appeal, *sb.* 602 B.

Apple, *sb.* RG. 283

Aprikie, *v. a.* == prick. RG. 553

April, *sb.* Wright's L. P. p. 27

Aquell, *v. a.* == quell or kill. Pol. S. 192. AS. a-cwellan

Aquench, *v. a.* Rel. S. i. 10. part. 'a-queynt' == quenched. Frag. Sci. 162. AS. acwencan

Ar, *sb.* == oar. HD. 1776. AS. ár

Ar, *adv.* == ere, before than. O. and N. 862. compar. 'erur.' O. and

N. 1736. AS. ǽr, ǽror

Arape, *adv.* == in haste. Alys. 4239. Fr. araper. Lat. arripere.

Arbalast, *sb.* RG. 377, 536

Arbalaster, *sb.* Alys. 2613

Arch, *sb.* RG. 415

Archbishop, *sb.* RG. 367

Archbishopric, *sb.* RG. 417

Archdeacon, *sb.* RG. 468

Archer, *sb.* RG. 199

Architemple, == chief church. RG. 74

Are, *adj.* == former. HD. 27

Are, *vb.* [aren], Wright's L. P. p. 34. See Be

Arear, *v. a.* == raise up; hence 'build,' of a church. 320 B.; to 'stir up,' as war. RG. 436; or dust. Alys. 4077

Areason, *v. a.* == talk to. Alys. 6751

Areche, *v. a.* == explain. K. Horn, 1258. AS. arecan

Areche, *v. n.* == extend, reach onwards to a thing. Rel. Ant. i. 110; reach, St Andrew, 92. AS. arǽcan

Aredde, *v. a.* == rid of. O. and N. 1569

Arehwe, *sb.* == fear. O. and N. 1714

Arenk, *adv.* == in a rank or row. 273 β

Areu, *sb.* == fear. O. and N. 1496. See Areȝ

Arewe, *adv.* == in a row. RG. 252

Arewe, *v. a.* == to rue. Pol. S. 188

Areȝ, *adj.* == afraid. O. and N. 407. AS. earh

Areȝthe, *sb.* == fear. O. and N. 404

Arge, *adj.* == slow. M. Ode, st. 10. AS. earh

Aright, *adv.* O. and N. 400

Arise, *v. n.* RG. 369, 379. 3 s. pret. 'aros.' RG. 560. 'arist.' Alys. 5760

Ark, *sb.* Ps. cxxxi. 8

Arm, *adj.* [areme] == poor, miserable. O. and N. 1160. AS. earm

Arm, *sb.* == a limb. 2136 B.

Arm, *v. a.* RG. 63, 511. part. 'y-armed.' RG. 386

Armour, *sb.* RG. 397

Arms, *sb.* 2087 B.

Arn, *v. n.* == run, pret. 'arnde.' RG. 397. 'orn,' 2158 B. See Urne

Arnement, *sb.* == ink? Alys. 6418. Lat. atramentum. Fr. attrament. Cotgr. This is Weber's conjecture, who refers to the Sevyn Sages, v. 2776, 'as blak as ani arnement,' in confirmation. And see Rel. Ant. i. p. 302

Arning, == destroying. Alys. 2165. Fr. arner == to enfeeble. Cotgr.

Aroom, *adv.* == aside, out of the way. Alys. 1637

Arost, *part.* == roasted. Pol. S. 151

Around, [aroun] *adv.* == in circumference. Alys. 6603

Arrive, *v. n.* RG. 371

Arrow, *sb.* RG. 394, 398

Arson, *sb.* == saddle. Alys. 4251. It is properly the bow of the saddle, from Fr. ars == arc, or bow

Arst, == erst, first. RG. 389, 393

Art, *vb.* O. and N. 642

Art, *sb.* [ars]. Alys. 74, 737

Arwe, *adj.* == arrant. Alys. 3340

Aryhed, == laboured. Ps. cxviii. 27. AS. erian, pres. erige

As, == ut. RG. 368

—— == where. RG. 555. St. Andrew, 16

Asad, *adj.* == sad. Pol. S. 212

Ascape, *v. n.* == escape. Pol. S. 190

—— *v. a.* == avoid. Alys. 3775

Aschewele, *v. a.* == frighten. O. and N. 1611. A 'shewel,' or 'shawel,' was a scarecrow. See O. and N. 1646

Aschend, *v. a.* == injure. 1356 B.

Ascoff, *adv.* == scoffingly. Alys. 874

Aseen, *part.* == seen. Alys. 847

Asele, *v. a.* == seal. RG. 510. [acele.] RG. 496

Asely, == to absolve. RG. 360. See 'assoil'

Asenk, *v. a.* == drown, make to sink, pret. 'asentte.' RG. 416; 'asencte.' ib. 489. Laȝamon, iii. 19, has 'aseingde.' AS. sencan

Aseven, *adv.* == in 7 parts. RG. 405

Ashes, *sb.* [aske]. RG. 536. [axen]. Pol. S. 203

21

Ash-wednesday. RG. 542

Ashunche, *v. a.* == shun, detest. Wright's L. P. p. 38. AS. ascunian

Asiwe, *v. a.* == follow. Alys. 2494

Ask, *v. a.* RG. 89. pret. 'ascode.' RG. 550. 'askede'

Aske, == ashes, *q. v.*

Asking, *sb.* == prayer. Ps. xix. 7

Aslawe, *part.* == slain. RG. 317

Asleep, *adv.* RG. 417, 547

Asoke, *vb. a.* == forsook. K. Horn. 69

Asluppe, *vb.* == slip away from. Wright's L. P. p. 38

Asperant, *adj.* == bold. Alys. 4871

Aspide, *sb.* == asp. Ps. xc. 13

Aspill, *v. a.* == spill. 356 B.

Aspy, *v. a.* part. 'aspie,' == aspied. RG. 553

—— *v. n.* RG. 549

—— *sb.* == spy. RG. 557

Ass, *sb.* RG. 404

Assail, *v. a.* [asayly]. RG. 394; part. 'asayled.' RG. 387

Assault, *v. a.* [asayly]. RG. 177

Assault, *sb.* [asayt]. RG. 380. [asaut]. RG. 409

Assay, *v. a.* == essay, try. RG. 34. [a-syghe]. Alys. 3879

Assemble, *v. a.* Pol. S. 188

Assent, *v. n.* RG. 96

—— *sb.* Alys. 1480

Asshreynt, *part.* == caught, deceived. Alys. 4819. AS. ascrencan

Assign, *v. a.* RG. 502. 347 B.

Assize, *sb.* == judicial inquest. RG. 429

—— *sb.* == commodities, goods. Alys. 7074

Assoign, *vb. a.* == excuse, hence as a legal term 'to put in a plea for delay and non-appearance.' RG. 539. Fr. essoiner

—— *sb.* == a plea for non-appearance at a trial. [asoyne, a sothne]. RG. 539

Assoil, *v. a.* == absolve. RG. 464, 501

Assoiling, *sb.* RG. 501

Assuage, *v. a.* 1454 B.

Assumption, *sb.* (Feast of the). RG. 570

Astand, *v. n.* == stand still, delay. [astonde] 1920 B. 3 pl. pret. 'astunte' RG. 546. 'astynte' RG. 128

Asteynte, *part.* == attainted. Alys. 880

Astiune, *sb.* == a precious stone. Cok. 88. Probably the 'astios' of Plin. H. N. xxxvii. 48

Astoned, == astonished. RG. 396

Astore, *v. a.* == store (a place). RG. 375, 385, 395

——— *adv.* == plentifully. Alys. 2110, 5002

Astrangle, *v. a.* == to strangle. RG 342

Astrengthy, *v. a.* == strengthen. RG. 342

Astride, *adv.* Alys. 4445

Astromyen, *sb.* == astronomer. Alys. 136

Astronomy, *sb.* Alys. 137

Astye, *v. n.* == move, or stir. RG. 317 AS. astígan

Asunde. See Aswunde

Aswink, *v. a.* == swink for, earn by labour. 1665 B.

Aswunde, *part.* == worn out, decayed. O. and N. 1478. 'asunde.' O. and N. 534. AS. aswindan

At, *adv.* == but. RG. 256, 372

——— with inf. == to. Ps. lxxvi. 16; lxxii. 23. ON. at

——— *prep.* == of time, 'at Alle Halwyn tide.' RG. 416

——— == of place, 'at Westmynstre.' 227 B.

Atake, *part.* == taken. 1963 B.

Atblenche, *v. a.* == shrink from, escape. Rel. S. v. 8

Atbroide, *part.* == seduced? O. and N. 1378. AS. æt-bredan

Ate. See Eat.

Atell, *v. a.* == reckon up. RG. 171

Ateliche, *adj.* == hateful, foul. O. and N. 1123. AS. átelic

Atfall, *v. n.* == fall. Rel. S. vii. 24

Atfly, *v. n.* == fly away. O. and N. 37

Atgo, *v. n.* == go away. Wright's L. P. pp. 48, 74

Athel, *sb.* == nobleman? Wright's L. P. p. 33. AS. æþel

——— *adj.* == noble. O. and N. 632

Atheling, *sb.* == nobleman. Rel. S. vi. 11. AS. æþeling

Athold, *v. a.* == retain. RG. 124; restrain. O. and N. 392

———— *v. n.* == hold still, remain faithful to. 2 s. pres. 'athalst.' RG. 193

Athrang, *adv.* == in a throng. Alys. 3409

Athree, *adv.* == in 3 parts. RG. 437

Atour, *adv.* == round about. Alys. 4511

Atprenche, *v. a.* == deceive. O. and N. 249, 812. ON. pretta, to deceive

Atraht, for 'at-raft.' == reaved or snatched away. Wright's L. P. p. 37

Atrute, *v. a.* == make a noise or disturbance. RG. 428. O. and N. 1166. See Route

Atscape, *v. a.* == escape. Wright's L. P. p. 75

Atschet, *vb. a.* == burst? O. and N. 44. AS. sceðan

Atschote, *vb. a. part.* == shot, destroyed by a shot. O. and N. 1621. AS. sceotan

Atsit, *v. a.* == withstand, oppose. RG. 174

Atstand, *v. a.* == withstand. RG. 44

———— *v. n.* == stand, remain. 2375 B. pret. 'atstode.' RG. 355

Attan, == at the, for 'at than.' 81 B.

Atte, == at the. RG. 285

Attercop, *sb.* == spider. O. and N. 600. Lit. 'poison-cup.' AS. attor-coppa

Attire, *v. a.* RG. 547

———— *sb.* Alys. 173

Attorn, *v. n.* == return. RG. 419, 539

Atwende, *v. a.* == put away, remove. O. and N. 1425

Atwit, *v. a.* == twit. RG. 33. pret. 'atwiste,' ibid. AS. edwitan

Atwo, *adv.* RG. 375

Atyl, *sb.* == array, dress. RG. 51. Fr. teile, toile

———— *v. a.* == array. RG. 191, 525

Aunt, *sb.* RG. 571. Fr. ante, tante. Lat. amita

Autors, *sb.* == ancestors. Alys. 4519

Avail, *v. a.* == bring down, lower. O. and N. 1683. Fr. avaler

Avail, *v. n.* == help, be of avail. Body and S. 188. Fr. valoir

Avenant, *adj.* == graceful. Alys. 6333. Fr. avenant

Avetrol, *sb.* == bastard. Alys. 2693. Fr. avoistre

Aveysé, *adj.* == wary. Alys. 5261

Avile, *v. a.* == render vile, with 'to.' RG. 495

Aviroun, *adv.* == round about. Alys. 2672. Fr. environ

Avise, *v. a.* == advise, inform. RG. 547

Avision, *sb.* == warning. RG. 255

—— == vision. 1101 B.

Avoi, *adv.* == away. 2061 B.

Avoirdupois. Rel. Ant. ii. p. 175

Avoth, == takes in, hear, from 'a-fón.' O. and N. 841

Avoué, *sb.* == protector. Alys. 3160. See 'Abowes'

Avowerie, *sb.* == help, patronage. Pol. S. 189

Await, *v. a.* == wait for. Pilate 17

—— == attend upon, observe. RG. 49

Awake, *v. n.* == pret. 'awok.' RG. 15. Alys. 356

Awaking, *sb.* RG. 557

Awaped, == amazed, angered. Alys. 899. AS. wafian

Aware, *adj.* == [iwar]. O. and N. 147

Awarie, *v. a.* == curse. Marg. 18. part. 'awariede.' Rel. S. v. 137. AS. awarian

Awarp, *v. a.* == cast away, render worthless. Rel. Ant. ii. p. 210. AS. awerpan

Away, *adv.* RG. 398

Awaybear, *v. a.* Ps. xlv. 10

Awayput, *v. a.* Ps. lxxxviii. 39; lxxxvii. 15

Awayward, *adv.* RG. 151

Awaywerp, *v. a.* == reject. Ps. lxxvii. 60

Awe, *sb.* [agh]. Ps. lxxxviii. 31

Awe, *v. a.* == own, possess. HD. 1291. AS. ágan

Awede, *v. n.* == go mad. O. and N. 1382. pret. 'awedde.' RG. 162. part. 'awed,' == mad. 1488 B. AS. awédan

Awend, *v. n.* == go. part. 'awend,' 1240 B. AS. awendan

Awene, *v. a.* == make to think or prompt? O. and N. 1256. part. 'awene.' O. and N. 239. AS. wenan

Awful, [aghful]. Ps. xlvi. 3

Awfully, [aghfulli]. *adv.* Ps. cxxxviii. 14

Awfulness, [aghfulness.] *sb.* Ps. cxliv. 6

Awhile, *adv.* 1243 B.

Awille, *adv.* == pleasingly, ex voto. O. and N. 1720

Awl, *sb.* == RG. 48. [owel]. O. and N. 80. AS. æl

Awlate, *v. a.* == disgust. RG. 485. AS. wlætian

Awonder, *v. a.* == cause to wonder. Alys. 1408, 5513

Awreke, *v. a.* == avenge. RG. 391. pret. 'awrete.' ib. 135

Awrothe, *v. n.* == become wroth, or evil. O. and N. 1276

Awuste, *v. a.* pret. == knew. M. Ode, 9

Axe, *sb.* RG. 490, 540

Ay, *sb.* == egg. Alys. 568. pl. 'ayren,' Alys. 4719. See Ey

Ayschelle, *sb.* == egg-shell. Alys. 577

Aye, *adv.* == ever. 884 B.

Ayke, *v. a.* == increase. Ps. civ. 24. AS. écan

Aysil, *sb.* == vinegar. Ps. lxviii. 22. AS. eisile. Germ. essig

Azure, *adj.* Ritson's AS. viii. 37

Aȝt, *adj.* == noble. RG. 377, 183, 459. AS. æht

Aȝte, *vb.* == ought. RG. 357

B.

Bac, *sb*. == a crown. Wright's L. P. p. 70. AS. beág

Back, *sb*. HD. 556

Backbite, *v. a.* Pol. S. 157. pret. 'backbate.' Ps. xxxvii. 21

Backbiter, *sb*. Rel. S. vii. 25

Bad, *adj.* RG. 108

Badly, *adv.* RG. 566

Baft, *sb*. == the hinder part. Ps. lxxvii. 66. AS. bæfta

Bag, *sb*. Pol. S. 150

Bagful, *sb*. St Swithin, 57

Bailiff, *sb*. RG. 473, 499. n. pl. 'baylis' RG. 129

Baillie, *sb*. == office, or duty. 202, 355 B.

——— == authority. Alys. 7532

Bait, *v. a.* (a bear). HD. 1840. ON. beita

Baker, *sb*. Rel. S. vii. 35

Balance, *sb*. == doubt. RG. 200

Bald, *adj.* [ballede]. RG. 377, 429

Baldelicker, == bolder. St Swithin, 69

Baldric, *sb*. == [baudry]. Alys. 4698. Fr. baldret. Lat. balteus

Bale, *sb*. == woe. HD. 327. AS. bealu

Baleful, *adj.* Wright's L. P. p. 53

Bali, == belly. *q. v.*

Ball, *sb*. Fragm. Sci. 89

——— == head. Alys. 6481. Compare our modern slang 'nob'

Balm, *sb*. [baum]. Wright's L. P. p. 35

Baloynge, == smoothness? Wright's L. P. p. 35. See Prompt. Parv. s. v. Balhew

Ban, *sb*. == message. RG. 188

——— == troop, army. O. and N. 390

——— *v. a.* == levy, or raise an army. O. and N. 1666

Band, *sb*. == chain, bond. [bende], RG. 379

Bandon, *sb*. == dominion, authority. Wright's L. P. p. 27. pl. bandons, == orders, commands. Alys. 3180

Baneur, *sb*. == ensign-bearer. RG. 361

Bank, *sb.* (of a river). Alys. 3495

Banker, *sb.* == cloth or covering for a bench. Ritson's AS. viii. 69. Fr. banquier. See Prompt. Parv. *s. v.* and Way's note there

Banner, *sb.* RG. 541, 542, 402

Banneret, *sb.* == a little banner. Alys. 5236

—— == knight-banneret. RG. 551

Baptize, *v. a.* RG. 86

Baptizing, *sb.* RG. 86

Bar, *sb.* HD. 1794

Barbary, *sb.* == foreign lands. Ps. cxiii. 1

Barbet, *sb.* == a hood, or muffler. Pol. S. 154

Barbican, *sb.* Alys. 1591. Fr. barbacan. *Vid.* Roq. s. v.; and see Phil. Soc. Proc. vol. iii. p. 156

Bare, *sb.* == tree. O. and N. 56. ON. Barr

Bare, *adj.* == naked. RG. 514

—— == mere, single. M. Ode, 70

—— == destitute, impoverished. RG. 511, 388

Barefoot, *adj.* RG. 434

Baret, *sb.* == quarrel. O. and N. 408. HD. 1932. ON. baratta

Barge, *sb.* Alys. 852

Bark, *v. n.* Alys. 1935

Barking, *sb.* Alys. 4966

Barm, *sb.* == yeast. Rel. S. vii. 30. AS. bearme

Barm, == bosom. K. Horn. 728. AS. bearm

Barman, *sb.* == kitchen-porter. HD. 868. See 'bermannen,' in Gloss. to Laȝ.

Barmhatres, == breast-cloths. Rel. Ant. ii. p. 176. AS. bearm, hæter

Barn, *sb.* RG. 496

Baron, *sb.* RG. 369, 511

Baronage, *sb.* [barnage]. HD. 2947

Barony, *sb.* == estate of a baron. RG. 479

—— == order of barons. RG. 535

Barrel, *sb.* Alys. 28

Barrow, *sb.* == wheel cart. 899 B.

Baru, *sb.* == a gelt boar. RG. 207

Basilisk, *sb.* == a kind of serpent. Ps. xc. 13

Basin, *sb.* == helmet. Pol. S. 189. Alys. 2333. Fr. bacinet

Basnet, *sb.* == a light helmet. Alys. 2234

Bast, == bastard. RG. 431, 516. Always preceded by 'a'

Bastard, *adj.* RG. 412

Baston, *sb.* == a kind of verse. Rel. Ant. ii. p. 175

Bat, *sb.* == club. Alys. 78

Batchelor, *sb.* RG. 453

Batchelry, *sb.* == order of batchelors, the youth. RG. 76

—— == prowess. RG. 192

Bate, *v. a.* == make to abate, put an end to. Body and Soul, 167

Bath, *sb.* RG. 7

Bathe, *v. a.* Alys. 2708

—— *v. n.* Rel. S. v. 210

Battailing, *sb.* == fighting. Alys. 100

Battailer, [batelur], *sb.* == warrior. Alys. 1433

Battle, *sb.* RG. 369, 514

Baudekyn, *sb.* == a stuff made of silk and gold, so called from Bagdad, Ital. Baldacco, where it was made. Alys. 202

Bawmed, == embalmed. Alys. 4670

Bay, *v. a.* == listen to, render fortunate. Wright's L. P. p. 27. Fr. bayer. Vid. Roq.

—— *v. a.* == to bait (a boar), pret. 'bede.' Wright's L. P. p. 27

—— *sb.* == baiting, 'bay of bor.' Alys. 4376

Bay, == boy. Alys. 4376

Be, *v. n.* 402 B. [beo], 403 B. [beon], 404 B. [bon], O. and N. 262. [ben], Wright's L. P. p. 24. [buen], ib. p. 25

—— *pres. ind.* 1 s. 'am.' O. and N. 276

2 s. 'art.' O. and N. 561. 'is.' Ps. 1. 6

3 s. 'is.' O. and N. 570. 'esse.' Ps. xci. 16. 'bes.' Ps. cxlvi. 10; cxxvii. 2

1 pl. 'buen.' Wright's L. P. p. 25

3 pl. 'aren.' Wright's L. P. pp. 34, 22; 'both.' O. and N. 568. 'beth.' RG 368. 'beoth.' 411 B.

—— *pres. subj.* 2 s. 'bo.' O. and N. 566

3 s. 'bo.' O. and N. 1376. 'beo.' O. and N. 1531

3 pl. 'be.' RG. 369. 'bo.' O. and N. 567

—— *pret. ind.* 1 s. 'wes.' Wright's L. P. p. 97

3 s. 'wes.' Wright's L. P. p. 25. 'was.' RG. 374

3 pl. 'were.' Rel. S. v. 178

—— *pret. subj.* 2 s. 'were.' O. and N. 1312

3 s. 'were.' O. and N. 1299

3 pl. 'were.' RG. 374

—— *imper. sing.* 'be.' Wright's L. P. p. 97

—— *part.* 'ibeo.' 434 B.

Beadle, *sb.* HD. 266. [budel.] Wright's L. P. p. 22. pl. 'bedeles.' 987 B. AS. bydel

Beam, *sb.* RG. 288

Bean, *sb.* RG. 497

Bear, *sb.* (the animal). HD. 573

Bear, *v. n.* == incline towards. 362 B.

Bear, *v. a.* == carry. RG. 375. pret. 'bar.' 224 B.

—— == pay, render. RG. 378

—— == produce (as fruit). RG. 352

—— == bring forth a child, part. 'i-bore.' RG. 516. O. and N. 716

Beard, *sb.* 611 β

Bearing, *sb.* == birth. Alys. 636

Beast, *sb.* RG. 375, 376

Beat, *v. a.* HD. 2763. RG. 453. 3 pl. pret. 'beoten.' St Andr. 69. part. 'bete' == beaten, of gold. Wright's L. P. p. 35

Beauty, *sb.* [bealté]. Wright's L. P. p. 53

Beaver, *sb.* M. Ode, 182

Bebled, == covered with blood. Alys. 3813

Beck, *sb.* == brook. Ritson's AS. viii. 63 AS. becc. Germ. bach

Beck, *v. n.* == beckon. Ps. xxxiv. 19

Beckon, [bocken] *v. n.* Pol. S. 149. AS. bécnan

Beclip, *v. a.* == embrace. RG. 469. Alys. 7416. AS. beclyppan

Becoll, *v. a.* == blacken. pret. 'becolmede.' K. Horn, 1096. AS. col

Become, *v. n.* == come into existence. RG. 15

—— == suit a person, with 'to.' RG. 36

Bed, *sb.* RG. 377

———— == bedfellow. O. and N. 1498

Bed, *v. a.* HD. 1237

Bedag, *v. a.* == bedew with mud; part. 'bydagged.' Alys. 5485. ON. dögg. Sw dagg. == dew. Not connected with 'dagged' == cut into slips; vandyked, as applied to clothing, which comes from AS. dág

Bede, *v. a.* == pray. RG. 547. 2 s. pres. 'byst.' RG. 337. 3 s. 'bit.' O. and N. 571. 3 pl. pret. 'baden.' Ps. cv. 19

———— == offer. Ps. lxxi. 10

———— *sb.* == prayer. RG. 571

Bedgang, *sb.* == going to bed. Ps. liv. 3

Bedsister, *sb.* == concubine. RG. 27

Bedyner, *sb.* == servant, officer. Wright's L. P. p. 49. Germ. bedienen

Bee, *sb.* Ps. cxvii. 12

Beech, *sb.* Alys. 5242. [breche]. O. and N. 14? Compare for the insertion or omission of the *r*, AS. 'spræcan,' Engl. 'speak,' 'gin' and 'grin' or 'grinew,' 'groom' and AS. 'guma'

Beef, *sb.* Alys. 5248

Beer, *sb.* [bor], O. and N. 1009

Befal, *v. n.* pret. 'bivel.' RG. 556

Before, *prep.*——of place. RG. 443

———— *adv.*——of time. RG. 443. [biforen] Wright's L. P. p. 24

———— == foreward, onward. O. and N. 774

Beget, *v. a.* == obtain. O. and N. 726. RG. 516

———— == procreate. RG. 516. part. 'byȝute.' RG. 388

Begetting, *sb.* Alys. 6866

Beggar, *sb.* Body and Soul, 139

Begin, *v. n.* RG. 380

Beginning, *sb.* RG. 384

———— == (of a country.) RG. 399

Begon, *part.* == adorned, or covered with. Ritson's AS. viii. 35. Cf. 'woebegone'

Begrown, *part.* [bi-growe]. O. and N. 27

Beguile, *v. a.* K. Horn, 328

Beh. See Bow, *vb.*

Behalve, *v. a.* == divide into two parts. HD. 1834

Behead, *v. a.* Pol. S. 213

Behest, *sb.* RG. 231

Behind, *prep.* O. and N. 594

—— *adv.* RG. 395

Behind, *sb.* == rump. O. and N. 596

Behold, *v. a.* == hold in the hand. O. and N. 1323

—— *v. n.* == look up. RG. 395; have regard. Ps. v. 3

—— *v. a.* Wright's L. P. p. 86

Behoof, *sb.* RG. 348. [byefþe], ib. 354

Behote, *sb.* == vow. Ps. cxv. 14

Behave, *v. n.* == RG. 177. Ps. cxiv. 18

Beigh, *sb.* == ring. Alys. 1572. AS. beág

Beigh, *v. a.* == bow, bend. Alys. 4373

Being, *sb.* == condition. Alys. 223

Beknow, *v. a.* == make known. Alys. 7472

—— == know thoroughly. Rel. S. i. 31

Belde, *v. a.* == protect? Wright's L. P. p. 24

Belie, *v. a.* O. and N. 837

Belay, *v. a.* == besiege. RG. 519

Belief, *sb.* == religious faith. RG. 73

Believe, *v. n.* RG. 229

Belive, or **Blive**, == quickly. RG. 50. SS. 'bilife.' Cf. Dan. 'oplive,' == to quicken, enliven, and the two senses of our Eng. 'quick'

Bell, *sb.* RG. 509, 541

Belly, *sb.* [bali]. Rel. S. v. 83

Bellows, *sb.* [bulies]. 467 β

Belock, *v. a.* == lock up. 3 s. pres. 'bi-luth.' O. and N. 1555. pret. 'bi-leck.' O. and N. 1079. part. 'bi-loken.' Rel. S. vii. 68

Beme, *sb.* == trumpet. Wright's L. P. p. 25. AS. béme

Bemoan, *v. a.* [bimene]. RG. 490

Bemoaning, *sb.* [bymening] == complaint. Alys. 534

Bemothered, == confused, perplexed. Pol. S. 158. Cf. Engl. prov. to

32

'mither' == to bother, perplex (the *i* is pronounced long). Probably connected with AS. méde == weary; Dutch, moeden

Bench, *sb.* Body and Soul, 153. [bink]. Ritson's AS. viii. 69

Bend, *v. a.* RG. 377, 536

Bende, *sb.* == bond. RG. 379

Bene, *sb.* == prayer. Wright's L. P. p. 58. AS. bén

Beneath, *prep.* O. and N. 910

—— *adv.* RG. 258, 491

—— [bi nither] == beyond, without. HD. 2025

Benim, *v. a.* == take away. RG. 375, 405, 443

Benison, *sb.* HD. 1723

Bequeath, *v. a.* RG. 301

Bequest, *sb.* [byquide]. RG. 384

Berain, *v. n.* K. Horn. 11

Berand, *sb.* == singing, sounding. Ps. xxvi. 6. See Bere

Bere, *sb.* == sound, voice. Alys. 550. O. and N. 923. [ibere]. O. and N. 222. SS. ibere. La3. iii. 25

Bereave, *v. a.* Wright's L. P. p. 101

Berfreyes, *sb.* == towers used in sieges, belfries. Alys. 2777

Berihed, == saved. Creed 63. Ps. xxvii. 9. AS. berigea, beorgan

Beryhing, *sb.* == protection. Ps. xxvii. 8

Berip, *v. a.* == strip (fruit off a tree). Ps. lxxix. 13

Bern, *sb.* == child. Wright's L. P. pp. 23, 58

Berne, *v. a.* == injure? K. Horn, 710

Berun, *part.* == overflowed (with tears). K. Horn, 670

Berwen, *v. a.* == defend, protect. HD. 697 2022. AS. beorgan.

Beryl, *sb.* Wright's L. P. p. 25

Beryng, *sb.* == bosom. Alys. 484. ON. bringa

Beryng, *sb.* == burying, *q. v.*

Besee, *v. a.* == provide for, see to. RG. 393, 505. Ps. v. 2; treat, 3 pl. pret. 'bysayen.' Alys. 4605

Beseech, *v. a.* RG. 480. 3 s. pres. 'bi-sehth.' O. and N. 1437

Beseeching, *sb.* Ps. cxviii. 159. Wright's L. P. p. 95

Beseem, *v. a.* == make to appear seemly or probable, in part. O. and N. 840

Besekandlik, == able to be besought, propitious. Ps. cxxxiv. 14

Beset, *v. a.* RG. 387

Beshine, *v. n.* K. Horn, 12

—— *v. a.* Fragm. Sci. 18

Beshit, *v. a.* — part. 'bishiten.' Alys. 5485

Beshrew, *v. a.* == curse. Rel. Ant. ii. p. 211

Beside, *prep.* of place, 'a toun biside Wircetre.' RG. 558

—— *adv.* of place, 'ther biside.' RG. 558

Beside, == in addition to. RG. 92

Besiege, *v. a.* RG. 387

Besmut, *v. a.* == defile. Ps. liv. 21

Bespeak, *v. a.* == speak against a thing. RG. 524, 550. AS. be-spræcan

—— == agree upon a thing. O. and N. 1736

Besprinkle, *v. a.* RG. 128

Best, *adj.* RG. 370, 504

Bestead, *part.* [bistad] == happened. Wright's L. P. p. 41

Bestir, *v. a.* Alys. 3079

Bestrew, *v. a.*—part, 'bistrete.' RG. 561

Bestride, *v. a.* HD. 2060. Alys. 706

Beswike, *v. a.* == deceive. Wright's L. P. p. 45. AS. be-swícan

Bet, *adj.* == better. RG. 375, 546

Bet, *v. a.* == lay a wager, part. 'y-bate.' Pol.

Bet of berne, == probably 'in labour with child.' Marg. 53, 71. AS. beátan?

Betake, *v. a.* == take. RG. 526

—— == give in charge to a person, i.e. cause another to take. RG. 201, 354; so 'was bitake four erles,' == was given in charge 'to four earls.' RG. 523; see p. 301. Hence == commend to a person, RG. 475; 'hand over to another,' HD. 203. AS. be-tæcan

Betaught, [bi-tahte] == taught. Rel. S. v. 124

Bete, *v. a.* lit. == 'make better;' hence, 'heal,' 'save.' Marg. 68

—— == 'recompense,' 'make amends for.' RG. 369. AS. bétan

Bete, *part.* == beaten. Vid. Beat

Beten, [y-beten] == overlaid, covered, as with silk, gold, &c. Alys. 1034, 1518

Beth, Beoth, &c. See Be

Bethink, *v. a.* == 'to bethink oneself' of a thing. RG. 368, 458

Betide, *v. n.* == happen. RG. 418, 14

Betime, *adv.* K. Horn, 995

Betoken, *v. a.* RG. 152

Betokening, *sb.* RG. 560

Betray, *v. a.* RG. 135

Better, *adj.* RG. 367, 422

—— *v. n.* == get the better. Ps xii. 5

Betterness, *sb.* Ps. li. 5

Between, *prep.* RG. 371, 513

Betwixt, *prep.* [bi-tuxen]. O. and N. 1745

Beverage, *sb.* == drink. RG. 26

—— == reward, consequence. RG. 299

Bewail, *v. a.* Alys. 4395

Beware, *v. n.* RG. 547

Beweep, *v. a.* O. and N. 972

Bewind, *v. a.* == entwine. part. 'bewound.' Christ on the Cross, 3

Bewray, *v. a.* == betray [by-wrye]. Alys. 4377. pret. 'bi-wro.' O. and N. 673. AS. wrégan.

Beyen, == are? Wright's L. P. p. 32

Beyond, *prep.* RG. 368, 420

Beyre, == of both, gen. pl. RG. 388, 398

Bezant, *sb.* == a piece of money. RG. 409. From Byzantium, or Constantinople, where they were originally used

Bible, *sb.* Rel. Ant. ii. p. 174

Bicast, *v. a.* == cast over, cover. 92 β

Bicatch, *v. a.* == deceive, ensnare. Alys. 258. K. Horn, 318

Bicharred, *part.* == deceived. Rel. Ant. ii. p. 211; M. Ode, 160. AS. becýrran

Bicherme, *v. a.* == chirp about or around. O. and N. 279. AS. cyrm

Bick, *v. n.* == fight. Alys. 2337

Bicker, *v. n.* == quarrel. RG. 540. Fr. becquer. W. bicra == to fight

Bicker, *sb.* == a quarrel, contention, battle. RG. 538, 543

Biclipe, Biclupe, *v. a.* == accuse. 365 B.

—— == appeal. RG. 473

Biclose, *v. a.* == enclose. RG. 558, 218

Bid, *v. a.* == ask. RG. 77. 3 pl. pret. 'badden.' Alys. 5823. See 'bede'

—— == command. RG. 29. pret. 'bad.' 683 B. part. 'y-bede.' RG. 383. AS. biddan

Bid, *v. a.* == offer, pret. 'bode.' RG. 379. 'beod'? O. and N. 1435. AS. beódan

Bid, *sb.* == asking, demand. Pol. S. 149

Bidding, *sb.* == demand, request. Pol. S. 150

Bide, *v. n.* == remain. Pol. S. 204

Bidene, *adv.* == presently. Ps. l. 4; ciii. 30

Bidelve, *v. a.* == bury. Rel. Ant. i. 116

Bidone, *part.* == 'bidun in grave.' Body and Soul, 97

Bier, *sb.* 128 B.

Bieren, *sb.* == a man. Ps. cxxvi. 5; cxxxix. 2. AS. beorn

Biflette, *v. n.* == flow past. K. Horn, 1457

Bifluen, *v. a.* == flee from. M. Ode, 77

Big, *v. a.* == build. Ps. xxvii. 5. AS. byggen. ON. byggja

Bigabbed, *part.* == deceived. Lit. 'talked over.' RG. 458. AS. gabban

Bigate, *sb.* == booty. Alys. 2138

Biggand, *sb.* == a builder. Ps. cxvii. 22

Biglide, *v. n.* Wright's L. P. p. 87

Bigrede, *v. a.* == lament. Alys. 5175. AS. grædan.

—— == call to. O. and N. 279

Bihaite, *v. a.* == behold? O. and N. 1320. AS. behawian. Or, possibly, == observe, regard. AS. hedan. Germ, behüten. See Gloss. Rem. on Laʒ. iii. 457

Bihalves, *adv.* == aside. St Kath. 13

Bihede, *v. a.* == regard. O. and N. 635

Bihemmen, *v. a.* == cover, cloak. O. and N. 672

Bihepe, *part.* == heaped up. O. and N. 360

Bihete, *v. a.* == promise, pret. 'bihet.' RG. 381. 'byheyghte.' Alys.

Bihoting, *sb.* == promise. Alys. 4000

Bike, *sb.* == cassia. Ps. xliv. 9. Literally 'pitch.' ON. bik

Bilace, *part.* == beset. Alys. 3357

Bilaue. See Bileve

Bilaucte. See Bilou

Bilede, *v. a.* == lead about. Pol. S. 155. O. and N. 68

Bilegge, *v. a.* == assert, allege. O. and N. 672

Bileve, *v. a.* == leave. RG. 421

—— *v. n.* == remain. RG. 372, 374. [bilaue]. Alys. 3541

Biliked, *part.* == rendered likely or probable. O. and N. 840

Bilime, *v. a.* == to mutilate. RG. 471, 560

Bilimp, *v. n.* == happen. M. Ode, st. 59 AS. belimpan

Bill, *sb.* (of a bird). O. and N. 79

—— == hatchet. Pol. S. 151

Bilou, *pret.* == laughed at. RG. 328. [bylaucte]. K. Horn, 681. [by lowe], RG. 299. [by low3]. RG. 64

Bimong, *prep.* == among. Wright's L. P. p. 35

Bind, *v. a.* Wright's L. P. p. 45. part. 'ibounde.' RG. 487

Binder, *sb.* HD. 2050

Binding, *sb.* == chain. Ps. cxxiv. 5

Bink, *sb.* See Bench

Bipahte, *pret.* == deceived. Rel. S. v. 128. AS. be-pæcan

Birade, *v. a.* == counsel. Alys. 3732

Birch, *sb.* == the tree. Alys. 5242

Bird, *sb.* RG. 177

Birde, *sb.* == lady. HD. 2760. A metathesis of 'bride'

Birst, == bruised. Body and Soul, 86. AS. berstan.

Birth, *sb.* == nation. Ps. lxxviii. 10

Birthman, *sb.* == man of good birth. HD. 2101

Birthtime, *sb.* [burtyme]. RG. 9, 443

Birue, *v. a.* == rue, repent. Fragm. Sci. 325

Bis, *sb.* == purple. Wright's L. P. p. 26. Fr. bis. Lat. byssus

Bisay, *v. a.* == recommend, say. RG. 422

Bisayen, == treated. See Besee.

Bischriche, *v. a.* == shriek at. O. and N. 67

Biscunien, *v. a.* == shun. M. Ode, 77

Bise, *sb.* == north wind. HD. 724. OHG. bísa

Bisend, *v. a.* == send after. RG. 491

Bishop, *sb.* RG. 376

Bishopric. RG. 414, 417

Bismere, *sb.* == blasphemy. Body and Soul, 110. [busemere]. RG. 12, 379. AS. bismér

Bisne, *adj.* == blind. O. and N. 78. AS. bisen

Bisoht, == sought out, got ready for. Pol. S. 220

Bisokne, *sb.* == beseeching. RG. 495

Bispel, *sb.* == proverb. O. and N. 127. AS. bispel

Bistad, *sb.* == a dwelling. Wright's L. P. p. 38

Bistand, *v. a.* == stand by a person; hence, to press or urge them. O. and N. 1436

Bistolen, *part.* == stolen, crept onwards. M. Ode, 9

Bisyhed, == the state of being busy. Alys. 3

Bit, *sb.* == a morsel. RG. 207

Bit, *sb.* == bottle. Ps. lxxvii. 13. [bite]. Body and Soul, 34. AS. bitte

Bitch, *sb.* Alys. 5394

Bite, *v. a.* Alys. 5435

Bite, *sb.* Alys. 5436

Bite, *v. a.* == drink. HD. 1731. Cf. bohem. 'piti,' potus; 'pitka,' potatio, &c. Gr. πίνω

Bitell, *v. a.* == excuse. O. and N. 263

Biti3t, == arrayed. O. and N. 1011. AS. biþæht. See Gloss. to La3. s. v.

Bito3e, == employed. O. and N. 702. AS. biteon. See Gloss. to La3. s. v.

Bitter, *adj.* Wright's L. P. p. 87

Biturn, *v. a.* == turn. RG. 210

Bituxen. See Betwixt.

Biwene, *v. a.* == discover, recognize. O. and N. 1507

Biwente, *vb.*—'hire bi-wente.' == turned her about. K. Horn, 329. In pass. 'þai bewent' == let them be turned back. Ps. vi. 11. AS. wendan

Biwere, *v. a.* == protect. O. and N. 1124. AS. bewerian

Biweved, == covered. RG. 338.

——— == woven? Alys. 1085

Biwin, *v. a.* == win. RG. 75, 420

Biwit, *adv.* == out of one's wits. RG. 528

Biwite, *v. a.* == defend. Rel. S. v. 252. AS. bewitan

——— == know? Alys. 5203

Biwrye, *v. a.* == cover. Alys. 6453. AS. wreon.

Black, *adj.* RG. 433, 522

Blacken, *v. n.* == become angry. HD. 2165

Blame, *v. a.* RG. 163

——— *sb.* RG 272, 432

Blandishing, *sb.* == blandishments. St Kath. 164

Blanis ? Alys. 6292

Blanket, *sb.* 1167 B. Fr. blanchet

Blast, *v. n.* == blow, puff. Alys. 5349

Blast, *sb.* Fragm. Sci. 190. Ps. cxlviii. 8

Blaze, *sb.* 1254 HD. AS. blǽse, blýsan

Blear, *v. n.* == become bleareyed. Rel. Ant. ii. p. 211

Bleat, *v. n.* Ps. lxiv. 14

Bled, blete, *sb.* == foliage. O. and N. 1040, 57. AS. blæd

Bleed, *v. n.* RG. 560

Bleike, *adj.* == pale. HD. 470. AS. blác. ON. bleikr

Blench, *sb.* == a trick? O. and N. 378. ON. blekkja

Blench, *v. n.* == avoid (a thing). O. and N. 170

——— == flinch from [blinche]. 2184 B.

——— == deceive. Ritson's AS. viii. 23

——— == give way? (of a ship) K. Horn, 1461. Another form of 'flinch.' AS. blinnan

Bleo, *sb.* == hue, complexion. O. and N. 152. Wright's L. P. p. 35. AS. bleo

Bless, *v. a.* RG. 406

Blessing, *sb.* RG. 421

Blete, *adj.* == bleak? O. and N. 616

Blete, *sb*. See Bled

Blike, *v. n.* == shine. Wright's L. P. p. 52 AS. blícan

Blinch. See Blench

Blind, *adj*. RG. 376, 407

—— *v. n.* == become blind. Rel. Ant, ii. p. 211

Blink, *sb*. 'to make blinks,' == deride a person. HD. 307. See Blench, sb.

Blin, *v. n.* == cease. RG. 566. pret. 'blenyte.' RG. 338. AS. blinnan

Bliss, *sb*. RG. 469

Blissful, *adj*. Wright's L. P. p. 52

Blissfully, *adv*. Ps. xcvi. 1

Blithe, *adj*. RG. 15

Blithely, *adv*. 89 β

Blitheful. Ps. cxi. 5

Blive, *adv*. == quickly. RG. 544. See Belive

Blode, *adj*. == pale, dried up. Rel. Ant ii. p. 210. Germ. blöde

Blood, *sb*. RG. 388, 416

Bloody, *adj*. RG. 304, 311

Bloom, *sb*. HD 63

Bloom, *v. n.* Ps. xxvii. 7

Blote, *adj*. == dried. Rel. Ant. ii. p 176

Bloute, *v. n.* == swell out? HD. 1910. ON. blautr. Eng. bloat

Blow, *v. a.* == as 'blow the fire.' HD. 385. Alys. 5030

—— *v. n.* pret. 'blew.' 524 β

Blow, *vb. n.* part. 'blowe,' == blown, in blossom. O. and N. 1634

Blowing, *sb*. 467 β

Blue, *adj*. [blo]. Wright's L. P. p. 86

Bo, == be. O. and N. 166, et passim. See Be

Bo, == both. *q. v.*

Boar, *sb*. RG. 133

Board, *sb*. == table. 122 β.; plank. Alys. 6415

Boast, *sb*. RG. 258. pomp. St Swithin, 43

Boast, *v. n.* Alys. 2597

Boasty, *adj*. == boastful. Fragm. Sci. 283

Bobance, *sb*. == boasting. Pol. S. 189 Fr. bobance

Bochevampe, (sic in MS.). == botched vamps or fronts of shoes. Rel. Ant. ii. p. 176

Bode, *sb.* == commandment. Ps. cxviii. 134, 128, et passim

Bode, *v. a.* == foretell. O. and N. 530

Boded ? Pol. S. 152

Boding, *sb.* RG. 416, 428

Bodeword, *sb.* == message. Ps. ii. 6

Body, *sb.* RG. 395, 547

Boffing, == swelling or puffing. RG. 414. Fr. buffer, to puff the cheeks

Boistous, *adj.* == coarse, rude. Alys. 5660. [boustes] Fragm. Sci. 273

Bold, *sb.* == a building. RG. 44. AS. bold

Bold, *v. a.* == embolden. Alys. 2468. [bald]. Ritson's AS. viii. 128

—— *adj.* RG. 383. 'bolder.' RG. 465

Boldhede, == boldness. O. and N. 514

Boldly, *adv.* RG. 500, 19

Boleax, *sb.* == large axe. Rel. Ant. ii. p. 176. ON. bolöxi

Bolken, *v. n.* == belch. Ps. cxliii. 13

Bollen, == swollen. Body and Soul, 31. 'ibolʒe.' O. and N. 145

Bolster, *sb.* Rel. S. v. 90

Bolt, *sb.* 'ʒoure bolt is sone ischote.' St Kath. 54

Bonde, *sb.* == bondman. Pol. S. 150

Bondman. RG. 370. HD. 32

Bone, *sb.* == os. RG. 446

Bone, *sb.* == prayer. RG. 14. AS. bén. SS. bone

Boned, [y-boned] == having bones. RG. 414

Bonére, *adj.* == debonair, graceful. Alys. 6732

Bonny, *adj.* Alys. 3903

Book, *sb.* RG. 374, 420

Boot, *sb.* == use, avail. Body and Soul, 92

—— == remedy, means (bote). RG. 277, 408. Pilate, 139

Booth, *sb.* Alys. 3457

Booze, *sb.* [bous] == drink. Wright's L. P. p. 111. Dutch, buysen

Booze, *v. n.* == drink. Rel. Ant. ii. p. 175

Bord, *sb.* == border. Alys. 1270

Borough, *sb.* [boru]. RG. 72

Borow, *v. a.* == defend. Wright's L. P. pp. 24, 25. part. 'iborȝe,' O. and N. 881

Borow, *sb.* == surety. RG. 472, 497

Borrow, *v. a.* RG. 393

Borstax, *sb.* == pick-axe. Pol. S. 151

Bosk, *sb.* == wood. RG. 547. Fr. bos, bosche

Boss, *sb.* == an ornament of dress. Pol. S. 154. Fr. bosse

Bote, *sb.* See Boot

Botemay, *sb.* == bitumen. Alys. 4763

Botfork, *sb.* == a crooked stick. Wright's L. P. p. 110

Both, *adj.* RG. 376, 445. 'both two.' Body and Soul, 120. [bo]. Wright's L. P. p. 58

Both, == are. See Be

In O. and N. 630, 633, the meaning of 'both' is uncertain; perhaps a mistake for 'doth'

Botheler, *sb.* == peasant, shepherd. Body and Soul, 144; from 'booth'?

Boting, *sb.* == recompense. Alys. 5711

Bough, *sb.* [bowe]. RG. 283. [boye], O. and N. 15

Bouk, *sb.* == body. Alys. 3946. [buc], O. and N. 1130. AS. búce. Germ. bauch

Bouked, *adj.* == protuberant. Alys. 6265

Boulder, *sb.* == a large stone. HD. 1790

Boun, *adj.* == ready. Wright's L. P. p. 100. Ritson's AS. viii. 149. ON. búinn.

Bound, *sb.* == boundary. Alys. 5593

Bouning, == making ready. Wright's L. P. p. 25

Bout, *sb.* == apparently some female ornament for the face. Pol. S. 154

Bow, *sb.* RG. 377, 541

Bow, *v. a.* == bend. pret. 'buyede.' RG. 475. 'beh.' Wright's L. P. p. 54. 'bed,' 2127 B.

—— *v. n.* == bow or bend. Wright's L. P. p. 70. AS. búgan.

Bowels, *sb.* Pol. S. 213. Alys. 4668. For the etymology of this word, see Phil. Soc. Trans. for 1856, p. 36

Bower, *sb.* HD. 2072. Wright's L. P. p. 114. AS. búr.

Bowermaiden, *sb.* == Rel. Ant. ii. p. 175

Bowiar, *sb.* == bow-maker. RG. 541

Bowl, *sb.* K. Horn, 1155

Bowman, *sb.* RG. 378

Bowshot, *sb.* Alys. 3491

Box, *sb.* RG. 456

Boy, *sb.* Pol. S. 237

Boy, == man. HD. 1899

Brag, *adj.* == boastful, bold. Wright's L. P. p. 24

Braid, *vb.* The following analysis of this difficult verb is taken from Egilson's Lex. Poet. Septent. s. v. bregða. All the senses here given are found in the O. Norse, while the AS. 'bredan' apparently is only used in those

43

marked with an asterisk.

* I. *act.* to weave, part. 'broiden.' O. and N. 645

II. *act.* to move a thing from its place. Hence,

α. to draw out, as a sword. HD. 1825. part. 'ybrad' == drawn, caught. Wright's L. P. p. 39

β. to brandish, as a sword or spear. Alys. 7373

γ. to pull down. RG. 22. [breide], Alys. 5856

* δ. to seize, or perhaps tear. Rel. S. v. 200. [brede]

III. *neut.* to change, as—

α. to awake out of sleep. HD. 1282

β. of any violent motion of body, as to leap. Body and Soul, 46

Braid, *sb.* ==

1. a quick motion, from III. β.; hence, 'at a breid' == in an instant. Body and Soul, 182. ON. bragð.

2. a violent struggle or wrench. RG. 22

Brain, *sb.* RG. 49, 446

Branch, *sb.* RG. 152

Brand, *sb.* == a burning mass. Body and Soul, 208

—— == torch. Alys. 5295. [brond]. AS. brand

—— == fire. Alys. 1856. [wilde bround]

Brased, *adj.* == of brass. Ps. cvi. 16

Brass, *sb.* RG. 2, 251

Bray, *sb.* == noise. Alys. 2175

Breach, *sb.* [bruch]. Wright's L. P. p. 30

Bread, *sb.* RG. 238

Breadth, *sb.* [brede]. RG. 385

Break, *v. a.* 47 B. part. 'i-broke' 1005 B.

—— *v. n.* pret. 'brake.' 2154 B.

—— == to break out (of flesh). 2421 B.

Breaking, *sb.* == breach, gap. Ps. cv. 23

Breast, *sb.* RG. 419

Breath, *sb.* Fragm. Sci. 203

Breathe, *v. n.* Fragm. Sci. 202

Breche, == beech? q. v.

Breech, *sb.* == rump. RG. 322

—— == breeches. 260 B.

Breed, *v. a.* (of a bird). 2 s. pres. 'breist.' O. and N. 1631. RG. 177. part. 'ibred' == brought up, educated. O. and N. 1722. Body and Soul, 81

Breed, *v. n.* == spring forth. Wright's L. P. p. 45

Breist, == breedest. See Breed

Breme, *adj.* == glorious, renowned. Wright's L. P. pp. 52, 32. AS. breme

—— == eager, lustful. O. and N. 202

Brenne, *sb.* == burning. HD. 1239

Breth, *sb.* == wrath. Ps. ii. 5; vi. 2. ON. brædi == anger

Breven, *v. a.* == write down. Pol. S. 156.

Brew, *v. a.* [browe]. RG. 26

Brewer, *sb.* Rel. S. vii. 35

Brewster, *sb.* Rel. Ant. ii. p. 176

Breȝe, *sb.* See Brow.

Breze, *sb.* == gadfly. Ps. civ. 34. AS. brimse

Briar, *sb.* RG. 331

Bridal, *sb.* Alys. 1071. K. Horn, 1064

Bride, *sb.* HD. 2131

Bridegroom, *sb.* [bridegome]. Ps. xviii. 6

Bride, *sb.* == bridle. Alys. 7626

Bridge, *sb.* RG. 399

Bridle, *sb.* RG. 396

Bright, *adj.* HD. 2131. Wright's L. P. p. 33

Brim, *sb.* == brink. 476 β

Brimstone, *sb.* Body and Soul, 219

Bring, *v. a.* RG. 379. pret. 'brought.' RG. 309. part. 'ybroȝt,' 'ibrouȝt.' RG. 376, 491

Brinie, *sb.* == cuirass. HD. 1775. Fr. brugne, brugnie. The root is 'brun' from 'brinnan,' to burn or shine; Cf. OHG. brunna

Brink, *sb.* Alys. 3491. K. Horn, 147

Brise, *v. a.* == bruise. HD. 1835

Bristle, *sb.* Alys. 6621

Bristled, *adj.* == having bristles. Alys. 5722

Britheling, == worthless, a rascal. Rel. S. vi. 11. Cf. O. Eng. 'brothell'

Brittene, == cut in pieces? HD. 2700. Cf. 'brittned,' in Gloss. to Ormulum. AS. bryttian

Broach, *sb.* (an ornament). RG. 489. Alys. 6842

Broad, *adj.* RG. 1. [brede], O. and N. 963

—— *v. a.* == make broad, part. 'ibroded.' O. and N. 1310

Broerh, *adj.* == brittle? Wright's L. P. p. 23

Brood, *sb.* RG. 70

Broodful, *adj.* Ps. cxliii. 13

Brook, *sb.* RG. 80

Broom, *sb.* (genista). Alys. 2492

Brost, *sb.* O. and N. 976, a mistake for 'prost,' i.e. 'priest.' The Jesus Coll. MS. reads 'preost'

Broth, *sb.* RG. 528

Brother, *sb.* RG. 371, 478

Brouke, *v. a.* == use, enjoy. HD. 311 AS. brúcan. Germ. brauchen

Brow, *sb.* Wright's L. P. p. 28. [bre3e]. Ib. p. 34

Brown, *adj.* RG. 429

—— *v. n.* == become brown. Alys. 3293

Brun, *sb.* == a brown jar. K. Horn, 1134

Brune, *sb.* == a burning. O. and N. 1153

Brust, *adj.* == rough, brusque. Pol. S. 151

Brut, *adj.* == rough? RG. 536

—— == bright. Body and Soul, 57

Bruthen, *adj.* == fierce, fiercely boiling, 'a bruthen led.' Rel. S. v. 242. Connected with 'breth,' and AS. brédan, to warm

Bu, *sb.* == buffalo. Alys. 5957

Bu, *vb.* See Buy

Buck, *sb.* Ritson's AS. iii. 8

—— == he-goat. Ps. xlix. 13

Buckle, *sb.* Wright's L. P. p. 35

Buckler, *sb.* Alys. 1190

Budel, *sb.* == messenger. O. and N. 1167. Wright's L. P. p. 22. AS. bydel

Bugging, *sb.* == a building, or lodging. Pol. S. 151. AS. byggan. ON. byggja

Bugle, *sb.* == buffalo. Alys. 5112

Buglehorn, *sb.* Alys. 5282

Build, *v. a.* RG. 439

Bulge, *sb.* == a lump, hump. Body and Soul, 185

Bulies, == bellows, q. v.

Bull, *sb.* (animal). RG. 116

Bull, (Pope's bull). RG. 473, 494

Bullock, *sb.* Ritson's AS. iii. 8

Bunting, *sb.* (the bird). Wright's L. P. p. 40

Burde, *sb.* == beard. Alys. 1164

Burdon, *sb.* == a pilgrim's staff. K. Horn, 1093. Fr. bourdon

Burel, *sb.* == sackcloth. Alys. 5475. Pol. S. 221. Fr. bure, burel. See Roq.

Burgess, *sb.* RG. 540, 541

Burial, *sb.* See Buryel

Burn, *v. a.* pret. 'barnde.' RG. 380, 511. 'brende.' RG. 536. part. pres. 'berninde.' RG. 534

Burn, *sb.* == rivulet. O. and N. 916. AS. byrnan, to burn. Cf. Lat. torrens, from torreo

Burst, *v. n.* pret. 'barst.' RG. 437

Burst, *sb.* == injury. Wright's L. P. p. 24. AS. byrst

Burthen, *sb.* HD. 807

Bury, *v. a.* RG. 123. part. 'y-bured.' RG. 382. AS. byrgan

Burying, *sb.* RG. 382. [beryng]. Alys. 4624

Buryels, *sb.* == a tomb, grave. RG. 204. AS. byrgels

Busemere, == blasphemy. See Bismere

Busily, *adv.* Ps. cxlii. 7

Busk, *v. a.* == array. Pol. S. 239

Busy, *adj.* Alys. 3906

But, *adv.* 43 B.

But, *prep.* == except [bote]. RG. 382. [butent]. Rel. S. ii. 25

——— == without [bute]. O. and N. 184. AS. bútan

But, *sb.* == a put, i.e. cast or throw, HD. 1040

But, *part.* == contended. HD. 1916. Fr. bouter

Butcher, *sb.* Pol. S. 192

Bute, *prep.* See But

Butler, *sb.* RG. 187, 438

Butte, *sb.* == a fish, probably a turbot. HD. 759. The Prompt. Parv. translates it by 'pecten;' the Pictorial Vocab., published by Mr Wright, p. 254, has 'hic turbo' == 'a but.' See N. and Q. 2d S. vi. 382. Sw. butta

Butter, *sb.* HD. 643

Button, *sb.* Pol. S. 239

—— *v. n.* == break out. St Swithin, 151. Fr. boutonner. Cotgr.

Buxomness, *sb.* == obedience. RG. 234, 318. AS. buhsomnes, from 'bugan,' to bow

Buy, *v. a.* [biggen]. Moral Ode, st. 33. [buggen]. O. and N. 1366. pret. 'bouȝte.' RG. 379, 496. 'bu,' imper. RG. 390

—— == to exact atonement for. K. Horn, 912

—— == redeem. Ps. xxv. 11

Buyer, *sb.* == redeemer. Ps. xviii. 15

Buzzard, *sb.* Alys. 3049

By, *prep.* == beside (of place). 1213 B. 'Nolde God that ich bi thé sete'

—— == according to. 169 B. 'bi his rede.'

—— == during (of time). 649 B. 'bi myn ancestors daye.' 2498 B. 'bi a Tuesdai'

—— == against. 871 B. 'bi the Bischop of L. thulke word he sede.' Cf. 1 Cor. iv. 4

—— == concerning, of. O. and N. 46

By. For verbs compounded with 'By,' see under 'Bi'

Bycase, *adv.* == by chance. RG. 490

Byefþe. See Behoof

Byquide. See Bequest

Byȝyte. See Beget

C.

Cable, *sb.* RG. 148

Cacherel, *sb.* == catch poll. Pol. S. 151

Cage, *sb.* Alys. 5011

Caitiff, *sb.* Body and Soul, 229

Cake, *sb.* Cok. 55

Cales, *sb.* == a kind of serpent. Alys. 7094

Calf, *sb.* (the animal). Alys. 6351

Call, *v. n.* Wright's L. P. p. 59

Call, *sb.* == cap worn on the head. Pol. S. 158. Fr. cale

Caluȝ, *adj.* == bald. Alys. 5950. AS. calo, caluw

Camel, *sb.* Alys. 854

Can, *vb.* == am able [con]. Wright's L. P. p. 82. [cunne]. 2 s. pres. 'cost.' Wright's L. P. p. 91. O. and N. 47. pret. 'cowþe.' RG. 29

—— == know [con]. RG. 443. [cunne]. O. and N. 48. 2 s. pres. 'canst.' O. and N. 560

Candle, *sb.* RG. 290, 561

Candlemas, *sb.* St Dunstan, 3

Canel, *sb.* == cinnamon. Wright's L. P. p. 27. Fr canelle. Lat. canna

Cankerfret, *adj.* RG. 299

Canon, *sb.* RG. 510

Capel, *sb.* == horse, nag. Cok. 32. Lat. caballus

Capelclawer, *sb.* == horse-scrubber. Pol. S. 239

Capital, *sb.* (of a column). Cok. 67

Carbuncle, *sb.* Alys. 5252. HD. 2145

Cardinal, *sb.* 1280 B.

Care, *sb.* RG. 457

Care, *v. n.* == be anxious. RG. 71. Wright's L. P. p. 54

Careful, *adj.* == full of care. 639 B.

Carie, *sb.* == carat. Alys. 6695

Carke, *v. n.* == pine away. Wright's L. P. p. 54

Carol, *sb.* RG. 53

Carol, *v. n.* Alys. 196, 1045

Caronye, *sb.* == carcass. RG. 265

Carp, *v. n.* == complain. Pol. S. 149

Carpenter, *sb.* RG. 537

Carrion, *sb.* (caraing). Pol. S. 203

Cart, *sb.* RG. 189

Cartload, *sb.* HD. 895

Cartstave, *sb.* RG. 99

Carve, *v. a.* RG. 560. == cut, flay. part. 'corven.' Wright's L. P. p. 35. 'curven.' HD. 189

Case, *sb.* == chance, event. RG. 528

—— == condition. Alys. 4428

Cast, *v. a.* RG. 511, 375

Castle, *sb.* RG. 371, 510; pl. 'kasteles' == tents. Ps. lxxvii. 28

Cat, *sb.* Alys. 5275

Catathleba (κατώβλεπας), == a noxious monster, mentioned in Alys. 6564. See Pliny, H. N. viii. 32

Catch, *v. a.* RG. 28. pret. 'caught.' RG. 375. part. 'cacchynge.' RG. 265

Cathedral, *adj.* RG. 282

Caudle, *sb.* RG. 561

Cauldron, *sb.* 158 β

Caution, *sb.* == surety. RG. 506

—— == quarter in battle. Alys. 2811

Cavenard, *sb.* == villain. HD. 2389. The form 'caynard' is found in Wright's L. P. p. 110. Fr. caignard. Cotgr.

Cayre, *v. a.* == turn. part. 'ycayred.' Wright's L. P. p. 37. AS. cerran. Germ. kehren

Caynard. See Cavenard

Cayser, *sb.* == emperor. HD. 1317. Wright's L. P. p. 32

Cayvar, *adj.* == hollow? Alys. 6062

Cedar, *sb.* Ps. ciii. 16

Cel, *sb.* == seal. RG. 77

Celadoyne, *sb.* See Celandine

Celandine, *sb.* == the flower. Wright's L. P. p. 26. Lat. chelidonium. It is the 'ranunculus ficaria' of botanists

Cell, *sb.* RG. 233

Cellar, *sb*. 287 B.

Cement, *sb*. Alys. 6177

Censer, *sb*. Marg. 75

Cerge, *sb*. == a taper. HD. 594. ON. kérti. Germ. kerze

Cert, *adv*. == certainly. Alys. 5803

Certain, *adj*. == fixed, ascertained. RG. 378, 552

Certés, *adv*. 898 B.

Cestred, == lodged, concealed. Ps. lxxiii. 20; cxxxviii. 12. AS. ceaster

Chaffare, *sb*. == merchandise. RG. 539. AS. ceápian

Chair, *sb*. RG. 321

Chaisel, *sb*. == a woman's upper garment. Alys. 279. 'espéce de vétement.' Roq. *s. v.* SS. cheisil. Fr. cheinsil, *v.* Roq. *s. v.* chainse, and Gloss. Rem. to La3. iii. 502

Chalandre, *sb*. == goldfinch. Cok. 95

Chalcedony, *sb*. Cok. 92

Chalen, *sb*. == chill, cold. Alys. 4834

Chalice, *sb*. RG. 489. HD. 187

Chalktrap, *sb*. == pit or snare. Alys. 6070

Challenge, *v. a.* RG. 279, 451

Chamber, *sb*. 452 B.

Chamberlain. RG. 390, 490

Champion, *sb*. HD. 1015

Chance, *sb*. == condition, fortune. RG. 465

——— == chance [cheance]. RG. 210

Chancellor, *sb*. RG. 540, 468

Chancellory, *sb*. == office of chancellor. 452 B.

Chane, *vb. pret.* == cleft. Alys. 2228. AS. cínan. perf. cán. The 'ch' appears in 'tochan,' the pret. of 'tocínan,' in La3amon, ii. 468. Weber wrongly derives the word from Fr. choir, and makes it mean 'fell'

Change, *sb*. RG. 493

Change, *vb. a.* RG. 548

Chantment, *sb*. == enchantment. RG. 28, 149

Chapel, *sb*. RG. 472, 473

Chapitle, *sb*. == chapter of a cathedral RG. 473

Chaplain, *sb*. 961 B.

Chapman, *sb.* RG. 539

Chapter, *sb.* (of a cathedral). 601 B.

Char, *sb.* == turn, movement. Body and Soul, 79. Hence 'ʒeynchar' == repentance. Wright's L. P. p. 46. SS. charren. AS. cérran, cérre. Germ. kehren

Charge, *v. a.* == load. RG. 13. part. 'icharged.' Pol. S. 195

—— *sb.* == load, weight. RG. 416

—— == expense. RG. 189

Charity, *sb.* Pol. S. 202. 'par charité.' 1811 B.

Charm, *sb.* == spell. Alys. 81

Charming, *sb.* == spell. Alys. 404

Charreye, *sb.* == car. Alys. 5097

Charter, *sb.* RG. 477, 498

Chase, *sb.* == hunting. RG. 6

Chaste, *adj.* 154 B.; [cheste]. Alys. 7050. 'chaster.' RG. 191

Chaste, *v. a.* == chastise. RG. 134

Chastise, *v. a.* RG. 420

Chasuble, *sb.* == priest's robe. 953 B. Fr. casule. Ital. casupola

Chasur, *sb.* == horse for hunting. Signa ante Jud. 110. Fr. chaceor

Chaterestre, *sb.* == a female chatterer. O. and N. 655

Chattels, *sb.* [chateus]. RG. 471, 569. Another form of 'cattle'

Chattering, *sb.* O. and N. 744

Chaumpebataile, *sb.* == battle-field. Alys. 5553

Chavling, *sb.* == jawing. O. and N. 284, 296

Chawl, *sb.* == jaw. Body and Soul, 189. Pol. S. 154. AS. ceafl. SS. chevele. pl. chæfles

Chawl, *v. n.* == to chide, jaw. Pol. S. 240

Cheap, *sb.* == haggling? Wright's L. P. p. 39

Cheap, *v. a.* == buy. Pol. S. 159. AS. ceápian

Cheaping, *sb.* == market. Pol. S. 151

Cheek, *sb.* Wright's L. P. p. 34

Cheer, *sb.* == comfort. 473 B.

—— == countenance. RG. 332

Cheese, *sb.* HD. 643

Chelde, *sb*. == chill, cold. Alys. 5501

Cheole, *sb*. == hair. M. Ode, 182. Fr. chevol

Chepe, Cheping. See Cheap, Cheaping

Chequer, *sb*. == chess. RG. 192; or perhaps 'the chessboard'

Cherde, *vb. pret.* == turned, came. O. and N. 1656. AS. cyrran, cérran

Chere, *adj.* == high? 'the chere men of the land.' RG. 166.

Cheson, *sb*. == occasion. Alys. 3930

Chess, *sb*. Alys. 2096

Chest, *sb*. == coffin. RG. 50

Cheste, *sb*. == strife. Alys. 29. AS. ceást

Chete, == a chewet, or pie. Wright's L. P. p. 31

Cheui, an error for 'cheve.' RG. 94

Cheve, *v. n.* == succeed in a thing. 856 B. Fr. chevir

Chide, *v. a.* 2 s. pres. 'chist.' O. and N. 1329. AS. cídan

—— *v. n.* RG. 390

—— == dispute. O. and N. 287

Chief, *sb*. == chieftain. 1003 B.

Chief, *adj.* == 'to hold in chief,' a law term, applied to those tenants who held their fiefs direct from the king; 'tenants in capite.' RG. 472

—— == principal. St Swithin, 22

Chieftain, *sb*. [cheventeyn]. RG. 386, 400

Chilce, *sb*. == childishness? M. Ode, 4. Formed from 'child,' as 'milce' from 'mild'

Child, *sb*. RG. 392, 441; [chil]. O. and N. 1438

Child, *v. n.* == bring forth a child. Alys. 604

Childbed, *sb*. RG. 379

Childering, *sb*. == bringing forth a child. Rel. S. ii. 7

Chill, *sb*. RG. 7

Chimbe, *sb*. == cymbal. Ps. cl. 5

Chime, *sb*. (of bells). Alys. 1852. Dan. kime

Chin, *sb*. 522 β

Chinche, *adj.* == niggardly. HD. 1763. Fr. chice == avarice

Chirchegong, == churchgoing. RG. 380. Cf. 'idelgong'

Chirm, *sb*. == chirping and screaming of birds. O. and N. 305. AS. cyrm

Chirurgeon, *sb.* RG. 566

Chivalry, *sb.* == prowess. RG. 413

Chivauché, *sb.* == an expedition, a body of men. Ritson's AS. viii. 141. Fr. chevauchée, from cheval.

Choice, *sb.* RG. 111

Chokering, *sb.* == a low chattering. O. and N. 504

Cholle, == shall. RG. 379, in the compound form 'ycholle'

Choose, *v. a.* RG. 400. pret. 'ches.' Marg. 2. part, 'chis.' Alys. 3294. 'ichose.' RG. 472

———— *v. n.* == have a choice. RG. 384

Christ, *sb.* == anointed person. Ps. civ. 15

Christen, *v. a.* part, 'icristened.' St Kath. 136

Christendom, *sb.* == sacraments belonging to Christianity. RG. 496

Christian, *adj.* 7 B.

Christmas, *sb.* 1932 B

Chrysolite, *sb.* Alys. 5682

Churl, *sb.* HD. 682. AS. ceorl

Church, *sb.* RG. 369, 381

Churchyard, *sb.* 2234 B.

Ciclaton, *sb.* == a rich stuff from India. Alys. 1964. Fr. ciglaton. Lat. cyclas

Cinqueports, *sb.* == the five havens of Dover, Sandwich, Romney, Hyde, Hastings. RG. 515

Citation, *sb.* == a summoning into court. RG. 473

City, *sb.* RG. 380; used adjectively as 'a city town.' Alys. 7543

Clack, *v. n.* == make a noise. O. and N. 81. AS. cloccan

Clad, *part.* == clothed. HD. 1354. AS. gecladed

Claht, == adhered, cleaved? Wright's L. P. p. 37

Clap, *v. a.* == strike. HD. 1821

Clarré, *sb.* == a kind of wine (claret?). HD. 1728

Clasp, *sb.* Pol. S. 222

Clastre, *v. n.* == to clatter. Pol. S. 157

Claw, *sb.* Body and Soul, 186. pl. 'clen,' Marg. 46. 'clees,' Ps. lxviii. 32. AS. clea

Clawed, *adj.* == having claws. Alys. 4969

54

Clay, *sb.* Wright's L. P. p. 85

Clay, *adj.* Rel. S. v. 73

Clean, *adj.* RG. 374

Cleanly, *adv.* RG. 434

Cleanness, *sb.* RG. 411, 434

Cleanse, *v. a.* [clansi]. O. and N. 610. Ps. l. 4. part, 'ycleansed.' RG. 43.

Cleansing, *sb.* Ps. lxxxviii. 45

Clear, *adj.* 1097 B.

Clearly, *adv.* 442 β

Cleave, *v. a.* == split. HD. 917. pret. 'clewyd' == cleft. Alys. 3790. 3 pl. 'clowen,' ib. 2765. AS. clúfan

—— *v. n.* == adhere to. HD. 1300. AS. clífan

Clench, *v. a.* == pinch, wither up. O. and N. 1204; the modern 'cling.' Compare Shakspere's 'Till famine *cling* thee.' Macb. v. 5 AS. clingan

Clench, *v. a.* == strike (as a harp). K. Horn, 1532

Clenyen. See Cling

Clergy, *sb.* == order of clergymen. RG. 563, 420

Clerk, *sb.* RG. 471, 472, 496

—— *adj.* == learned. St Kath. 4

Cleten ? K. Horn, 1433; probably a mistake for 'clenten' == clung

Cleve, *sb.* == cottage. HD. 557; a room, chamber. Ps. iv. 5. AS. cleafa. ON. klefi

Cliff, *sb.* Ps. cxiii. 8

Climb, *v. n.* RG. 410, 527. pret. 'clam.' RG. 333

Cling, *v. n.* Wright's L. P. p. 85. Alys. 2903; [clenyen], Wright's L. P. p. 37

Cling, *v. n.* == wither. Rel. Ant. ii. p. 211. Pilate, 215. AS. clingan

Clinglich, == cleanly? Cok. 15

Clink, *v. a.* == make to sound. Pol. S. 189

Clip, *v. a.* == embrace. RG. 14. [cluppede] 288 B. [clupte]. AS. clyppan

Clipie, *v. a.* == call. 472 B.; [clipen]. 1182 B.; [clupe]. RG. 410. pret. 'clepude.' RG. 10. part. 'yclepud.' RG. 10. AS. clypian

Clivers, *sb.* == claws, talons. O. and N. 78. AS. clîfrian, to scratch

Clod, Clot, *sb.* (of earth). Rel. S. v. 73; [clut]. O. and N. 1165

Clog, *sb.* == a sort of female ornament. Pol. S. 154

Cloister, *sb.* 2089 B

Close, *v. a.* == enclose. HD. 1310

—— == shut. RG. 566

Close, *sb.* RG. 7

Cloth, *sb.* RG. 7, 389 (523 β). == clothing. Cok. 29

'Clothes,' pl. == garments. RG. 566. HD. 586

Clothe, *v. a.* RG. 557

Clothing, *sb.* == garment. Ps. ci. 27

Cloud, *sb.* HD. 207. 1415 B.

Clout, *sb.* Alys. 4459

Clowe, *sb.* == clew, small ball. O. and N. 178. AS. clíwe

Club, *sb.* HD. 1927

Clude, *sb.* == rock, hill. O. and N. 999. AS. clúd

Clupe, *sb.* See Clipie

Clutch, *sb.* == claw. Body and Soul, 183

—— *v. n.* Rel. Ant. ii. p 211

Coal, *sb.* Ps. xvii. 9

Coalblack, *adj.* O. and N. 75

Coat, *sb.* HD. 1141

Cocle, *sb.* == war. Ps. cxliii. 1. See Cock. *vb.*

Cock, *sb.* (animal). 1090 B.

Cock, *sb.* == cockboat? HD. 873

Cock, *v. n.* == cut? Pol. S. 153; or contend? Cf. Cocle, ubi sup. AS. cocor, a sword

Cod, *sb.* == codpiece, or scrotum? O. and N. 1122

Coffer, *sb.* 1925 B.

Cog, *sb.* ? O. and N. 86

Coinoun, *sb.* == robber. Alys. 1718. [konioun]. Ib. 7748

Cokedrill, *sb.* See Crocodile

Cold, *adj.* RG. 1. Wright's L. P. p. 24

—— == cruel. RG. 131

Cold, *sb.* HD. 416

Colfer, *sb.* == dove. RG. 190. AS. culfre

Collar, *sb.* == neck. RG. 223

Collation, *sb.* == feast. Cok. 143

Colle, *sb.* == collar. Pol. S. 157

Colmie, *adj.* for 'collie.' == black, coaly. K. Horn, 1114

Colour, *sb.* == hue. RG. 24

——— == pretext. RG. 313

Colt, *sb.* Alys. 684. AS. colt

Columbine, *sb.* (the flower). Wright's L. P. p. 26. The 'aquilegia vulgaris' of botanists

Comb, *sb.* [kambe]. == honeycomb. Ps. xviii. 11

Come, *v. n.* pret. 'come.' RG. 367. part. 'icumen.' Ritson's AS. iv. 1

——— == become, suit. Leg. of St Cuthbert cited in Warton, H. E. P. vol. i. p. 14, n.

Come, *sb.* == coming. Creed of St Athan. 79

Comely, *adj.* Alys. 6055

Comet, *sb.* RG. 416, 548

Comfort, *v. a.* RG. 139

Coming, *sb.* Alys. 5541

Commandment, *sb.* 2022 B.

Common, *adj.* 'common right.' RG. 500. 'the common bell.' RG. 541

Common, *sb.* == the commons, plebs. Pol. S. 188

——— == 'commons,' i.e. food. RG. 528

Commonalty, *sb.* 1302 B.

Commonly, *adv.* == all in common, universally. Fall and P. 46

Commune, *v. n.* RG. 571

Companage, *sb.* == sustenance. Pol. S. 240

Companion, *sb.* RG 552

Company, *sb.* == band of men. RG. 544, 370

Compass, *v. a.* == seek after a thing by design. Pol. S. 202. part. 'ycompassed.' RG. 109

Compassment, *sb.* Alys. 1345

Compline, *sb.* == the last service in the day. 2090 B. Fr. complie

Con, *v. a.* == know. pret. 'couthe.' RG. 559; 'kuthe.' O. and N. 663; part. 'cud.' Wright's L. P. p. 27.

Con, *v. a.* == acknowledge, [kan]. HD. 160. 'to kan thank'

Conceive, *v. n.* == bear oneself, behave. Alys. 2204

Concubine, *sb.* RG. 27

Conduct, *sb.* == guidance. RG. 40

Coney, *sb.* [cunig]. M. Ode, 182

Conferment, *sb.* == confirmation. RG. 349

Confessor, *sb.* 2341 B.

Confirm, *v. a.* RG. 440, 446

Confirming, *sb.* RG. 277

Conger, *sb.* Rel. Ant. ii. p. 174

Conjure, *v. a.* == adjure a person to do a thing. 2330 B.

Conjurison, *sb.* == sorcery. Alys. 81

Conscience, *sb.* 426 β

Consent, *v. n.* RG. 526

Consistory, *sb.* [constory]. Pol. S. 159

Consonant, *sb.* Rel. Ant. ii. p. 174

Constable, *sb.* RG. 538

Contek, *sb.* == strife. RG. 470, 509. Fr. contencer

—— *v. n.* == to strive. RG. 259

Contecker, *sb.* == a striver. 196 B.

Convent, *sb.* RG. 433

—— == the body of people in the convent. 225 B.

Cook, *sb.* HD. 903

Coot, *sb.* [cote]. Body and Soul, 201

Cop, *sb.* == head. Pol. S. 70. Rel. Ant. i. 144. AS. copp.

Cope, *sb.* RG. 566. HD. 429

Copener, *sb.* == paramour. O. and N. 1340. AS. copenere

Coral, *sb.* Wright's L. P. p. 25

Cord, *sb.* St Andrew, 66

Corn, *sb.* RG. 13, 372

Cornel, *sb.* == embrasure. Alys. 7210

Corour, *sb.* == courser. Alys. 2475

Corporas, *sb.* == a cloth on which the elements were laid at the Eucharist. HD. 188

Corpse, *sb.* RG. 145

Corrin, *sb.* == a churn, or vessel? Rel. Ant. ii. p. 175. AS. cyrin

Cost, *sb.* == expenditure. RG. 297; expense. RG. 183

—— *vb. a.* pret. 'costenede.' RG. 390

Cost, == couldest or canst. See Can

Costage, *sb.* == a sum of money deposited by way of surety. RG. 391

Cot, *sb.* == cottage. Pol. S. 152

Coufle, *sb.* == a basket. RG. 265. AS. cowel, cawl

Could, *vb.* See Can

Coulter, *sb.* == ploughshare. Pol. S. 152. Lat. culter

Council, *sb.* RG. 495

Councillor, *sb.* RG. 417

Counsel, *sb.* RG. 412, 371

Counsel, *v. n.* == take counsel, consider. RG. 91

—— *v. a.* == give counsel. Wright's L. P. p. 95

Counseller, *sb.* Alys. 7118

Count, *sb.* == account. Pol. S. 152

Countenance, *sb.* == appearance, demeanour. 187 B.

—— == courage. Pol. S. 216

Counter, *sb.* == reckoner. RG. 538

Countess, *sb.* RG. 370, 510

Country, RG. 368, 510

County, [countene] *sb.* Pol. S. 157

Coupe, *v. n.* == buy or aby? HD. 1800. ON. kaupa

Courageous, *adj.* RG. 453

Courant, == running. Alys. 3461

Couren. See Cower

Courser, *sb.* == steed. Alys. 4056

Court, *sb.* == courtyard. RG. 525

—— == of a king. 165 B.

—— == of law. RG. 471

—— == courtesy—to 'pay court.' 204 B.

Courteous, *adj.* RG. 385, 525

Courtesy, *sb.* RG. 189, 516

Couth, *adj.* == known. RG. 514, 455. AS. cuð

Couthe, *v. a.* == make known. O. and N. 90. pret. 'ykud.' RG. 57. AS. cýðan

Couwe, *v. n.* == cower? Rel. Ant. ii. p. 211

Cove, *adv.* == quickly. O. and N. 379. AS. cóf

Covel, *sb.* == coat. HD. 547. AS. cufle == cowl

Covenant, *sb.* RG. 179

Cover, *v. a.* == recover. RG. 49

—— == take care of [coverye]. Alys. 7533

Coverture, *sb.* == bedclothes. K. Horn, 716

Covet, *v. a.* RG. 306

Covetise, *sb.* RG. 46

Covetous, *adj.* Fragm. on Seven Sins, 23

Cow, *sb.* Alys. 6333. pl. 'kye.' Ps. lxvii. 31

Coward, *adj.* RG. 455. Fr. coard

—— *v. a.* == dishearten, make fearful. Alys. 3344

—— *sb.* Alys. 2053

Cower, *v. n.* Alys. 2053. 'couren,' == cowering. Pol. S. 157

Cowl, *sb.* 2246 B. AS. cufle

Crab, *sb.* Alys. 4943

Crack, *v. a.* == break in two. HD. 568

—— == discourse, 'reisons craken.' Alys. 6991. Cf. our Engl, 'to crack jokes'

Crack, *v. n.* == snap short. Alys. 4436

Cradle, *sb.* RG. 107

Craft, *sb.* == art. O. and N. 757; skill. Wright's L. P. p. 35

Craftfully, *adv.* Rel. Ant. ii p. 176

Craftilich, *adj.* Rel. Ant. ii. p. 175

Cram, *v. a.* Pol. S. 238

Cramp, *v. a.* [crempe] == interrupt, stop. O. and N. 1786

Crane, *sb.* HD. 1726

Crave, *v. a.* HD. 633. part, 'cravand.' Ps. cxviii. 121

Craver, *sb.* Ps. lxxi. 4

Craving, *sb.* == desire. Ps. cxviii. 134

Creator, *sb.* Fall and P. 51

Creature, *sb.* 2255 B

Creed, *sb.* Pol. S. 204

Creek, *sb.* [krike] == creek of the sea. HD. 708. AS. creeca

Creep, *v. n.* RG. 296; part, 'crepand.' Ps. lxviii. 35

Crice, *sb.* == rima podicis. HD. 2450

Crices, in the phrase 'Nai crices.' St Andrew, 31. This is evidently an interjection, and may possibly be the same as our vulgar 'crikey'

Crisp, *adj.* Fragm. Sci. 282

Crocodile, *sb.* [cokedrill], Alys. 5720

Croke, *sb.* == bend double. Rel. Ant. ii p. 211

Croll, *sb.* == curly. Alys. 1999. Dut. krol

Crook, *v. a.* == distort. Marg. 53

Crook, *sb.* == wile. Wright's L. P. p. 105. Alys. 4819

Crooked, *adj.* Alys. 7099. Fragm. Sci. 326. part, 'icroked.' O. and N. 1674

Crop, *sb.* == belly. Pol. S. 208. AS. cropp

———— == produce of a plant. Wright's L. P. p. 100

Cross, *sb.* [croys], RG. 392

Cross, *v. a.* == mark with the cross [croice]. RG. 480

Crosslet, *sb.* == piece of armour [croisliʒte]. K. Horn, 1353

Croude, *v. a.* == press down, keep back. Alys. 609. AS. crydan

Croud, *part.* == crowded, oppressed? HD. 2338

Croupe, *sb.* == crupper. Alys. 2447

Crouthe, *sb.* == fiddle. Wright's L. P. p. 53

Crow, *sb.* == the bird. RG. 490

Crow, *sb.* == cockcrow. 1090 B.

Crow, *v. n.* Pol. S. 238. O. and N. 336

Crown, *sb.* RG. 376

Crown, == top of the head. HD. 568

Crown, *v. a.* RG. 383. part. 'ycrouned.' ibid.

Crowning, *sb.* RG. 367. HD. 2948

Crownment, *sb.* RG. 433

Croyserie, **Creyserie**, *sb.* == crusade. RG. 346, 502

Crude, *v. a.* == creak? K. Horn, 1333

Cruel, *adj.* RG. 417

Cruets, *sb.* 313 β. Fr. cruche

Crupper, *sb.* (of a saddle). Alys. 3421

Crus, *adj.* == wrathful. HD. 1966. Fr. cruz. See Hall. *s. v.* Crous

Crust, *sb.* Pol. S. 204

Cry, *v. n.* RG. 381, 495

Cry, *sb.* Alys. 5410. HD. 2772. Ps. ci. 2

Crystal, *sb.* Fragm. Sci. 66

Cubur, *sb.* == cover. Alys. 2359

Cuckingstool, *sb.* Rel. Ant. ii. p. 176

Cuckold, *sb.* == O. and N. 1592. Fr. cocul

Cuckoo, *sb.* Ritson's AS. iii. 2

Cucube, *sb.* == cubeb. Cok. 76

Cumberment, *sb.* Alys. 472

Cummin, *sb.* Alys. 6797

Cumrade, == relation. See Kindred

Cundut, *sb.* == religious service. O. and N. 483. Fr. conduis

Cunig, == coney, *q. v.*

Cunne, *vb.* See Can

Cup, *sb.* RG. 117

Cure, *sb.* (of souls). 857 B.

Curne, *v. a.* == form grains, ripen (said of corn). RG. 490

Curreye, *sb.* == waggon-train. Alys. 5118

Curse, *v. a.* 550 β

Curtain, *v. a.* Alys. 1028

Curven. See Carve

Cusse, *v. a.* == kiss. *q. v.*

Cust, *sb.* == dignity. O. and N. 9. AS. cyst

—— == choice. O. and N. 1396. AS. cýst

Custom, *sb.* RG. 470

Cut, *v. a.* [citte]. HD. 942. part, 'ykyt.' Alys. 2709

—— == destiny, remove. Ps. cxviii. 39

Cypress, *sb.* Alys. 5785

Cytoling, *sb.* == playing on the 'cytol' or guitar. Alys. 1043

D.

Dab, *v. a.* == strike. Pol. S. 192

Dab, *sb.* == a blow. Alys. 2306

Dahet, *sb.* == a curse. O. and N. 99. See Datheit

Dainty, *sb.* 1202 B. Fr. dain. Cotgr. W. dantaeth

—— == daintiness [deynté], Alys. 7070

—— == fondness [deynté]. St Dunstan.

Dais, *sb.* == a raised seat. RG. 536. Alys. 1039

Daisy, *sb.* [dayes-eʒe]. Wright's L. P. p. 43

Dale, *sb.* RG. 362

Damage, *sb.* Alys. 959

Dame, *sb.* RG. 560

Damn, *v. a.* == judge. Wright's L. P. p. 100

Damsel, *sb.* RG. 432

Dance, *v. n.* Alys. 5213

—— *sb.* Alys. 6990

Danger, *sb.* RG. 78

Dangerous, *adj.* Rel. Ant. i. 115

Dank, *v. a.* == make wet [donke]. Wright's L. P. p. 44. 'Dank' is probably another form of 'damp.' Cf. 'dimple' and 'dingle'

Dar, *vb. impers.* == it needs. RG. 317. See Thar

Dare, *v. n.* 'durre.' O. and N. 1704. pret. 'dorste.' RG. 367

—— *v. n.* == stare, gaze. Wright's L. P. pp. 50, 54. O. and N. 384. See note to Prompt. Parv. *s. v.* 'daryn'

Dark, *adj.* RG. 560

Dark, *v. a.* == darken. part. 'idurked.' 1416 B.

Darkhood, *sb.* [derkhede] == darkness. RG. 560

Darling, *sb.* 56 β

Dash, *v. a.* RG. 51, 540. ON. daska

—— *v. n.* == burst in. Alys. 2837

Datheit, *adj.* == cursed. HD. 296. Fr. dehait (haïr)

Daughter, *sb.* RG. 368, 509

Dawn, *sb.* [dawing]. RG. 208

Dawn, *v. n.* [dawe]. Pol. S. 238. Wright's L. P. p. 45; [dawen]. Ib. p. 96; [dagen]. Fragm. in Warton H. E. P. p. 21

Dawning, *sb.* == dawn. RG. 557

Day, *sb.* RG. 505, 368; 'bi hys daye' == 'in his time.' RG. 376; pl. 'dawes.' RG. 383; 'to bring out of dawe,' == put to death. 622 B.; 'daies,' *gen. abs.* == in the daytime. O. and N. 1588

Dayred, *sb.* == dawn. Rel. S. iv. 17

Dayrim, *sb.* == break of day. O. and N. 328

Dayspring, *sb.* Alys. 4290

Daystar, *sb.* O. and N. 328

Daystern, *sb.* == daystar. Ps. cix. 3

Dead, *adj.* 1826 B.

Deadly, *adj.* RG. 195. == dead. Ps. xliii. 2

Deaf, *adj.* RG. 352

Deal, *sb.* == part. RG. 368, 509

Deal, *v. a.* == 'distribute to.' RG. 383; 'scatter,' as to 'deal words.' O. and N. 952; 'give.' Pol. S. 204

Dealing, *sb.* == a part, Ps. cxxxv. 13

Dealtakand, *sb.* == participator. Ps. cxviii. 63

Dealtaking, *sb.* == participation. Ps. cxxi. 3

Dear, *adj.* == precious. RG. 390

Dearworth, *adj.* == precious. Wright's L. P. p. 52

Dearworthly, *adv.* Wright's L. P. p. 54

Dearth, *sb.* [dere]. RG. 416

Death, *sb.* RG. 375, 382; 'deathes,' *gen. abs.* == 'dead,' or 'in death.' O. and N. 1630

Debonair, *adj.* RG. 167, 374

Debruise, *v. a.* RG. 410, 529, 537. Fr. debriser

Debt, *sb.* RG. 473

Deceit, *sb.* Alys. 7705

Decline, *sb.* == decay. Pol. S. 154

Dedayn. See Disdain

Deduit, *sb.* == pleasure. RG. 564

Deed, *sb.* RG. 369, 501

Deem, *v. a.* == condemn. RG. 504

—— == judge. O. and N. 188

Deemer, *sb.* == a judge. Ps. vii. 12

Deep, *adj.* RG. 6, 233

Deeply, *adv.* HD. 1417

Deepness, *sb.* Ps. xxxv. 7

Deer, *sb.* == beast [deor, duer]. Wright's L. P. pp. 44, 45; [dor]. O. and N. 1321, 493

—— == stags, &c. RG. 439

Default, *sb.* RG. 456, 457

Defence, *sb.* RG. 214

Defend, *v. a.* == guard, protect. RG. 536, 542

Defensible. RG. 549

Defiance, *sb.* Alys. 5545, written 'defence' in Alys. 7237

Defoul, *v. a.* RG. 536

Defy, *v. a.* Alys. 7014

Deign, *v. n.* RG. 557

Del. See Devil

Delay, *sb.* RG. 156, 421

Delay, *v. a.* RG. 495

Delice, *sb.* RG. 195

Delicious, *adj.* Alys. 38

Delight, *v. a.* Alys. 5802

Delightable, *adj.* 26 β

Deliver, *v. a.* RG. 430, 382, 524

Delve, *v. n.* == dig. pret. 'dolve,' RG. 395. AS. delfan

Demain, *v. a.* == manage. Alys. 603. Fr. démener

Demand, *sb.* RG. 500

Demay, *v. a.* == dismay. RG. 156

Demember, *v. a.* == dismember. RG. 559

Demere, *v. n.* == tarry. Alys. 7295. Fr. demeurer

Demorance, *sb.* == delay. Alys. 4123

Den, *sb.* Alys. 5400. AS. denn

Denchax, == Danish axe. RG. 299

Dene, *sb.* == valley. Ps. cvii. 8. AS. denu

Denkless, == poor? Body and Soul, 198

Depart, *v. a.* == separate. RG. 394, 466

—— *v. n.* == break up, separate (neut.). 483 B.

Departing, *sb.* == separation. Alys. 912

Deraign, *v. a.* == try, prove. RG. 285. Fr. desraigner

Deray, *sb.* == fight, quarrel. Alys. 1177; prowess. Alys. 2722. Fr. deroi

Derayne, *sb.* == battle. Alys. 7353. Fr. desraigner

Dere, *sb.* == dearth, *q. v.*

Dere, *v. a.* == injure. Alys. 6191. HD. 574; [derven], Marg. 38. part. 'idorve.' O. and N. 1156. AS. derian

Derenge, a mistake for 'drynge.' Alys. 2534

Dern, *adj.* == secret. RG. 114. AS. dearn

Derne, == dearly? K. Horn, 1385

Dernely, == secretly. 27 B.

Derven. See Dere

Desclander, *v. a.* == slander. 2050 B

Desclander, *sb.* 2061 B.

Describing, *sb.* == description. RG. 60

Deserie, *v. a.* == disinherit. RG. 85

Desert, *sb.* == merit. RG. 253

Deserve, *v. a.* Fragm. Sci. 371

Desire, *v. a.* 225 B.

Despeple, *v. a.* == publish. RG. 517, 568

Despise, *v. a.* RG. 31

Despite, *sb.* RG. 566

Destance, *sb.* == strife. RG. 511, 570

Dester, 'in dester' == on the right hand. A steed led by the squire 'in dester' was the 'destrier' or 'dextrarius,' or war-horse. Body and Soul, 18. See Roq. *s. v.* Destrier

Destining, *sb.* == destiny. Alys. 6867

Destroy, *v. a.* part, 'destrud.' RG. 372. pret. 'destrude.' RG. 376

Destroying, *sb.* == destruction. Alys. 2888

Destuted, == destitute, wanting. Alys. 2199

Deus! an *interj.* == O God! hence our 'deuce.' HD. 2096, 2114. Fr. deus

Deus, *adj.* == sweet. HD. 1312. Fr. doux

Deutyraun, *sb.* == some monstrous animal. Alys. 5416

Devil, *sb.* RG. 411; [del]. Wright's L. P. p. 111

Devilness, *sb.* == demon. Ps. xcv. 5

Devise, *v. a.* == contrive. 876 B.

—— == describe. Alys. 7377

Devotion, *sb.* RG. 405, 456

Devout, *adj.* RG. 369

Dew, *sb.* Fragm. Sci. 232. Wright's L. P. p. 72. [dewyng.] Alys. 914

Dewdrop, *sb.* Wright's L. P. p. 114

Dewing, *sb.* See Dew

Diadem, *sb.* 2161 B.

Diamond, *sb.* Wright's L. P. p. 25

Dicce, *v. n.* == shudder, tremble? Signa ante Jud. 24. Cf. 'didder,' in Halliwell, and Phil. Soc. Proc. vol. v. p. 39

Dice, *sb.* [deys]. Alys. 3297

Die, *v. n.* RG. 530

Dight, *v. a.* == set in order, govern. RG. 424; 'compose,' applied to the voice of a bird. O. and N. 1653; 'attack.' Pol. S. 223. part. 'idiȝte.' Rel. Ant. ii. p. 217. AS. dihtan

Digne, *adj.* == worthy. RG. 132

Dignity, *sb.* 244 B.

Dike, *sb.* == ditch. Body and Soul, 120

Dim, *v. a.* Ps. lxviii. 24

—— *v. n.* Christ on the Cross, 7

Dim, *adj.* == dusky. O. and N. 577. AS. dim

Dimness, *sb.* Ps. xvii. 10

Din, *v. a.* [denie]. K. Horn, 606. Ps. xlv. 4. AS. dýnian

—— *sb.* Ps. xli. 5

Dine, *v. n.* RG. 558. AS. dýnan

Ding, *v. a.* == strike. HD. 215. part. 'dungen.' HD. 227. Sw. danga. ON. dángla

Dint, *sb.* == blow. 2138 B. AS. dýnt

Discharge, *v. a.* == deprive of a charge or office. Alys. 3868

Disciple, *sb.* RG. 232

Discipline, *v. a.* 2384 B.

—— *v. n.* Rel. Ant. ii. p. 175

Discomfort, *v. a.* RG. 212

Discord, *sb.* RG. 195

Discording, *sb.* == discord. RG. 255

Discoverte, *sb.* == an unguarded part. Alys. 7418

Disdain, *sb.* [dedayn]. RG. 172

Disguise, *v. a.* Alys. 121

Dish, *sb.* HD. 919

Disherison, *sb.* [diserteison]. 1872 B.

Disherit, *v. a.* RG. 327, 375

Disherit, *sb.* [deseryte] == a disinherited person. RG. 452, 563

Dishonor, *sb.* Alys. 3867

Dismay, *v. a.* [demay]. RG. 156

Disordain, *v. a.* == deprive of holy orders, unfrock. RG. 473

Dispence, *sb.* == equipment. Alys. 2616

Disport, *sb.* Ritson's AS. xviii. 15

Dispute, *v. n.* St Kath. 74

Disraying, *sb.* == irregular fighting. Alys. 673

Distance, *sb.* 1287 B.

Distinction, *sb.* == distinguished person. Alys. 112

Distrain, *v. a.* 742, 752 B.

Distress, *sb.* RG. 460, 442, 568

Disturb, *v. a.* RG. 396, 436

Disturbance, *sb.* RG. 429, 436

Disturber, *sb.* 1110 B.

Ditch, *sb.* RG. 408, 549

Ditched, *adj.* [ydyched] == surrounded by a ditch. Alys. 2658

Dite, *v. a.* == indite. Rel. Ant. ii. p. 176

Ditement, *sb.* == indictment. Pol. S. 198

Ditty, *sb.* Rel. Ant. ii. p. 175

Divers, *adj.* == several. RG. 378

Diȝele, *adj.* == secret. O. and N. 2. AS. digel

Do, *vb. a.* 19 B. part. 'ydo' == done. RG. 369. == finished (of winter). RG. 371

———— == place. pret. 'dude.' 259 B.

———— == cause. Wright's L. P. pp. 69, 71

———— *vb. abs.* 'do' == act. RG. 501. [done]. RG. 377. 2 s. pres. 'dost.' RG. 428. 3 s. pret. 'dude.' RG. 369

—— *vb. aux.* RG. 429. 'dost chese'

—— 'doth' used to represent a preceding verb. Wright's L. P. p. 34

Dod, *v. a.* == chop, cut. Pol. S. 192. Probably another form of 'dock'

Dog, *sb.* RG. 69

Dogged, *adj.* Pol. S. 199

Dole, *sb.* == portion. RG. 165

—— == grief [del]. RG. 392; [deol]. RG. 381

Doleful. [deolvol]. RG. 414; [delvol]. RG. 558

Dolefully, *adv.* 1448 B.

Dolphin, *sb.* Alys. 6576

Doom, *sb.* RG. 53

Doomsday, *sb.* HD. 748

Doomsman, *sb.* == judge. Rel. S. vi. 3

Door, *sb.* RG. 508, 495

Doorpin, *sb.* K. Horn, 1003

Doppe, *sb.* == a round ball, knob. Alys. 5776. ON. doppa

Dor. See Deer

Dorre, *v. n.* == need. RG. 457. Germ. bedürfen

Dosil, *sb.* == a spigot of a barrel. RG. 542. Fr. doisil. See the Prompt. Parv. *s. v.* dotelle, and note there

Dotance, *sb.* == doubt, fear. Alys. 582

Double, *adj.* 417 B.

Double, *v. a.* 598 β. part. 'idoubled.' 295 β

Doubt, *sb.* == fear. RG. 89, 402

Doubt, *v. n.* == be afraid. 395 B.; feel doubt. St Swithin, 105

Doubt, *v. a.* == fear. 289 β

Doughtily, *adv.* Alys. 7382

Doughty, *adj.* Wright's L. P. p. 27

Douthe, == 'might,' or 'availed,' perf. of 'dow,' to avail, prosper, be able. (See Phil. Soc. Proc. ii. 158.) HD. 833, 1184. part. 'ydought.' Alys. 5906. AS. dugan

Douzepairs, *sb.* == the twelve peers of France, [dosse pers], RG. 188. [dozzepers]. RG. 200

Dove, *sb.* Ps. liv. 7

Down, *sb.* == open heath. RG. 144; [dune]. O. and N. 830. AS. dún

70

Down, *adv.* HD. 2291

Downcast, *v. a.* == cast down. pret. 'douncaste.' Ps. lxxiii. 6

Downcome, *v. n.* Ps. cxliii. 5

Downer, == lower. Alys. 6619

Downfall, *v. n.* == fall down, in part. 'downfalland.' Ps. xvii. 9

Downfalling, *sb.* Ps. li. 6

Downgo, *v. n.* == go down. Ps. cvi. 26. part, 'downgaand.' Ps. cvi. 23

Downright, *adv.* Ps. cv. 18

Downshear, *v. a.* == cut down. pret. 'douneschare.' Ps. lxxiii. 6

Downward, *adv.* RG. 362

Dozen, *sb.* Pol. S. 229

Dragon, *sb.* == (animal). RG. 131

—— == a war standard. RG. 303, 216, 545

Dragonet, *sb.* == a small dragon. Alys. 602

Drake, *sb.* HD. 1241. Wright's L. P. p. 44

—— == dragon. Alys. 553

Drapery, *sb.* Rel. Ant. ii. p. 175

Draught, *sb.* == drawing. Body and Soul, 43

Draw, *v. a.* RG. 367

—— == cut down, 'hang and draw.' 724 B. part. 'drawe' (of a sword). RG. 536

Draw, *v. n.* == draw towards a thing, approximate to. RG. 369; [drey3e]. Wright's L. P. p. 34

Drawbridge, *sb.* Alys. 1205

Dread, *sb.* RG. 401, 457

Dread, *v. n.* pret. 'dradde.' 127 B.

Dreadful, *adj.* Wright's L. P. p. 50

Dreadly, *adj.* Body and Soul, 6

Dream, *sb.* HD. 1284

—— *v. n.* HD. 1284, 1304. ON. dreyma

Drearied, == sorrowful. Ps. xxxvii. 7

Dreary, *adj.* RG. 351; [drury], Alys. 4389. Cf. La3. ii. 184

Dreg, *sb.* Ps. xxxix. 3

Dreme, *sb.* == song, melody. Wright's L. P. p. 57; [dreim]. O. and N. 21. AS. dreám

Drench, *sb.* == a potion. RG. 151. AS. drenc

Drench, *v. a.* == to drown. Wright's L. P. p. 113. part. 'dreynt.' Ibid. p. 111

Dreng, *sb.* == chieftain, gentleman. HD. 31. AS. dreng

Drepen, *v. a.* == slay. HD. 1783. pret. 'drape.' Ps. xciii. 6. AS. drepan

Dribil, *sb.* == moisture, dribble. Rel. Ant. ii. p. 210

Drie, *v. a.* == endure. Marg. 52; [dreeg]. Ritson's AS. viii. 157. AS. dreógan

Drink, *sb.* RG. 289, 389

—— *v. a.* pret. 'dronc.' RG. 165. part. 'ydronke.' RG. 43

Drinker, *sb.* Fragm. Sci. 285

Drit, *sb.* == dung. Cok. 177. ON. drit. AS. gedritan; used as a term of abuse. HD. 682

Drive, *v. a.*

RG. 367. part, 'ydrive.' RG. 97. pret. 'drave.' Ps. xlii. 2. 'To drive a plea of law.' RG. 471

—— *v. n.* == come or move rapidly. RG. 407. 'a wel driving flod.' RG. 20

Driȝte, *sb.* == the Lord Jesus Christ. K. Horn, 1354. Alys. 6139. AS. drihten

Drogman, *sb.* == dragoman, interpreter. Alys. 3401

Dromedary, *sb.* Alys. 3407

Dromoun, *sb.* == a swift ship. Alys. 90. ON. drómundr. Fr. dromon

Drop, *sb.* RG. 560

Drop, *sb.* == aloes. Ps. xliv. 9

Droukening, *sb.* == slumber. Body and Soul, 1. ON. druckna

Droupne, *v. n.* == droop, faint. Wright's L. P. p. 54. ON. driúpa

Drove, *v. a.* == disturb. Ps. iii. 2; vi. 3. AS. drífan

Droving, *sb.* == persecution. Ps. ix. 22

Druery, **Drury**, *sb.* == gallantry, courtship. RG. 191

—— == love, delight. Alys. 2999. Fr. drue, a mistress

Drunke, *sb.* == drinking. M. Ode, 128

Drunken, *v. a.* == make drunk. Ps. lxiv. 10

Drunness, *sb.* == drunkenness? O. and N. 1397

Drury, *adj.* == dreary, *q. v.*

Dry, *adj.* RG. 531

—— *v. a.* part. 'idriid.' Rel. Ant. ii. p. 193

—— *v. n.* == become dry. Ps. xxxvi. 2; 3 s. pres. 'druith.' Rel. Ant. ii. p. 210

Dryhed, *sb.* == dryness. Ps. lxv. 6

Dub, *v. a.* HD. 2038. AS. dubban

Dubbing, *sb.* K. Horn, 499

Duelsing, *sb.* == deceit. St Swithin, 105

Duke, *sb.* RG. 367

Dumb, *adj.* RG. 131

—— *v. n.* == become dumb. Ps. xxxviii. 3

Dung, *sb.* RG. 310; [ding]. Rel. Ant. ii. p. 191. Serm. 7

Dunge, *sb.* == dungeon. Body and Soul, 236

Dungheap, *sb.* Wright's L. P. p. 103

Dure, *v. n.* == endure. RG. 403; [duyre]. Alys. 3258

Durwe, *sb.* == dwarf. Alys. 6266. AS. dweorg

Dusi, *adj.* == foolish. O. and N. 1464. AS. dýsig

Dust, *sb.* RG. 137

Dute, *sb.* == pleasure. Cok. 9. Fr. deduit

Dutten, *v. a.* == close, dite. Wright's L. P. p. 110. AS. dyttan

Duty, *sb.* [devyte]. RG. 316

Duȝethe, *sb.* == manhood. O. and N. 634. AS. duguð

Dwel, *sb.* == space of time. Rel. Ant, ii. p. 191

Dwele, *v. a.* == deceive. Ps. lvii. 4. AS. dwelian

Dwell, *v. n.* HD. 4. ON. dvelja

—— == delay. HD. 1351

Dwelle, *sb.* == folly. Serm. 13

Dwelling, *sb.* delay. Alys. 5208. HD. 1352

Dwole, *sb.* == error, trick. O. and N. 823, AS. dwola

—— *adj.* == false, deceitful. O and N. 924

E.

Each, *adj.* RG. 369

Eachone. RG. 374

Eager, *adj.* RG. 80

Ear, *sb.* (of corn). RG. 490. AS. eár

Ear, *sb.* (of the body). RG. 492. AS. eáre

Eardingstowe, *sb.* == dwelling-place. O. and N. 28. AS. eardungstow

Earl, *sb.* RG. 370

Earldom, *sb.* RG. 523

Early, *adj.* 905 B.

Earn, *v. a.* == gain, realize. O. and N. 1202. AS. earnian

Earnest, *sb.* == earnestness. RG. 121, 401

Earth, *sb.* == the world. Wright's L. P. p. 68.

—— == the ground. HD. 2657

—— == mould. HD. 740

—— *v. n.* == to dwell. HD. 739. AS. eardian

Earthgrine, == earthquake. RG. 530. AS. grynd, an abyss

Earthgrythe, *sb.* == earthquake. RG. 414. ON. gríð == vehemence, violent motion

Earthly, *adj.* 440 B.

Ease, *sb.* 1473 B.

Easily, *adv.* 395 B.

East, *sb.* 35 β

Easter, *sb.* 546 B.

Eastward, *adv.* RG. 41

Easy, *adj.* == slack. Body and Soul, 115

Eat, *v. a.* 143 β. pret. 'at.' 274 B. 'ete.' RG 408. part. 'y-ete.' 311 β

Ebb, *v. n.* Fragm. Sci. 253

Ech, *adj.* == eternal. O. and N. 742. AS. éce.

Eche, *v. a.* == increase. Rel. S. v. 126. AS. eácan

Eche, *sb.* == aches. M. Ode, st. 100

Ederlyng, *sb.* == ancestor? Alys. 1711

Edged, *adj.* [i-egged] (of a sword). RG. 274

Edict, *sb.* RG. 568

Edissehen, *sb.* == quail. Ps. civ. 40. AS. edisc-hen, from 'edisc,' a park

Edmod, *adj.* == mild, humble. Fragm. in Warton, H. E. P. vol. i. p. 21. AS. eádmod

Edneth. Rel. Ant. i. 114; possibly a mistake for 'endeth,' i.e. comes to an end

Edwyt, *sb.* == scorn. RG. 379. AS. edwíte

—— *v. a.* == reproach. Ten. Comm. 8

Eel, *sb.* HD. 897. Alys. 5792

Effte, *vb. a.* == gave. RG. 367

Efne, == in the evening. O. and N. 313

Eft, *adv.* == after. RG. 367

Eft, *sb.* pl. 'evetis.' Alys. 6126; 'eveten.' M. Ode, 138. AS. efete

Eftsoon, *adv.* RG. 397

Egging, *sb.* == incitement. Wright's L. P. p. 106. AS. eggian

Ehte, *sb.* == goods, property. Alys. 1507; [ei3te]. O. and N. 1151; [eyghtis]. Alys. 1573. AS. æht

Eight. RG. 1, 385

Eighth, *adj.* RG. 473

Eighteen. RG. 407

Eighteenth, *adj.* RG. 436

Eighty. RG. 478

Eirmonger, *sb.* == eggseller. St Swithin, 69

Eisliche, *adj.* == fearful. M. Ode, 142. AS. egeslíc

Either, *adj.* [eithe]. RG. 62; [aither]. 434 β

Eke, *adv.* == also. RG. 374, 378; [ekyn]. RG. 165

Eke, *v. a.* == increase. See Eche.

Eker, *sb.* == watercress, weed. Alys. 6175. AS. eácerse

Eke, *v. a.* == to avenge? RG. 474. Probably an error for 'wreke.' See the parallel passage in the Life of Beket, 1948 B., where the reading is 'wreke'

El, == else. *q. v.*

Elbow, *sb.* Fragm. Sci. 322

Elde, *sb.* == age. RG. 379, 421

—— *v. n.* == become old [ealdi]. M. Ode, st. 1

Elder, *adj.* RG. 367

Elders, *sb.* [elderne]. RG. 11

Eldest, *adj.* RG. 370, 381

Eldrynges, *sb.* == elders. Alys. 4948

Element, *sb.* Fragm. Sci. 124

Elephant, *sb.* == the animal. Alys. 854

—— == a horn of ivory. Alys. 1182

Eleven, [enlene]. RG. 441

Eleventh, *adj.* [endlefte]. RG. 414, 408

Elf, *sb.* pl. 'elvene.' RG. 130

Elidelik, *adj.* ('eldelike' in MS.) == elderly. Ritson's AS. viii. 39

Eling, *adj.* == wretched. 637 β. Dan. elendig. ON. eligr

Ell, *sb.* RG. 429

Else, *adv.* [elles]. Wright's L. P. p. 36. [el]. RG. 451. 'El' is the old nominative, of which 'else' or 'elles' is the genitive used absolutely. Cf. the old Lat. gen. 'alias'

Elsewhere, *adv.* RG. 395

Ely, *sb.* == oil. Marg. 60

Embe, *prep.* == concerning, for; 'embe no3t' == in vain. St Kath. 214

Emcristen, *sb.* == equal or even Christian. M. Ode, st. 148

Eme, *sb.* == uncle. HD. 1326. AS. eám.

Emerald, *sb.* Alys. 7030. Wright's L. P. pp. 26, 35

Emperor, *sb.* RG. 440

Empery, *sb.* == empire. RG. 85

Empoison, *v. a.* RG. 463

Empress, *sb.* RG. 440, 442

Emprise, *sb.* == attempt. Body and Soul, 144

Enchanter, *sb.* RG. 28

Enchantment. RG. 10

Enchantry, *sb.* RG. 10, 148

Encheson, *sb.* == occasion. RG. 452, 454. Fr. enchaison

Encounter, *v. a.* 411 β

—— *sb.* RG. 391

End, *sb.* RG. 377

—— *v. n.* RG. 370

——— *v. a.* part. 'y-ended' 1770 B.

Endday, *sb.* == last day of life. 1574 B AS. endedæg

Enderday, *sb.* 'this enderday,' == this past day, the day which has now come to an end. Wright's L. P. p. 94

Endelong, *adv.* == along, in length. HD. 2822

Ending, *sb.* Wright's L. P. p. 59

Endless, *adj.* RG. 152

Ene, *adv.* == only? 882 B.

Enes, *adv.* == once. RG. 376, 411

Enferm, *v. a.* == fortify. RG. 552

Engine, *sb.* == device, plot. Body and Soul, 125. Wright's L. P. p. 58

Engineful, == ingenious. Alys. 4869

Enhance, *v. a.* RG. 458

Enherit, *v. a.* == give as an inheritance. Alys. 7153

Enjoin, *v. a.* RG. 234

Enke, *sb.* == ink. *q. v.*

Enlegiance, *sb.* == allegiance. RG. 85

Enliance, *sb.* == alliance. RG. 12

Ennesure, *sb.* == game, play. Alys. 5543. Fr. enveysure, enveyser—to be joyous

Enough, *adv.* [inou]. RG. 519. [ynou]. RG. 83

Enquest, *sb.* 348 B. Pilate, 196

Enqueyntance, *sb.* RG. 330

Enquire, *v. n.* RG. 508

——— *v. a.* Pilate, 52

Enquiry, *sb.* RG. 373

Enreson, *v. a.* == to reason with. RG. 321

Ensample, *sb.* RG. 446

Ensent, *v. n.* == RG. 171, 446. part, 'ensentan' == assenting. RG. 239

Entail, *sb.* == sculpture. Alys. 4762

Entempri, *v. a.* == to temper. Fragm. Sci. 290

Entent, *v. n.* == attend to. Alys. 2834

——— *sb.* == intent. RG. 140

Ententively, *adv.* == attentively. 460 B.

Enter, *v. n.* 640 B.

Entrail, *sb.* Alys. 3628. Fr. entrailles. Lat. internalia

Envenom, *v. a.* Alys. 5436, 5611

Envy, *sb.* Body and Soul, 129

Eode, *vb.* == went. RG. 417

Epetite, *sb.* == bloodstone, apatite. Cok. 92. The hepatitis of Pliny, HN. xxxvii. 71; from Gr. ἧπαρ, the liver

Epiphany, *sb.* Wright's L. P. p. 96

Er, *adv.* == early. Wright's L. P. p. 99

Erde, *v. n.* == dwell. Ps. xxi. 4; xxiv. 13. AS. eardian

Ere, *adv.* == before than. 52 B.

—— *v. a.* == plough. RG. 21. AS. erian

Eremig, *sb.* == pitiful creature. O. and N. 1109. AS. earm

Eri, *sb.* == tillage. Pol. S. 196. AS. erian

Ermine, *sb.* RG. 191. M. Ode, 182

Erming, *sb.* == grieving. Alys. 1525. AS. earming, yrmian

Ern, *sb.* == eagle. RG. 177, 215. AS. earn

Ernde, *v. a.* == intercede, gain for another by intercession. Wright's L. P. p. 62. AS. ærendian

Ernding, *sb.* == intercession. Wright's L. P. p. 58; [herendinge]. Rel. S. iv. 86

Erne, dat. of adj. 'er,' == early; 'on erne morowe.' Alys. 5458

Erne, *v. n.* == run. Wright's L. P. p. 81. AS. yrnan

Erre, *sb.* == a wound, scar. Ps. xxxvii. 6. ON. ör. Dan. ar

Errand, *sb.* RG. 501. AS. ærend

Erst, == first. Wright's L. P. p. 32

Erur, *adv.* == before. O. and N. 1736. AS. æror, from ær

Esle, *v. a.* == ask. RG. 453

Esmyte, *v. n.* == smite, 'to gader esmyte,' (of two armies). RG. 215

Esse, *v. a.* == ask. RG. 374, 498

Este, *sb.* == ford, provisions. O. and N. 358. AS. ést

Este, *adj.* == mild, kindly. O. and N. 997.

—— == dear. Rel. Ant. i. 111. AS. este. ON. ást

Estellation, *sb.* == astrology. Alys. 589

Estre, *sb.* == condition. Alys. 5467

Ete, *sb.* == eating. M. Ode, 130

Eth, *adj.* == easy. M. Ode, 188. RG. 327; [ythe]. K. Horn, 61. AS. eáð

Eðlete, *adj.* == what is lightly thrown away, worthless. M. Ode, 75, 78. AS. eáð, lǽtan

Evangelist, *sb.* RG. 67, 348

Eve, *sb.* RG. 415, 532

Even, *adv.* with 'as,' == just as, or when. RG. 535

—— *adj.* == equal. Creed, 77

—— == straight, level. Wright's L. P. p. 35

—— *sb.* == peer, equal. Pol. S. 157

—— *v. a.* == compare. 1631 B.

Evenforth, *adv.* == forward. 2186 B.

Evening, *sb.* == equal, peer. Alys. 3008

Evenmette, *adj.* == coëqual. Creed, 58. Ps. xlviii. 13

Evenness, *sb.* == equity. Ps. ix. 8

Evensong, *sb.* RG. 369

Ever, *adv.* RG. 535, 370; [everne]. RG. 74

Evereft, *adv.* 54 B

Evermore, *adv.* Wright's L. P. p. 29. Ritson's AS. viii. 160

Every, *adj.* [everyche]. RG. 374

Everyldele, *sb.* == every part. RG. 408

Evil, *sb.* == sickness. HD. 114; misfortune. Ps. lxxxix. 15; [uvel], RG. 472

—— *adj.* [uvele]. 413 B.

—— *adv.* O. and N. 1204. 404 B.

Evilness, *sb.* Ps. xxxv. 5; li. 5

Ewt, *sb.* See Eft

Executor, *sb.* Fragm. on Seven Sins, 42

Ey, *sb.* == egg. RG. 404. pl. 'eiren.' St Swithin, 57. Germ. ei. AS. æg. ON. egg

Eye, *sb.* == awe. RG. 469, 507. AS. ége

Eye, *sb.* == organ of sight. RG. 376. AS. eáge

Eyebrow. Pol. S. 239

Eyful, *adj.* == proud. [heyvol]. RG. 377

Eyre, *sb.* == journey, circuit. RG. 517. Lat. iter

F.

Fabling, *sb.* == fable, story. Ps. cxviii. 85

Face, *sb.* RG. 476

Fadme, *v. a.* == embrace. HD. 1295. AS. fæðmian

Fagen, *adj.* == glad, fain. Fragment in Warton, H. E. P. vol. i. p. 31. AS. fægen

Fail, *v. n.* == wither (of fruit). RG. 414. 3s. pres. 'falt.' O. and N. 37; part. 'ifailled.' Pol. S. 202

Fail, *sb.* RG. 369

Fain, *v. a.* == be glad, rejoice. Ps. xix. 6

Fain, *adj.* RG. 349; [vawe]. RG. 218

Fainness, *sb.* == gladness. Ps. iv. 7

Faint, *adj.* Wright's L. P. p. 25

Faintise, *sb.* == cowardice. RG. 39

Faintly, *adv.* RG. 515

Fair, *adj.* == beautiful. RG. 383

——— == light, pale (of colour). RG. 429. 'fairer.' RG. 395; 'fairest.' 133 β

——— *v. n.* == become fair. Alys. 2903

Fairhede, *sb.* == fairness. RG. 118

Fairly, *adv.* == pleasantly, easily. RG. 446

Fairy, *sb.* == enchantment. Alys. 6924. Fr. faérie, faé

Faith, *sb.* [fei]. 2074 B.

Falcon, *sb.* Wright's L. P. p. 26

Fale, *adj.* == many. RG. 416, 146. AS. feala

Falewe, *v. a.* == become yellow. Wright's L. P. p. 50. AS. fealo.

Falewi, *sb.* == yellowness. O. and N. 456

Fall, *v. n.* RG. 6. pret. 'fell.' RG. 401. part. 'ifallen.' O. and N. 514. 'it falleth not to thee,' == it is not thy duty or lot. Leg. of St Cuthbert, cited in Warton, H. E. P. vol. i. p. 14, n.

—— *v. a.* == make to fall. part. 'yfalle.' Alys. 7183

Fallows, *sb.* == fields. HD. 2509. AS. fealh

False, *adj.* RG. 385

Falsehood, *sb.* RG. 454

Falseleke, *sb.* == falsehood. Wright's L. P. p. 32

Falsely, *adv.* Wright's L. P. p. 31

Falseness. Pol. S. 150

Falseship. Pol. S. 212

Fame, *sb.* RG. 367

Fanding, *sb.* == temptation. Ps. xvii. 30

Fanger, *sb.* == taker, lifter up. Ps. ii. 4

Far, *adv.* [ver]. RG. 502; [feor]. O. and N. 921

Farant, *adj.* == walking. Alys. 3460

Fare, *v. n.* == go, journey. 657 β. pret. 'fore.' Ps. civ. 13

—— == succeed, turn out. 918 B. part. 'ifare.' O. and N. 400

—— == behave. 2076 B.

—— == fare, live. 20 B.

—— *sb.* == journey. RG. 52

—— == custom, proceeding. Alys. 7072. Ritson's AS. viii. 158, 188

Farforth, *adv.* == far. RG. 448

—— == entirely [ferforth]. RG. 242

Farm, *v. a.* RG. 378

Farthing, *sb.* == the coin so called. RG. 507

Fast, *adj.* == firm, sure. Wright's L. P. p. 37

—— *adv.* == quickly. RG. 490; strongly. Id. ibid.

Fast, *v. n.* == abstain from food. 2512 B. part, 'fasting.' RG. 545. AS.

fæstan

—— *sb.* 2511 B.

Fasten, *v. a.* Pol. S. 214. Ps. xcii. 1

Fasting, *sb.* RG. 405

Fastlic, *adv.* == firmly. Creed of St Athan. 101

Fastness, *sb.* == castle. Ps. xvii. 3

—— == firmness. Ps. lxxii. 4

Fastrede, *adj.* == firm in counsel. O. and N. 211

Fat, *adj.* RG. 429

—— *v. a.* == fatten. Pol. S. 150

Father, *sb.* RG. 382

Fatherless, *adj.* RG. 142

Fatte, == fetched. See Fetch

Fathom, *sb.* [fedme]. Alys. 546

Fatness, *sb.* Ps. cxlvii. 14

Fawning, *sb.* == flattery, deceit. Wright's L. P. p. 23

Fax, *sb.* == hair. Wright's L. P. p. 33. AS. feax

Fayly, *adj.* == base, vile. Pol. S. 157. Fr. failli. Vid. Roq.

Fear, *sb.* RG. 402

Feast, *sb.* == festival. RG. 376

Feather, *sb.* RG. 487

Feathered, *adj.* Alys. 5406

Feblesse, *sb.* == feebleness. RG. 442

Fedme, == fathom. *q. v.*

Fee, *sb.* == money. RG. 565. AS. feoh

—— == cattle [feh], Wright's L. P. p. 48. Pol. S. 152

Feeble, *adj.* RG. 379, 380. 'feebler.' RG. 372

—— == bad. 'feble wede.' HD. 323

Feebly, *adv.* 1178 B.; [feblelike]. HD. 418

Feed, *v. a.* RG. 375. pret. 'fedde.' 273 B. part. 'ifed.' 300 β

—— == obtain, conquer. Alys. 3064

Feel, *v. a.* part. 'yvelde.' RG. 185

Feeling, *sb.* == sense of feeling. Fragm. Sci. 333

Fei, == faith. *q. v.*

Feide, *sb.* == feud, league. Alys. 97

Feign, *v. a.* == pretend. RG. 421

—— == form. 3 s. pres. 'feinyhes.' Ps. xciii. 9, 20. Lat. fingere

Feintise, *sb.* == deceit, feigning. RG. 39

Fel, *sb.* == skin. RG. 208. AS. fell

Felawrede, *sb.* == fellowship. Alys. 6199

Fele, *adj.* == many. 571 B. AS. feala

Felefold, *v. a.* == multiply. Ps. xi. 9. part. 'felefolded.' Ps. iii. 2

Fell, *adj.* == cruel. Body and Soul, 228. AS. fell

—— *v. a.* RG. 415, 526

Felle, *v. a.* == fulfil? or perhaps a mistake for 'telle.' K. Horn, 1292

Fellow, *sb.* RG. 397, 524

Felon, *sb.* 565 B.

Felony, *sb.* RG. 526

Fen, *sb.* == marsh. RG. 6

—— == mud, dirt. Ps. xvii. 43

Fenestre, *sb.* == window. RG. 312

Feng, *v. a.* == take. RG. 36. 3 pl. pret. 'fongon.' RG. 36

Fenge, *sb.* == a grapple. O. and N. 1283. AS. feng

Fenge, *sb.* == a girl. Wright's L. P. p. 36. ON. fenna

Fennel, *sb.* Wright's L. P. p. 44. AS. fenol

Feoff, *v. a.* RG. 369, 370

Feorne, *adj.* == ancient. Alys. 6356. AS. fyrn

Feorre, *adv.* == from far. O. and N. 1321

Fer, *adv.* See Far

Ferblet ? Fragm. Sci. 275, 280

Ferd, *sb.* == army. RG. 19, 204. AS. fyrd

Ferdness, *sb.* == fear. Ps. lxxxviii. 41

Fere, *v. a.* == carry. Fragm. on Seven Sins, 41

Fere, *sb.* == companion, equal. Wright's L. P. pp. 24, 36. AS. fera, gefera

Fered, *adj.* == afraid. Wright's L. P. p. 24

Feres, *vb. impers.* == it becomes, suits. Ps. lxiv. 2

Ferhede, *sb.* == company. RG. 138

Ferinkli, *adv.* == suddenly. Ps. lxiii. 6. AS. færinga

Ferlich, *adv.* == wonderfully. RG. 299, 509. AS. færlic

—— *adj.* == fearful. Rel. Ant. ii. p. 176

Ferly, *sb.* == a wonder. Ritson's AS. viii. 14

Ferth, *sb.* == road. RG. 8. AS. faran. W. ffordd

Festel, *sb.* == a chain. Ps. cxlix. 8. AS fetel

Fet, *sb.* == vat, vessel. Marg. 61. AS. fæt

Fetch, *v. a.* RG. 437. pret. 'fette.' RG. 15. 'fatte.' Pol. S. 152. AS. feccan

Fetter, *v. a.* HD. 2758

83

—— *sb.* HD. 2759

Few, *adj.* [vewe]. RG. 402, 368. pl. 'fone.' Ps. cvi. 39

Fewness, *sb.* Ps. ci. 24

Fewté, *sb.* == fidelity, fealty. Alys. 2911. Fr. feuté

Feye, *adj.* == near to die. Wright's L. P. p. 28. AS. fæge

Feynes, *sb.* == phœnix? Wright's L. P. p. 36

Fickle, *adj.* HD. 1210. AS. ficol

Fiddle, *sb.* 185 β

Field, *sb.* RG. 380, 565

Fiend, *sb.* HD. 2229

Fierce, *adj.* [fers]. RG. 486, 543

Fiery, *adj.* [fury]. RG. 340, 334

Fifteen. RG. 416

Fifteenth, *adj.* RG. 522

Fifth, *adj.* RG. 400

Fifty. RG. 382

Fight, *v. n.* RG. 455; [feȝe]. Pol. S. 154. pret. 'foȝte.' RG. 400. part. 'yfaȝt.' RG. 208

—— *sb.* RG. 173; [fyth]. Wright's L. P. p. 23

Fighter, *sb.* Alys. 5703

Fighting, *sb.* RG. 299

Fightlac, *sb.* == conflict. O. and N. 1697. AS. feohtlác, from 'lác' == play, sport.

Figure, *sb.* [vigour] == an image, idol. Alys. 1524. Ps. xcvi. 7

Fikele, *v. a.* == flatter. RG. 31, 36. AS. ficol

Fikeling, *sb.* == flattery. RG. 30

Fildore, == made of gold thread. Wright's L. P. p. 33. Fr. fil d'or

File, *sb.* == a vile person. HD. 499

Fill, *v. a.* [fulle]. RG. 13. part, 'yfuld.' RG. 120

—— == fulfil. Wright's L. P. p. 99

Fille, *sb.* == thread. RG. 128, 297. Fr. fil

—— == wild thyme. Wright's L. P. p. 44. AS. fylle. Lat. serpyllum

Fillet, *sb.* Pol. S. 154

Filth, *sb.* Alys. 6370

84

Filthhede, *sb.* RG. 290

Fin, *sb.* Alys. 6591

Find, *v. a.* RG. 463. pret. 'founde.' RG. 374. part, 'yfounde.' RG. 87

Finder, *sb.* Alys. 4794

Finding, *sb.* == invention. Ps. lxxx. 13

Fine, *sb.* == end. RG. 413

—— *v. n.* == cease. 129 B.

—— *v. a.* == pay a fine. RG. 528, 511

Finger, *sb.* 1194 B.

Fining, *sb.* == end. Alys. 8015

Fire, *sb.* [fuyr]. RG. 151; [fir]. RG. 108

Firebrand, *sb.* Alys. 6848

Fired, *adj.* == fiery. Ps. cxviii. 140

Fireiron, *sb.* [furire] == a steel for striking a light. 639 β

Firmament, *sb.* 243 β

Firren, *adj.* == made of fir. HD. 2078

First, *adj.* 119 B.

—— *adv.* 101 B.; [vorst]. RG. 383

Firstkinned, *adj.* == first-born. Ps. civ. 36

Fish, *sb.* RG. 1, 6

—— *v. n.* St Andrew, 3

Fisher, *sb.* [vyssare]. RG. 265

Fishing, *sb.* St Andrew, 4; [vysseth]. RG. 264

Fist, *sb.* [fust]. RG. 345

Fitte, *sb.* == match, equal. O. and N. 782. The Prompt. Parv. gives 'Fyt or mete—equus, congruus'

Five. RG. 383, 518

Flaune, *sb.* == pancake. HD. 644. Fr. flan

Flay. See Flea

Flea, *sb.* Pol. S. 238

Flea, *v. a.* == flay [flo]. HD. 612. pret. 'flow.' HD. 2502; part. 'yflawe.' Alys. 894

Flecche, *v. n.* == flinch. 951 B.

Flee, *v. a.* == escape from. RG. 367

—— *v. n.* == flee away. RG. 380, 501; 3 pl. pret. 'flodeden,' == fled.

85

Alys. 2441; part. 'flen,' == made to flee. RG. 258

Fleet, *adj.* == swift [flette]. Alys. 3740

Fleme, *v. a.* == banish. RG. 562, 547; part. 'yfloynd.' RG. 328; 'fleme.' Wright's L. P. p. 44; 'flemed.' Ritson's AS. viii. 178. AS. flyman

Flescher, *sb.* == fleece. Ps. lxxi. 6

Flesh, *sb.* RG. 406, 514

Fleshly, *adj.* Wright's L. P. p. 72

Fleshhede, *sb.* == the Incarnation. Creed of St Athan. 66

Flet, *adj.* == flat, i. e. stupid. Wright's L. P. p. 47

Flette, *sb.* == a floor, flat. Alys. 1105; [flitte]. Rel. Ant. ii. p. 192. AS. flett

—— == ground. Alys. 2884

—— == battlefield. Alys. 2378

Fleur-de-lis, *sb.* Pol. S. 190

Fling, *v. n.* == rush hastily. Alys. 1165; pret. 'fleng.' Ib. 6084. Sw. flänga

—— *adv.* ? == rashly. Alys. 4602

Flint, *sb.* HD. 2667. AS. flint

Fliting, *sb.* == scorn. Ps. cvi. 40. AS. flitan

Flitte, *v. n.* fly. Rel. Ant, ii. p. 192

Float, *v. n.* [flete]. RG. 261; pret. 'flet.' Pilate, 251

Flock, *sb.* == company. HD. 24

Flon, *sb.* == arrows. RG. 394. AS. flán

Flood, *sb.* RG. 20, 416

Floor, *sb.* RG. 288

Flosche, *sb.* == pit. Ps. xxvii. 1; xxix. 4; [flask]. Ps. cxlii. 7. ON. flaska, diffindere

Flouren, *adj.* == made of flour. Cok. 55

Flow, *v. n.* 3s. pres. 'floh.' O. and N. 918. AS. flówan

Flower, *sb.* RG. 433; virginity. Fall and P. 52

—— *v. n.* == bloom. Alys. 2904

Flum, *sb.* == stream. Alys. 3402. AS. flum. Lat. flumen

Flumbardyng, *sb.* == a fiery, hot-tempered man. Alys. 1788. Fr. flambard, a torch

Fly, *sb.* (the insect). RG. 428

Fly, *v. n.* == to fly with wings; pret. 'fleʒ' 184 β; part, 'yflowe.' RG. 29

―――― == to fly away, escape; pret. 'flowe.' RG. 372; 'flew.' RG. 18

Fnaste, *v. n.* == breathe. HD. 548. AS. fnæst

―――― *sb.* == breath or windpipe? O. and N. 44

Fo, *v. a.* == take. O. and N. 179; [vone]. RG. 204; [ifo]. O. and N. 612; 3s. pres. 'ifodh.' O. and N. 1643. AS. fón

Foam, *sb.* 404 β. AS. fám

―――― *v. n.* RG. 208

Fode, *sb.* == child. K. Horn, 1384. AS. fëdan

Foder, *sb.* == producer, mother. Alys. 645

Foe, *sb.* pl. 'fon.' RG. 401; 'fan.' Ps. xli. 11; 'ivo.' O. and N. 1714; 'faas.' Ps. xxx. 12

Foeman, *sb.* Wright's L. P. p. 104

Foh, *adj.* == particoloured (of dress). Rel. S. iv. 28. AS. fáh

Foil, *v. a.* == defile. Alys. 2712

Foison, *sb.* == plenty. Alys. 1012. Fr. foison. Lat, fusio

Fold, *sb.* == sheepfold. Pol. S. 152. AS fald

Fold, *sb.* == earth. Wright's L. P. p. 24. AS. folde

Fold, *v. a.* == bend. Wright's L. P. p. 47. AS. fealdan

Folewen, *v. a.* == baptize. Marg. 58. AS. fullian, to whiten, baptize

Folht, *sb.* == baptism. Pol. S. 157. AS. fulluht

Foliot, *sb.* == folly. O. and N. 866

Folk, *sb.* RG. 376, 377

Folliche, *adv.* == foolishly. 647 B.

Follow, *v. a.* Wright's L. P. p. 48; pret. 'fulied.' O. and N. 1237

―――― == persecute. 3 pl. pres. 'filiyhen.' Ps. cxviii. 157; 'fylegh.' Ps. vii. 6; pret. 'filiyhed.' Ps. cxviii. 161; part. 'filyhand.' Ps. vii. 2

Folly, *sb.* 156 B.

Fond, *v. a.* == try. RG. 455; part. 'yfonded.' RG. 102. AS. fandian

Fonge, *v. a.* == take up, resume. Pol. S. 216. AS. fón, fangen

Fontstone, *sb.* RG. 247

Food, *sb.* Wright's L. P. p. 69

Fool, *adj.* == foolish. RG. 568

―――― *sb.* 768 B.

Foot, *sb.* RG. 490; pl. 'fet.' RG. 508

Footfast, *adj.* == captive. Ps. ci. 21

Footfastness, *sb.* == captivity. Ps. civ. 18

For, *prep.* == on account of. RG. 58

—— == during (of time). 11 B.

—— *adv.* == because. RG. 366. 16 B.

Forasmuch, *adv.* RG. 454

Forban, *v. a.* == summon. O. and N. 1091

Forbear, *v. n.* RG. 526

—— *v. a.* == space. Alys. 4509

Forbearing, *sb.* Alys. 3826

Forbeode, *v. a.* == expect, Wright's L. P. p. 23

Forberne, *v. n.* == burn. O. and N. 419. Rel. S. iv. 11

—— *v. a.*—part, 'verbarnd.' RG. 378

Forbid, *v. a.* RG. 494

Forbisen, *sb.* == example, fable. O. and N. 244. Pol. S. 197. AS. fórebysen

Forbisening, *sb.* == parable. Ps. xlviii. 5

Forbreak, *v. a.* == break. RG. 375; part. 'forbroken,' == corrupt, Ps. xiii. 1

Forbreaking, *sb.* == destruction. Ps. xiii. 3

Forbreide, *v. a.* == offend against, O. and N. 1381. Dan. for-bryde

—— *v. n.* == commit a crime. O. and N. 510

Forbrode, Forbroide, *adj.* == criminal. O. and N. 1379. RG. 21, 205

Forby, *prep.* == beyond. Ps. xx. 7; xliv. 3

Forcast, == cast. Ps. xxi. 11

Force, *v. a.* == take care, heed. Leg. of St Wolstan in Warton, H. E. P. vol. i. p. 16

Forcleave, *v. a.* == cleave. RG. 17, 401

Forcling, *v. n.* == wither; pret. 'forclonge.' Pilate, 216

Forcome, *v. a.* == anticipate. Ps. xvi. 13.

—— *v. n.* == come before. Ps. cxviii. 147

Forcrempe, *v.* == to be convulsed, furious? O. and N. 510. Dan. krampe, a spasm or convulsion

Fordeme, *v. a.* == condemn. O. and N. 1096

Fordit, *part.* == shut up. Body and Soul, 236. AS. fordyttian

Fordo, *v. a.* == destroy. Wright's L. P. p. 71

—— == put away. Ps. lxxxviii. 45

Fordred, *adj.* == afraid. Wright's L. P. p. 88

Fordrue, *v. n.* == become dry. O. and N. 820. AS. fordrugan

Fordwine, *v. n.* == dwindle away. Pilate, 215. AS. fordwinan

—— *v. a.* == cause to wither; part. 'fordwinnen.' Rel. Ant. ii. p. 211

Fore, *adv.* == before. 31 B.

Fore, *sb.* == track. O. and N. 815. AS. fór

—— == business, proceeding? 'hys fore was no3t' == it was all over with him. RG. 386

Forehead, *sb.* 2217 B.

Foremost, *adj.* Wright's L. P. p. 41

Forene, *adj.* == interior, hidden; 'chambre forene' == a privy chamber. RG. 310. Fr. foreins. Vid. Roq.

Forest, *sb.* RG. 375

Forester, *sb.* RG. 499

Foretoken. Ps. lxxvii. 43

Foretokening, *sb.* Ps. lxx. 7

Foreward, *sb.* == compact, agreement. RG. 391, 514. AS. fóreweard

Forfare, *v. a.* == destroy. Marg. 4; part, 'furfarne.' Marg. 53; 'forfaren.' HD. 1380. The AS. 'forfaran' appears to be only used in the neuter sense == to perish, but 'furfare' is used actively in La3amon

Forfret, *v. a.* == devour. RG. 8. AS. fretan

Forget, *v. a.* RG. 446

Forgetelnes, *sb.* == forgetfulness, oblivion. Ps. ix. 19

Forgive, *v. a.* 1002 B.

Forgiveness, *sb.* RG. 58

Forgnide, *v. a.* == destroy, pret. 'forgnode.' Ps. civ. 16; cvi. 16. AS. forgnidan

Forgo, *v. a.* RG. 290. pret. 'foreode.' Wright's L. P. p. 23

Forgraythe, *v. a.* == prepare. Ps. xx. 13

Forgraything, *sb.* == preparation, design. Ps. ix. 38

Forgulte ? RG. 1

Forhaht, == despised, hated? Wright's L. P. p. 37. AS. forhiegan?

Forheaded, == beheaded. Alys. 1366

Forhele, *v. a.* == conceal, part. 'forhole.' Alys. 6967. In v. 7349, it seems to be used adverbially, and to mean 'secretly.' AS. forhelan

Forheler, *sb.* == a concealer. Ps. xvii. 31

Forheling, *sb.* == concealment. Ps. xvii. 19

Forhenge, *v. a.* == hang. HD. 2724

Forhoght, *sb.* == contempt. Ps. cxviii. 22

Forhone, *v. a.* == scorn, despise. Ps. xliii. 6. AS. hýnan, forhohnes

Forhoȝe, *v. a.* == despise. O. and N. 1600. AS. forhogian

Fork, *sb.* Alys. 1191

Forlaped, *adj.* == tired with lapping or drinking? Pol. S. 238

Forlength, *v. a.* == lengthen. Ps. cxxviii. 3

Forlere, *v. a.* == learn. O. and N. 924

Forleose, *v. a.* == lose. O. and N. 1664. part. 'forlore.' RG. 243

Forlest, *v. a.* == destroy. Ps. xx. 11. AS. læstan

Forlet, *v. a.* == leave alone. 1997 B. part. 'forlet' == desert. Alys. 2889

—— == allow. Ps. cxxiv. 3

Forleteness, *sb.* == contempt. Ps. cxxii. 3

Forleting, *sb.* == contempt. Ps. cxxii. 4

Form, *sb.* == manner. RG. 388; shape. Pilate, 125

Formanging, *sb.* == changing. Ps. liv. 20. AS. margian

Forme, *adj.* == first. O. and N. 818. AS. forma

Formeward, **Formerward**, *sb.* = vanguard. Alys. 5733, 7786

Forn, *sb.* 'þat forn.' == therefore. Creed of St Athan. 7. Cf. 'þer forne.' Ps. xvii. 3

Fornomen, *part.* == carried away. Ps. cviii. 23. AS. forniman

Forpine, *v. n.* == languish. 2402 B.

Forrede, *v. a.* == deceive. Body and Soul, 131

Forshaken, *part.* == shaken. Ps. cviii. 23; cxxvi. 4

Forsake, *v. a.* RG. 411

Forsee, *v. a.* == overlook, neglect. Ps. ix. 22

—— == see. pret. 'forsegh.' Ps. xci. 12

Forset, *v. a.* == place. Ps. cxxxvi. 6

Forsetting, *sb.* == proposition, discourse. Ps. xlviii. 5

Forsleuthed, *vb. pret.* == grew slothful. RG. 197

Forspeak, *v. a.* == speak against. Ps. xliii. 17

Forspread, *v. a.* == spread. Ps. xxxv. 11

Forswallow, *v. a.* == swallow [vorsuolwe]. RG. 206; [forswolehen].
Rel. S. v. 215

Forswarted, *part.* == blackened, swarthy. Pilate, 227

Forswat, *part.* == covered with sweat. Pol. S. 158

Forswear, *v. a.* == give up a thing. RG. 387

——— == perjure, part. 'forsworn.' RG. 446, 457

Forswelte, *part.* == suffocated. Alys. 7559. AS. forsweltan

Forswolehen. See Forswallow

Forte, *adv.* == until. RG. 463

Forth, *adv.* RG. 554

Forthbring, *v. a.* Ps. lxxvii. 26

Forthcall, *v. a.* == challenge. Ps. lxxvii. 58

Forthcast, *v. a.* Ps. xlix. 17

Forthcome, *sb.* Ps. civ. 38

Forther, == forwarder. 639 β

Forthern, *vb.* See Further

Forthferred, *part.* == gone forth. Ps. cxix. 5

Forthgang, *sb.* Ps. cxliii. 14

Forthfollow, *v. n.* Ps. lxviii. 32

Forthgo, *v. n.* part. 'forthgaand.' Ps. lxxxviii. 42

Forthi, *adv.* == therefore. Wright's L. P. p. 28. AS. forþi

Forthlead, *v. a.* Ps. lxviii. 32

Forthlook, *v. n.* Ps. xiii. 2; lxxxiv. 12

Forthrist, *v. a.* == smash, crush. Ps. xlvii. 8. AS. forþræstian

Forthshew, *v. a.* Ps. cxliv. 4

Forthward, *adv.* RG. 245

Fortnight, *sb.* 2327 B.

Fortread, *v. a.* == tread down. Ps. vii. 6. pret. 'fortrade.' Ps. lv. 2

Fortress, *sb.* Alys. 2668

Forty. RG. 419

Forwake, *part.* == having been long awake. Wright's L. P. p. 28

Forwerp, *v. a.* == throw away, reject. Ps. l. 13. AS. forweorpan

Forworthe, *part.* == destroyed, made worthless. O. and N. 548

Forwleynt, *part.* == puffed up. Wright's L. P. p. 24. AS. wlanc

Forwondred, *part.* == astonished. Ps. xlvii. 6

Forwounded, *part.* RG. 56, 306

Foryield, *v. a.* == recompense. Ps. cxxxvi. 8; xvii. 21

Foryielding, *sb.* == reward. Ps. xviii. 12; cxxx. 2

Foster, *v. a.* HD. 1434. Ps. liv. 23

Fother, *sb.* == a weight of 19 cwt. of lead, thence 'a large quantity.' Alys. 1809; 'a lump.' Alys. 6467. AS. foðer

Fou, *sb.* == yellow or tawny fur? M. Ode, 182. Rel. Ant. ii. p. 192. Fr. fauve

Foul, *adj.* RG. 380, 490

—— *v. a.* == defile. O. and N. 96

Found, *v. a.* part. 'ifounded.' RG. 469

Foundling, *sb.* K. Horn, 234

Four. RG. 389

Fourscore. RG. 382

Fourteen. RG. 383

Fourteenth, *adj.* RG. 408

Fourth, *adj.* [verthe]. RG. 415

Fous, *adj.* == eager. Wright's L. P. p. 50. AS. fús

Fox, *sb.* RG. 570

—— *adj.* == crafty. Rel. S. i. 15. ON. fyx, crafty

Fowl, *sb.* == bird. RG. 1; [fuȝele]. O. and N. 64

Foȝe, *sb.* == agreement. O. and N. 184. AS. fog

Fraist, *v. a.* == try. Ps. xi. 7. ON. fresta

Frame, *sb.* == profit. Wright's L. P. p. 71. AS. freme. ON. frami

Franchise, *sb.* RG. 47, 499

Franklin, *sb.* RG. 36

Free, *adj.* RG. 474

—— == liberal, noble. RG. 420. AS. freó

Freedom, *sb.* HD. 631

Freeman, *sb.* HD. 628

Freeze, *v. a.* part. 'yfrore.' RG. 265. 'frore.' Wright's L. P. p. 25

—— *v. n.* Wright's L. P. p. 110; 3 s. pres. 'frost.' O. and N. 620

Freitour, *sb.* == friar's room. 275 β

Freke, *sb.* == champion. Alys. 2161. AS. freca

Frely, *adj.* == noble, beautiful. Wright's L. P. pp. 45, 46

Fremd, *adj.* == foreign. HD. 2277. AS. fremed

Freme, *v. a.* == perform. HD. 441. AS. fremman

Freondrede, *sb.* == friendship. Alys. 1488

Fresh, *adj.* == active [versse]. RG. 395, 397

—— == inhabiting fresh water (of fish). RG. 1

—— == new, untired. Alys. 2405

Fret, *v. a.* == tear, devour. RG. 417; pret. 'frate.' Ps. lxxix. 14; part. 'ifrette.' Pol. S. 201. AS. fretan

Friar, *sb.* RG. 492, 545

Friday. RG. 229

Frie, *v. a.* == blame. HD. 1998. ON. frýja

Friend, *sb.* RG. 388, 502

Friendless, *adj.* RG. 343

Friendship, *sb.* RG. 35

Friendsome, *adj.* Ps. lxviii. 17

Friendsomeness, *sb.* Ps. lxiv. 12

Fright, *sb.* Body and Soul, 172

Frith, *sb.* [fryht] == a wood. Wright's L. P. pp. 36, 26. Low Lat. 'fretum.' SS. frið. See Laȝ. iii. 287

Fro, *adj.* == good. Wright's L. P. p. 100. AS. from

Frog, *sb.* RG. 69; [frosk]. Ps. civ. 30. AS. frosc

From, *prep.* [fram]. RG. 501, 500; [fron]. O. and N. 1612

Frome, *sb.* == beginning. O. and N. 477. AS. fruma

Fromward, *adv.* 885 B.

Fronst, *adj.* == shrivelled. Alys. 1630. Fr. froncer

Front, *sb.* == brow. 1195 B.

Frontel, *sb.* == frontlet. Pol. S. 154

Frosk. See Frog

Frost, *sb.* RG. 416; [forst]. O. and N. 524

Frother, *vb.* == comfort. AS. frófre

Frouri, *v. a.* == comfort. O. and N. 535. AS. frófrian

Frouȝ, *adj.* == wicked, froward. Body and Soul, 150. AS. fræc

Frude, *sb.* == ferret. M. Ode, 138. Fr. furet. Dut. foret

Fruit, *sb.* RG. 372, 378

Fruitful, *adj.* Ps. cxlviii. 9

Frusche, *v. a.* == smash. Alys. 1814. Fr. froisser, fruisser

Fuatted. Probably a mistake for 'flatted.' Alys. 6447

Fuel, *sb.* RG. 568

Fulfil, *v. a.* M. Ode, st. 150 (Hickes), but the Egerton MS. st. 156, reads 'fulð'

Fulhede, *sb.* == fulness. Ps. xxxv. 9

Full, *adj.* RG. 33, 380; [fulli]. Ps. cxxxviii. 22

Full, *v. a.* == baptize, lit. 'whiten.' part. 'yvolled.' RG. 239; 'ifulled.' St Kath. 141. AS. fullian

Full, *sb.* == the whole. Pol. S. 151

Fuller, *sb.* Pol. S. 188

Fully, *adv.* [follyche]. RG. 371; [fuliche], O. and N. 128

Fulmake, *v. a.* == complete, perfect. Ps. xvi. 5

Fundament, *sb.* (of the body). RG. 310, 526

Fundement, *sb.* == foundation. RG. 130

Fur, *sb.* Alys. 3295

Furchures, *sb.* == legs. Alys. 4995

Furford, *part.* for 'forfared' == perished. Alys. 3814; where the first 'ymad' should be omitted

Furlong, *sb.* Pol. S. 69

Furred, *adj.* Alys. 5474

Furrow, *sb.* HD. 1094

Further, *v. a.* [forthern]. Wright's L. P. p. 99

—— *adj.* 2360 B.

Furthermore, *adv.* Ritson's AS. viii. 42

Fyger, *sb.* == fig-tree. Alys. 5784

Fyke, *v. a.* == deceive, flatter. Wright's L. P. p. 46. Cf. 'fikele,' and AS. fácen

G.

Gabbe, *v. n.* == chatter, joke. Pol. S. 204. AS. gabban

—— *sb.* == talking. Wright's L. P. p. 49

Gabbing, *sb.* == talking. 'bi my gabbyng.' Pol. S. 158. (Cf. 'on my word.')

—— == idle talk. O. and N. 626. AS. gabbung

Gadeling, *sb.* == lit. 'companion;' thence afterwards a term of reproach, vagabond. RG. 310. See Gloss. Rem. to Laʒ. iii. 485. AS. gædeling

Gaff, *sb.* == an iron hook. Rel. Ant. ii. p. 174. Fr. gaffe

Gage, *sb.* == pledge. Alys. 7236. Fr. gage. Lat. vadium

Gain, *adj.* == elegant, gainly. Wright's L. P. p. 29. ON. gégn. Su. Goth. gen

Gain, *v. a.* == obtain. Pol. S. 151

Gainsay, *sb.* == contradiction. Ps. lxxix. 7

Gale, *sb.* == banquet or dance. Wright's L. P. p. 26. Fr. gale. AS. gál

—— == chattering, noise. Alys. 2047; a song. Alys. 2548. AS. galan

Galegale, *sb.* == noise, twittering. O. and N. 256

Galek, *sb.* Cok. 103; a mistake for 'garlek,' which is the reading of MS. Harl. 913

Galingale, *sb.* == the sweet cyperus. Cok. 71. Fr. galangue

Gall, *sb.* Wright's L. P. p. 99

Gallon, *sb.* K. Horn, 1155. Rel. S. vii. 37

Gallop, *v. n.* Alys. 461. Goth. 'hlaupan.' with 'ga' prefixed

Gallows, *sb.* HD. 1161

Gallowtree, *sb.* HD. 43

Gambison, *sb.* == a stuffed doublet, Alys. 5151. Fr. gambais. Goth. wamba. See Burguy, *s. v.* gambais

Game, *sb.* == sport. RG. 567, 375; [gome]. O. and N. 521

Gamen, *sb.* == sport, pleasure. HD. 2135. AS. gamen

Gan, *vb.* == began. 98 B.; [gonne]. RG. 371

Gange, *v. n.* == go. HD. 1057. AS. gangan

—— *sb.* == going, footstep. Ps. xvi. 5

Gangle, *v. n.* == jangle. Alys. 7413

Gaoler, *sb.* Pilate, 218

Gardener, *sb.* Fragm. in Warton, H. E. P. vol. i. p. 20

Gargaze, *sb.* == throat. Alys. 3636. Fr. gargate

Garland, *sb.* Pol. S. 218. Fr. garlande, from Lat. gyrus

Garlic, *sb.* Cok. 103

Garner, *sb.* Pol. S. 238. AS. gearo, ready

Garnet, *sb.* Wright's L. P. p. 25. Fr. grenat

Garste, *v. a.* == terrify. See Gast

Garyson, *sb.* == reward, payment. RG. 409, 413. Fr. garison

—— == care, office. 790 B.

Gast, *v. a.* == terrify. Wright's L. P. p. 90; [garste]. Pol. S. 222

Gaste, == ghost. *q. v.*

Gate, *sb.* == way. Ps. i. 6; 'thus gate,' == this way. HD. 2586. ON. gata

—— == manner, fashion. HD. 2419

Gate, *sb.* == entrance to a house. RG. 539, 394. AS. geát

Gateward, *sb.* == doorkeeper. K. Horn, 1099

Gather, *v. a.* RG. 380, 505

—— *v. n.* part. 'gaderyng.' Rel. Ant. ii. p. 175

Gaveler, *sb.* == usurer. Ps. cviii. 11. AS. gafel

Gavelock, *sb.* == javelin. Alys. 1355. Ps. liv. 22. AS. gafeloc

Gay, *adj.* Wright's L. P. p. 52

Gear, *sb.* == dress, appearance. Wright's L. P. p. 36. AS. gearwa

Geld, *adj.* == impotent, barren. Rel. Ant. ii. p. 210. Ps. cxii. 9

Geld, *v. a.* Wright's L. P. p. 24

Geldhede, *sb.* == barrenness. Ps. xxxiv. 12

Gem, *sb.* [zimme]. RG. 489

General, *adj.* RG. 495

Genge, *sb.* == family. HD. 790

—— == host, army; [gyng]. Alys. 922

—— == nation. Ps. ii. 8. AS. genge

Gent, *adj.* == gentle. RG. 24

Gentle, *adj.* == noble. RG. 420

Gentleman, *sb.* [gengylman]. RG. 323

Gentrise, *sb.* == nobleness, RG. 46, 434

Georre, *sb.* == anger. M. Ode, 139. AS. eorre, which is the reading of one MS.

Geoter, *sb.* == a caster of metals. Alys. 6735. AS. geótan

Gersoun, *sb.* == treasure. Rel. Ant. ii. p. 217. AS. gersume. ON. gérsemi

Gest, *sb.* == gesture, appearance. Alys. 6413

Gest, *sb.* == a tale. HD. 2328. Fr. geste. Lat. gestum

Gestning, *sb.* == hospitality. Alys. 1779

Geswinc, *sb.* == toil. M. Ode, 98. AS. geswinc

Get, *v. a.* == obtain. HD. 792; part. 'igotte.' Pol. S. 203

—— == take. HD. 2762

Geting, *sb.* == generation. Ps. xiii. 6

Ghost, *sb.* == a spirit. RG. 130

—— == spirit, as opposed to body. O. and N. 1396

—— == Holy Ghost. [Gaste]. Ps. i. fin.

Giant, *sb.* RG. 15

Gibbet, *sb.* Alys. 4722

Giddily, *adv.* == foolishly. O. and N. 1280

Giddy, *adj.* == foolish. RG. 68. AS. gidig

Gift, *sb.* 570 B.; [give]. HD. 357

Giglot, *sb.* == a loose girl. Pol. S. 154. AS. gagol

Gigour, *sb.* == a musician, properly a player on the wind instrument called a 'gige.' K. Horn, 1528. Vid. Roq. *s. v.* Gigueour

Gihte, *sb.* == manner? M. Ode, 192. See Gate

Gildert, *sb.* == a snare. Ps. ix. 31. Fr. guille

Gileyspeke, *sb.* == a cunning trick. RG. 553. Fr. guille

Gilmins, *sb.* == some order of Friars? Rel. Ant, ii. p. 175

Gilt, *part.* Alys. 927

Gin, *sb.* == device. RG. 402, 549. AS. grin

Gin, *vb.* == begin. 753 B.

Ging, *sb.* == army. See Genge

Ginger, *sb.* Alys. 6797; [gyngyvre]. Wright's L. P. p. 27

Gird, *v. a.* == cingere. RG. 435; part. 'ygurd.' RG. 174

—— *sb.* == girdle. Alys. 2272

Gird, *v. a.* == strike, smite. Alys. 2299. AS. gyrd, a staff

Girdle, *sb.* Wright's L. P. p. 35

Give, *sb.* See Gift

Give, *v. a.* [ȝeve]. RG. 12; pret. 'ȝaf.' RG. 17; imper. 'ȝef.' Wright's L. P. p. 59; part. 'iȝive.' O. and N. 551; 'yȝyne.' RG. 430

Giveled, *part.* == heaped together. HD. 814. Fr. gavelé. Sir F. Madden also suggests Dut. 'villen,' to flay, as a possible origin of this word. Others have proposed the Germ. gefüllt

Giving, *sb.* Alys. 839

Glad, *adj.* RG. 371; 'gladden.' 1066 B.

—— *v. n.* == be glad. RG. 265

—— *v. a.* == make glad. 1204 B.; part. 'igladed.' Pilate, 130

Gladden, *v. n.* == be glad. Ps. xcvi. 8

Gladful, *adj.* Ps. xlvi. 2

98

Gladly, *adv.* RG. 112

Gladness, *sb.* RG. 195, 530

Gladship, *sb.* Wright's L. P. p. 38

Glaive, *sb.* == a sword. RG. 203. Fr. glaive. Lat. gladius

Glass, *sb.* Wright's L. P. p. 31

—— == a mirror. Alys. 4408

Gleam, *sb.* HD. 2122

—— *v. n.* Wright's L. P. p. 36

Glede, *sb.* == live coal. HD. 91. AS. gléd

Glee, *sb.* RG. 272

Gleeman, *sb.* HD. 2329

Gleowinge, *sb.* == gleeing or singing. K. Horn, 1524

Glew, *adj.* == skilful. O. and N. 193. AS. gleáw

Glewe, *vb.* See Glow

Glide, *v. n.* HD. 1851; pret, 'glyt.' Alys. 4252

Glisten, *v. n.* Wright's L. P. p. 36

Gloterie, *sb.* == gluttony. Body and Soul, 93

Glove, *sb.* Fragm. on Seven Sins, 16

Glow, *v. n.* Fragm. Sci. 141; [glewe]. Wright's L. P. p. 38

Gloze, *v. n.* == flatter, be deceitful. RG. 510; part. 'glozyng.' RG. 497; AS. glesan

Glue, *v. a.* Alys. 6180

Glutton, *sb.* HD. 2104. Lat. gluttus, the throat

Gluttony, *sb.* RG. 330

Gnaist, *v. n.* == rage. Ps. ii. 1. ON. gnista

Gnat, *sb.* Ps. civ. 31

Gnaw, *v. a.* RG. 404, 417. AS. gnagan

Gnede, *adj.* == niggardly. HD. 97. Body and Soul, 20. AS. gneðen

Gnide, *v. a.* == dash to pieces. Ps. xvii. 43; pret. 'gnode.' Ps. lxxxviii. 45. AS gnidan

Gnoste, *sb.* == noise or clamour? Pol. S. 237. ON. gnaust

Go, *v. n.* RG. 13; [gon]. 74 B.; 2 s. pres. 'gest.' O. and N. 836, 536; 3 s. pres. 'goth.' Wright's L. P. p. 61; 'gas.' Ps. lxxxix. 6; pret. 'eode.' RG. 417; 'wende.' RG. 368; 'wode.' 1481 B.; 'ʒeode.' 99 B.; part, 'going.' RG. 538

Go, == good. *q. v.*

Goad, *sb.* [gad]. HD. 279. AS. gád

Goat, *sb.* pl. 'geet.' Pol. S. 198

God. RG. 468

Goderhele, *sb.* == happiness. RG. 368

Godhede, *sb.* == goodness. Alys. 7060

Godly, *adj.* Wright's L. P. p. 38

Godness, *sb.* == God-head. Creed of St Athan. v. 62

Godson, *sb.* 21 β

Gold, *sb.* RG. 1, 383

Golnes, *sb.* == lasciviousness. O. and N. 492. Ps. lxvii. 14. AS. gál

Goldfinch, *sb.* Alys. 783

Golokes. Rel. Ant. ii. p. 176; perhaps another form of 'galker' == a tub for wort. See Phil. Soc. Trans. for 1855, p. 267

Gome, *sb.* == a man. Wright's L. P. p. 38. AS. guma

Gome, *sb.* == care, thought. RG. 454, 537. AS. gýmen

Gome, *sb.* See Game

Gonfanon, *sb.* == banner. Alys. 1963

Goninde, *part.* == gaping, yawning. Marg. 43. AS. geonan

Gonnylde, *adj.* == foolish? Pol. S. 237. See Hall. *s. vv.* Goneil and Gomerill

Good, *adj.* RG. 375, 384; acc. 'godne.' K. Horn, 753

—— *sb.* 19 B. 'to do good'

—— *adv.* == will. Alys. 6267

Goods, *sb.* [god]. RG. 495

Goodman, *sb.* == husband

—— == a good man. RG. 257

Goodness, *sb.* RG. 434, 436

Goose, *sb.* HD. 702

Gore, *sb.* == a narrow slip let into a woman's dress, hence the dress itself, as in the phrase 'geynest under gore.' Wright's L. P. p. 29. ON. gára, to rend

Gorge, *v. a.* == devour, feed. Alys. 5625

—— *v. n.* Alys. 5625

Gorger, *sb.* == gorget. Alys. 3636

Goshawk, *sb.* Alys. 483

100

Goshorne ? Rel. Ant. ii. p. 176

Gospel, *sb*. RG. 470

Gothele, *v. n.* == make a noise, as water does when a hot iron is placed in it. Fragm. Sci. 140. ON. gutla

Goule, *v. n.* == howl. HD. 164, 454. ON. góla

Gout, *sb*. RG. 564, 564

Govern, *v. a.* RG. 398

—— *sb.* == government. 1792 B.

Grace, *sb*. 'year of grace.' RG. 382

—— == pardon. RG. 563

Gracious, *adj*. Wright's L. P. p. 52

Grade, *sb*. == a cry. Alys. 5740

Grain, *sb*. [grein]. == a small piece. Wright's L. P. p. 38

Gram, *adj*. == angry. HD. 2469, 214. AS. gram

Grame, Grome, == anger. Pol. S. 199

—— == sorrow. Pol. S. 219. AS. grama

Grandsire, *sb*. RG. 311

Grange, *sb*. HD. 764. Fr. grange, from Lat. granum

Grant, *v. a.* RG. 447, 477, 208

Grape, *sb*. 417 β

Grass, *sb*. RG. 43

Grasshopper, *sb*. [gressop], Ps. lxxvii. 46; civ. 34

Grate, *sb*. == firegrate. Body and Soul, 204

Graueth, *vb*. == clothes? Wright's L. P. p. 61. Rel. Ant. ii. p. 217. AS. gerǽdian?

Grave, *v. a.* == dig. Ps. vii. 16

—— == bury. HD. 613; part 'graven.' HD. 2528

—— *sb.* == sculpture. Ps. lxxvii. 58

—— == image. Ps. cv. 19

Grave, *sb*. Body and Soul, 98

Gravel, *sb*. K. Horn, 1521. Gael. gairbheil. See Phil. Soc. Proc. vol. iv. p. 257

Grayking, *sb*. == graying, or early dawn. Alys. 5413; 'griking.' Ps. xlv. 6

Grease, *sb*. RG. 410

Great, *adj.* RG. 377; [grot]. RG. 26; 'great heart,' == anger. RG. 309

—— *v. n.* == become great. Alys. 452

Greave, *sb.* == magistrate. HD. 266. AS. geréfa

Grede, *v. n.* == cry out. RG. 559; pret. 'gradde.' O. and N. 934. AS. grædan

Grede, *sb.* == breast of a mantle. Alys. 4187; [i-grede]. O. and N. 1641. AS. greada

Greding, *sb.* == crying. Alys. 7882

Green, *adj.* RG. 419

—— *sb.* == an open grass lawn. HD. 2840; in pl. 'greens,' == herbs. Ps. xxxvi. 2

Greet, *v. a.* == salute. RG. 554. AS. grétan

Greet, *v. n.* == weep; part 'i-gret.' HD. 163, 164; 'graten,' Ib. 241; 'igroten,' Ib. 285. AS. grætan

Greeting, *sb.* == salutation. 1238 B.

Greeting, *sb.* == weeping. HD. 166

Greme, *v. a.* == displease. Wright's L. P. p. 36; part 'i-gremet,' O. and N. 931

—— *v. n.* == be displeased [grom]. O. and N. 870. AS. gremian

Grene, = desire? HD. 996. AS. geornan

Greneris, *sb.* == green branches, hence 'greene-ry.' Cok. 8

Grenne, *sb.* == grin; 'thou list grenne,' == thou liest a-grin or grinning. Body and Soul, 56

Gressop. Grasshopper. *q. v.*

Grete, *sb.* == weeping. Ps. ci. 10

Grey, *adj.* RG. 440, 498

—— *sb.* == gray fur. M. Ode, 183. Rel. Ant. ii. p. 192

Greyhound, *sb.* [grif-hound]. Alys. 5284

Greyn, *sb.* == edge. Alys. 6537

Greythe, *v. a.* == make ready. RG. 371, 434. ON. greiða

Grieve, *v. a.* RG. 563; part. 'igreved.' St Swithin, 120

Grievance, *sb.* Alys. 965

Grievous, *adj.* RG. 202

Grill, *adj.* == sharp, unkind. Body and Soul, 34. ON. gríla

—— *sb.* == sorrow. Wright's L. P. p. 91

Grim, *adj.* HD. 155; 'grim or gore?' HD. 2497

Grimful, *adj.* Signa ante Jud. 156

Grimly, *adv.* RG. 347

Grin, *v. n.* 987 B.

Grind, *v. a.* Pol. S. 69; [gryngen]. Alys. 4443; part. 'ygrounde.' Alys. 5872

Grine, *sb.* == gin, snare. O. and N. 1057; [grinew]. O. and N. 1054

Grip, **Gripe**, *v. a.* == seize hold of. RG. 22; [grope]. Alys. 1957

Grip, *sb.* == griffin. HD. 572. Alys. 5667

Grip, *sb.* == ditch. HD. 1924

Grise, *v. a.* == agrise, frighten. Body and Soul, 96. AS. a-grýsan

Grisful, *adj.* Signa ante Jud. 16

Grisly, *adj.* RG. 415, 566; 'grisloker,' == grislier. RG. 590. AS. grislíc

Grith, *sb.* == peace. HD. 61, 511. AS. gríð

Grithbruch, *sb.* == breach of the peace. O. and N. 1043

Grithsergeant, *sb.* HD. 267

Gro, *sb.* == a rich fur. Wright's L. P. p. 26; [groy]. Rel. Ant. ii. p. 217

Groan, *v. n.* RG. 380

Grom. See Greme.

Gromyl, *sb.* == the herb 'gromwell,' or Lithospermum officinale. Wright's L. P. p. 27

Grone, *sb.* == a part of a woman's dress. Wright's L. P. p. 27. Fr. giron. Vid. Roq., and compare 'gronet in grene' in the Anturs of Arthur, at Tarne Wathelan. st. 47

Groom, *sb.* == boy or infant. HD. 790. AS. guma

Grope, *v. a.* == investigate. Alys. 6642

Grope, == feel. O. and N. 1494. AS. gropian

Grotes, *sb.* == grouts, small pieces. HD. 472. AS. grút

Grouer, *sb.* == grosvair, a kind of fur. Rel. Ant. ii. p. 217

Ground, *sb.* RG. 22

—— *v. a.* == bring to ground. RG. 372

—— == form, constitute. Ps. viii. 4

Groundly, *adv.* == deeply [grundlike]. HD. 651

Groundstathelnes, *sb.* == foundation. Ps. cxxxvi. 7

Groundwall, *sb.* == foundation. Ps. lxxxvi. 1

Grow, *v. n.* RG. 21; pret. 'greu.' RG. 470

Gruche, *v. n.* == murmur, grumble. Rel. Ant. ii. p. 211. Fr. groucer

Grudge, *v. n.* Ps. lviii. 16

Grudging, *sb.* O. and N. 423

Grulde, *vb.* == struck. O. and N. 142. Probably from AS. 'grillan,' to provoke, and hence to keep on touching or striking, so as to irritate. Cf. the ἐρεθίζειν μάγαδιν of Telestes, ap. Ath. 637 A.

Grund, or **Ground**, used as an intensifying prefix—'grund-stalworthe.' HD. 1027

Grunt, *v. n.* Alys. 5846

Grys, *sb.* == a kind of fur. Wright's L. P. p. 26. Fr. gris. See the Prompt. Parv. *s. v.* Gryce, and the note there

Guede. A mistake for 'gnede.' *q. v.*

Guile, *sb.* RG. 538

—— *v. a.* == deceive. Rel. Ant. p. 116

Guiling, *sb.* == deceit. Alys. 3475

Guilt, *v. n.* == sin, become guilty. Ps. cxviii. 67

Guilt, *sb.* 827 B.

Guiltless, *adj.* RG. 327, 509

Guilty, *adj.* 2123 B.

Guise, *sb.* == fashion. Pol. S. 221

Gulte, *vb.* == offends? O. and N. 1521

Gun, *sb.* Alys. 3268

Guodded, *vb.* == stained. Alys. 2374. Fr. guede, woad

Gut, *sb.* RG. 446, 526

Gutter, *sb.* == waterpipe [goter]. Ps. lxxi. 6

Gwinris, *sb.* == guides. Alys. 7244. Fr. guioneres

Gylofre, *sb.* == gilliflower. Wright's L. P. p. 27

Gyng, *sb.* == host, army, our 'gang.' See Genge

Gyngyvre. See Ginger

Gyour, *sb.* == a guide. Alys. 4810. Fr. guicour. Sec Roq. *s. v.*

Gysceres. M. Ode, 135. Probably a mistake for 'gyveres,' avaricious. AS. gífer

Gyve, *sb.* Pol. S. 221. W. gefyn

Gywise, *sb.* == judgment. St Kath. 9

H.

Habit, *sb.* == dress. RG. 150, 434

—— == custom. Rel. Ant. ii. p. 175

Hack, *v. a.* RG. 216. Ps. liv. 4

Hahe, == courtyard. See Haȝe

Haie, == wall of a yard. See Haȝe

Hair, *sb.* RG. 560

—— == hairshirt. 259 B.

—— == sackcloth. Ps. xxxiv. 13

Hail, *adj.* == wholesome. Alys. 7036. AS. hǽl

Hail, *sb.* Fragm. Sci. 216. AS. hagol

—— *v. n.* [haweli]. 683 β

Hake, *sb.* (the fish). Wright's L. P. p. 31

Hal, *adj.* == whole. HD. 2370

Hale, *sb.* == a hollow. O. and N. 2. AS. hal, hol

Half, *adj.* RG. 3

—— *sb.* == side. Pol. S. 217

—— *v. a.* == divide in half. Ps. liv. 24

Half, *sb.* == behalf. 1688 B.

Halfendele, *sb.* == half part. RG. 390, 5

Halfman, *sb.* RG. 401

Halfpenny, *sb.* Alys. 3116

Halidom, *sb.* == sacrament. 2290 B. AS. háligdóm

Halihingness, *sb.* == sanctification. Ps. xcv. 6

Halimote, *sb.* == court, Pol. S. 154. AS. halle gemót

Halke, *sb.* == corner. K. Horn, 1119. AS. heal

Hall, *sb.* RG. 390

Hallow, *v. a.* pret. 'halwede.' RG. 469; 'halewe.' 319 B.; part. 'y-hallowed.' RG. 416

Halo, *sb.* [halewe]. 2166 β

105

Halt, *v. n.* == walk lamely. Wright's L. P. p. 48

Halter, *sb.* 1174 B.

Halwe, *sb.* == the Saints. RG. 82, 255

Halwei, *sb.* == balsam. Cok. 82. See Laȝ. iii. 501. AS. hæl and hwæg, == whey

Hame, *sb.* == skin. Alys. 391. ON. hamr

Hammer, *sb.* RG. 99

Hand, *sb.* RG. 369; 'to go on hand,' == to attempt to deceive. O. and N. 1649

Handaxe. RG. 26. HD. 2553

Handfull, *sb.* Ps. cxxv. 6

Handiwork, *sb.* Wright's L. P. p. 60

Handle, *v. a.* RG. 435. St Swithin, 60

Handmaiden, *sb.* Ps. cxxii. 2

Handtame, *adj.* == mild, mansuetus. Ps. xxxiv. 9

Handtameness, *sb.* Ps. xliv. 5

Handwork, *sb.* Ps. cxxxvii. 8

Hang, *v. a.* 3 s. pres. 'hoth.' O. and N. 1121; pret. 'honge.' RG. 473; part. 'yhonge.' RG. 174

———— == make to hang down. Pol. S. 154

———— *v. n.* Wright's L. P. p. 68

Hans, *sb.* == a quantity. Alys. 1571. MG. hansa

Hap, *sb.* RG. 447. ON. happ. W. hap

Harat, *sb.* == stable or stud of horses. Cok. 35. Fr. haras. Probably from Lat. 'hara.' See the Prompt. Parv. *s. v.*

Hard, *adj.* RG. 391

———— *v. a.* == harden; part, 'yharded.' RG. 352

Hardily, adv. RG. 375

Hardish, Hardy, *v. a.* == encourage. RG. 426. Alys. 3343

Hardissy, *sb.* == boldness. RG. 204

Hardy, *adj.* RG. 452

Hare, *sb.* RG. 376

Harlas, *sb.* == plinth. Cok. 67. Fr. orle. See Cotgr. and Roq. *s. v.*

Harle, *vb.* See Hurl

Harlot, *sb.* == used of a man. Pol. S. 237. W. herlawd

106

Harm, *sb.* RG. 409, 377

Harmless, *adj.* RG. 335, 509

Harness, *sb.* Alys. 7479. Fr. harnas

Harp, *sb.* RG. 272

—— *v. n.* RG. 272. Alys. 1043

Harper, *sb.* RG. 272

Hart, *sb.* RG. 376

Harvest, *sb.* RG. 414, 500

Has, == ars, art? Alys. 444

Hasp, *sb.* Body and Soul, 199. AS. hæps

Haste, *v. n.* RG. 305

—— *sb.* Ps. lxxvii. 33

Hastiness, *sb.* RG. 475

Hastily, *adv.* RG. 382

Hasty, *adj.* RG. 414, 458

Hat, *sb.* == a command. Pol. S. 158. AS. hátan

Hatch, *sb.* == a small door. O. and N. 1056. AS. hæca

Hatch, *v. a.* pret. 'haȝte.' O. and N. 105; part, 'y-haht.' Pol. S. 237

Hatchet, *sb.* Pol. S. 223

Hate, *sb.* 1667 B.; [hete]. O. and N. 167

—— *v. a.* Wright's L. P. p. 90. RG. 437

Hatred, *sb.* Pol. S. 157

Hattest. See Hight

Hattren, *sb.* == clothes. Wright's L. P. p. 110. Alys, 4264, 7054. AS.
hæter

Hauberk, *sb.* RG. 99, 174, 297. Fr. hauber. See Roq.

Haught, *adj.* [haȝt], == haughty. RG. 418

Haughtiness, *sb.* RG. 29

Haul, *v. a.* Alys. 992; part, 'ihauled.' 1499 B. ON. hala

Haumudeys, *sb.* == a purse. Alys. 1707. Fr. aumoniére (Weber)

Haunt, *v. a.* == frequent. RG. 534

—— == practise. Alys. 7496

—— *sb.* Alys. 6531

Hautain, *adj.* == haughty. RG. 66

Have, *v. a.* pres. 'abbe.' RG. 423; 2 s. pres. 'havest.' O. and N. 1148; 3 s. pres. 'ath.' RG. 368; pl. 'habbeth.' RG. 9; pret. 'adde.' RG. 368

—— *vb. aux.* Rel. S. ii. 13, 31

Haven, *sb.* RG. 423; [have]. RG. 134

Haver, *adj.* == clever, Pol. S. 155. ON. hagr

Haw, *sb.* == the fruit of the hawthorn. RG. 524. AS. hagan

Hawe, *sb.* == care, attention. Marg. 18

Hawk, *sb.* RG. 275

Hay, *sb.* RG. 406

Hayward, *sb.* == 'a person who guarded the corn and farmyard in the night time.' Halliwell. Wright's L. P. p. 110. Pol. S. p. 149

Hazardry, *sb.* RG. 195

Haȝe, *sb.* == courtyard of a house. O. and N. 585; [hahe]. O. and N. 1610

—— == wall of a yard. Ps. lxxxviii. 41. Fr. haie. AS. haga

Haȝt, *adj.* == haughty, *q. v.*

HE, *nom.* RG. 367, 443; gen. 'his.' RG. 367; dat. 'him.' RG. 367; acc. 'him.' RG. 367; 'hine.' O. and N. 1372

Heo, Ho, == she. RG. 13; [ȝoe]. RG. 436; [he]. Wright's L. P. pp. 27, 95; gen. 'hire.' RG. 13; dat. 'hire.' RG. 13; acc. 'here.' RG. 12; 'hire.' Marg. 44; 'hine.' Ps. lxviii. 37

Hit, == it. [he]. O. and N. 21; [het]. O. and N. 21

—— *pl. nom.* 'hii.' RG. 367; 'ho.' Marg. 61; 'he.' HD. 152; 'heo.' RG. 4, 45; 'hue.' Wright's L. P. p. 105; 'thei.' 494 B.; 'thai.' Ps. xxi. 5

—— *gen.* 'here.' O. and N. 936; 'her.' RG. 369; 'hor.' RG. 467; 'heore.' Rel. S. iv. 18; 'thare.' O. and N. 140; 'hore.' O. and N. 280; 'huere.' Wright's L. P. p. 41; 'tho.' Wright's L. P. p. 29, with 'of'

Hit, *dat.* 'heom.' O. and N. 1380; 'hem.' RG. 381

—— *acc.* 'heom.' O. and N. 1515; 'hom.' O. and N. 913; 'hem.' RG. 385

He, *adj.* == high. Fragm. Sci. 283

Head, *sb.* RG. 23, 402

Headlong, *adv.* [hedlyng]. Alys. 2261

Heal, *v. a.* RG. 151

Healing, *sb.* == health. Ps. lxvi. 3

Health, *sb.* [hele]. RG. 151. Ps. xxi. 2

Healer, *sb.* Ps. xxiv. 5

Heap, *sb.* 443 β. Sermon, 34

Hear, *v. a.* [i-here]. O. and N. 544; [i-hure]. RG. 556; pret. 'hurde.' RG. 391; part. 'y-herd.' RG. 87

Hearing, *sb.* == rumour. Ps. cxi. 7

Hearken, *v. n.* RG. 1

—— *v. a.* == listen to. RG. 308

Heart, *sb.* HD. 479; [hurte]. 22 B.

Heartily, *adv.* RG. 1347. HD. 1347

Heartsblood, *sb.* HD. 1819

Heat, *sb.* 62 β

—— *v. n.* == become hot. pret. 'hatte.' K. Horn, 622

Heathen, *sb.* RG. 396

Heathenesse, *sb.* == heathens. RG. 480

—— == heathenism. RG. 529

Heave, *v. a.* [hebbe]. RG. 17. AS. hebban

Heaven, *sb.* RG. 405; [hoven]. O. and N. 860

Heavenriche, *sb.* == sky. Cok. 6

—— == heaven. M. Ode, st. 31

Heaviness, *sb.* Fragm. Sci. 110

Heavy, *adj.* Wright's L. P. p. 102

—— *v. a.* == make heavy. Ps. xxxi. 4

Hechil, *sb.* == a hackle, for carding flax. Rel. Ant. ii. p. 176. Dut. hekel

Hedge, *sb.* RG. 211. AS. hege

Hedy ? Wright's L. P. p. 22. Probably a mistake for 'hendy.' Cf. Ib. p. 27

Heed, *sb.* Wright's L. P. p. 112

—— *v. a.* HD. 2389

Heel, *sb.* HD. 898

Heelspor, *sb.* == footstep. Ps. xlviii. 6; lv. 7

Heifer, *sb.* Pol. S. 239

Height, *sb.* Wright's L. P. p. 110

109

Heir, *sb*. RG. 377, 469

Heisugge, *sb*. == hedge-sparrow. O. and N. 505. AS. hege-sugge. Bosworth on the authority of More gives 'Sugga,' a bird which feeds on figs. Lye explains 'hege-sugge' as 'cicada,' 'vicetula'

Helde, *sb*. == loyalty. RG. 285. AS. held, heol (see Beowulf, 2459). Germ. hold

—— == virtue? Wright's L. P. p. 37

Helde, *v. n*. == incline, lean to. Wright's L. P. p. 24. Ps. lxi. 4; AS. healdan, hyldan

Hele, *v. n*. == drink health to a person? Alys. 1048

Hele, *v. a*. == cover [hile]. HD. 2082; part, 'y-heled.' RG. 305, 457; 'hole.' Alys. 4203. AS. hélan

Heling [hiling], *sb*. == cover. Ps. lx. 5

—— == lurking-place [heolyng]. Alys. 6188

Hell, *sb*. RG. 322

Helm, *sb*. == helmet. RG. 186, 401

Help, *sb*. RG. 556

—— *v. a*. RG. 3; part. 'y-hoppe.' RG. 405

Helper, *sb*. Ps. li. 9

Helpless, *adj*. RG. 134, 237

Helplich, *adj*. == helpful. Fall and P. 4

Heme, *sb*. == man. Pol. S. 156; O. and N. 1113. Fr. homme

Heme, *adj*. == pleasant, agreeable? Wright's L. P. p. 32. Perhaps for 'queme,' 'q-heme,' the first letter being dropped to preserve the alliteration

Hemming, *sb*. == fringe. Ps. xliv. 14

Hemp, *sb*. HD. 782. AS. hænep

Hen, *sb*. RG. 404

Henceforth, *adv*. [heþenforth]. Ps. cxii. 2

Hence, *adv*. [henne]. RG. 476; [hunne], Fragm. Sci. 98; [honne], O. and N. 879. Probably an old gen. of 'hen' (cf. Germ. 'hin'), used absolutely

Hende, *adj*. == kind, courteous. RG. 404. See on this word Gloss. Rem. to Laȝ. iii. 445

Hende, *sb*. == duck. HD. 1241. ON. önd. AS. ened

Hendely, *adv*. == well, cleverly. 167 B.

Hene, *adj.* == abject. Pol. S. 150. AS. hean

Hente, *v. a.* == take. RG. 460; part. 'yhent.' RG. 185. AS. hentan

Henyng, in Wright's L. P. p. 36, a misprint for 'hevyng.' See Hoving

Heowes, == high men? Wright's L. P. p. 114. AS. heáh

Herb, *sb.* 41 β

Herbarewen, *v. a.* == harbour, lodge. Pol. S. 240; part. 'herborwed.' HD. 742. ON. herbergja, Fr. herbergier

Herbegi, *sb.* == a lodging. Signa ante Jud. 168

Herber, *sb.* == arbour, garden. Alys. 331. Lat. herbarium

Herboru, *sb.* == lodging. HD. 742

Herd, *sb.* Ps. lxiii. 3

—— *v. a.* == keep, preserve. Ps. xlix. 19; lvii. 3. AS. hyrdan

Here, *adv.* RG. 369; 'here and there.' 42 B.

Here, *sb.* == army. Alys. 2101, 5266. AS. here

Here, *vb.* == to bless, praise. See Herie

Herebefore, *adv.* 1239 B.

Hereby, *adv.* 938 B.

Hereof, *adv.* RG. 364

Hereto, *adv.* 137 B.

Hergonge, *sb.* == invasion. O. and N. 1189. AS. heregang

Herie, *v. a.* == praise. Ps. xcix. 4; [here]. Body and Soul, 200. AS. hérian

Herigaus, *sb.* == cloaks. RG. 548. Pol. S. 156. Fr. hergaut

Heritage, *sb.* RG. 431, 523

Hermit, *sb.* 610 β

Hermitage, *sb.* 1139 B.

Hernes, *sb.* == brains. HD. 1808; necks? Ps. cxxviii. 4. ON. hjarni. AS. hærnes

Hernpan, *sb.* == brain-pan. HD. 1991

Herre, == higher. See High

Herring, *sb.* HD. 758. Alys. 6589

Hert, == heart? Wright's L. P. p. 31

Herte, == highest. See High

Herying, *sb.* == praise. Ps. cxliv. 21

Hest, *sb.* == command. RG. 493, 556; [hes]. M. Ode, 174

Hestris, *sb.* == condition. Alys. 7611. Fr. estre

Hete, *sb.* == hate. *q. v.*

Hethe, *v. a.* == threaten. Wright's L. P. p. 37. ON. hæta. Sw. höta

Hethe, *v. a.* == command; pret. 'hettede.' HD. 551. AS. hátan

Hethele, *sb.* == hot iron. Body and Soul, 204. Cf. the Yorkshire 'hottel'

Hething, *sb.* == contempt, scorn. Ps. lxxviii. 4. ON. háðung

Heving. See Hoving

Heving, *sb.* == lifting up. Ps. cxl. 2

Hew, *v. a.* Wright's L. P. p. 110; 3 s. pres. 'hoȝeth,' O. and N. 455. AS. héawan

Hide, *v. a.* [hude]. Pol. S. 150; pret. 'hudde.' Alys. 2489; part. 'y-hud.' RG. 87; 'hyd.' Wright's L. P. p. 40

Hide, *sb.* == a skin. RG. 116, 404

—— == a measure of land. RG. 374; a field. Alys. 458. In Wright's L. P. p. 31, 'in hyde' seems to mean 'in a hiding-place or retreat'

Hidel, *sb.* == hiding-place. Ps. xxvi. 5. AS. hidels

Hiding, *sb.* [huding] == concealment. 1381 B.

Hie, *v. n.* RG. 544; pret. 'hied.' RG. 387. AS. higan

High, *adj.* [heye]. RG. 367; [hoh]. HD. 1361; [he]. Fragm. Sci. 283. Comp. 'herre.' RG. 473; sup. 'hexte.' RG. 6, 397; 'herte.' RG. 509

Highman, *sb.* [heyme], RG. 288

Highmaster, *sb.* Alys. 270

Highness, *sb.* == high thing. Ps. xli. 8

Hiht, == caught? Pol. S. 150. Dut. 'hechten,' apprehendere (Kil.)

Hill, *sb.* RG. 398

Hilt, *sb.* == handle of a shield. Alys. 1270

Hind, *sb.* (animal). RG. 376

Hinder, *adj.* == posterior. 638 β

Hindforth, *adv.* == backwards. Alys. 4710

Hindward, *adv.* Ps. xxxix. 15

Hine, *sb.* == low fellow, servant. RG. 485, 540. AS. hína

Hinehed, *sb.* == society. Ps. xxi. 28; ciii. 14. AS. hynden

Hip, *sb.* (part of the body) [hupe]. RG. 322. AS. hyp

Hip, *sb.* == fruit of the wild rose. Alys. 4983. AS. heope

Hippopotamus, *sb.* [ypotamos]. Alys. 5166

Hird, *sb.* == shepherd. Wright's L. P. p. 96

Hire, *v. a.* 1173 B.

—— *sb.* HD. 908

Hire, *sb.* == hireling, man. HD. 997. AS. hýra.

Hirmon, *sb.* == servant, domestic. Wright's L. P. p. 50. Pol. S. 157. AS. hýr-man

Hit, *v. a.* pret. 'hutte.' Alys. 2155

Hither, *adv.* 1329 B.

Hitherward, *adv.* RG. 505

Hiȝte, *v. n.* == rejoice. O. and N. 436. AS. hyhtan

Hlad. O. and N. 1574. Perhaps a mistake for 'hald' or 'halt,' == holdeth

Hoar, *v. n.* == become hoary. Alys. 1597

—— *adj.* == hoary. Alys. 5031

—— *sb.* == an old man. Alys. 6752

Hoard, *sb.* Wright's L. P. p. 54. O. and N. 1222

Hoarfrost, *sb.* Fragm. Sci. 232

Hoarse, *adj.* [hose]. O. and N. 504. AS. hás

Hog, *sb.* Alys. 1885

Hohful, *adj.* == full of care. O. and N. 1290. AS. hohfull

Hoke, *v. n.* == move tortuously? O. and N. 377. ON. hoka

Hoker, *sb.* == scorn. RG. 272, 285. AS. hocer

Hokerly, *adv.* RG. 417

Hoket, *sb.* == a plaything. Alys. 7000. Fr. hochet

Hold, *adj.* == firm. HD. 2780; friendly. RG. 456, 383. AS. hold

Hold, *sb.* [i-hold], == a hold, residence. O. and N. 621

Hold, *v. a.* RG. 368; 3 s. pres. 'hal' == holds. RG. 289; 'halt.' RG. 12, 36; pret, 'huld.' RG. 367; part, 'halle.' Alys. 2327

—— *v. n.* == to hold with a person. Wright's L. P. p. 32

Holde, *sb.* == plenty. Ps. xviii. 11

Hole, *sb.* HD. 1813

Holer, *sb.* == adulterer, libertine. RG. 26. Fr. holier. See Roq.

Holiness, *sb.* RG. 332

Hollow, *adj.* RG. 131, 251

113

Holm, *sb.* == holm oak. Alys. 4945

Holy, *adj.* RG. 392, 503; comp. 'holier.' RG. 239

Holyday, *sb.* Rel. S. vii. 62

Holyman, *sb.* RG. 255

Homage, *sb.* 'do homage.' RG. 388

Home, *sb.* RG. 375; [ham]. O. and N. 1529; [heom]. O. and N. 1532

Homeward, *adv.* RG. 260, 269

Honest, *adj.* == honourable. Alys. 158

Honey, *sb.* Cok. 44

Honour, *sb.* RG. 20

——— *v. a.* RG. 80, 367

Hood, *sb.* == state, person, or hypostasis. Creed of St Athan. 15. AS. hád

Hood, *sb.* == covering for the head. Wright's L. P. p. 52

Hooded, *adj.* [ihoded]. O. and N. 1175

Hook, *sb.* HD. 752

Hooked, *adj.* [i-hoked]. O. and N. 1673

Hop, *v. n.* == go [huppe], RG. 537. AS. hoppian

——— == hop; 3 s. pres. 'hupth.' O. and N. 379; pret. 'hupte.' O. and N. 1634; 'hoppede.' RG. 278

Hope, *sb.* RG. 404

——— *v. n.* pret. 'hopede.' RG. 182, 558

——— == to hope to, trust in. M. Ode, st. 15

Hopper, *sb.* == a large basket. Ps. lxxx. 7. From AS. hóp, an osier

Hore, *v. a.* == pray. Wright's L. P. pp. 37, 50. Fr. horer.

Hori, *adj.* == filthy. Rel. Ant. ii. pp. 176, 191. AS. hórig

Horn, *sb.* HD. 700

Horned, *adj.* Ps. xcvii. 6

Horre, *sb.* Rel. Ant. ii. p. 177, possibly a filthy place, cavern. AS. hóru

Horse, *sb.* RG. 375, 404

Horsebere, *sb.* == litter. RG. 163. AS. hors-bær

Horseknave, *sb.* == horseboy. Pol. S. 237

Horseman, *sb.* Pol. S. 189

Horwyla, *sb.* == groom, equerry. Cok. 34. AS. hors-weálh, an

Hose, *sb.* RG. 390

Hosed, *adj.* Wright's L. P. p. 111

Hospital, *sb.* 84 B.

Host, *sb.* == an army. RG. 387, 459. Lat. hostis

Host, *sb.* == an entertainer, landlord. 1188 B. Fr. hôte. Lat. hospes

Host, *v. a.* == to lodge a person; part. 'y-osted.' RG. 52

Hostage, *sb.* RG. 367, 563

Hostel, *sb.* == hospitality. Alys. 7171

Hot, *adj.* RG. 7, 531

Hote, *v. n.* == be called. RG. 93; 2 s. pres. 'hattest.' O. and N. 256; pret. 'het.' RG. 556; 'hatte.' RG. 89; part. 'y-hote.' RG. 89. AS. hátan

Hote, *v. a.* == command. 479 B. O. and N. 777; pret. 'het,' RG. 381; 'hat,' Pol. S. 158; part. 'ihote.' 701 B. AS. hátan

—— *sb.* == a command. Ps. lv. 12

—— == a vow. Ps. lxiv. 2

Hotfoot, *adj.* == in hot haste. Body and Soul, 211

Houdsithe, *sb.* == outgoing journey. O. and N. 1584. AS. ut-sið

Hound, *sb.* RG. 275

Houndfly, *sb.* == locust. Ps. lxxvii. 45; pl. 'hundflegh.' Ps. civ. 31

Hour, *sb.* Wright's L. P. p. 71

House, *sb.* RG. 20, 370

—— *v. a.* RG. 21

Housel, *v. a.* == to administer the Sacrament to a person. RG. 392. AS. húsl

Houue, *sb.* == cap. Rel. Ant. ii. p. 175. AS. húfe. In Body and Soul, 123, 'houue' seems to mean 'covering' generally

Hove, *v. n.* == remain, stop, or hover. Fragm. Sci. 216. RG. 547, 172

—— == float? 368 β See the Prompt. Parv. *s. v.* hovyn

Hoventinge, == encircling? (as a haven does ships). O. and N. 999. Probably another form of 'hovening' or 'havening,' a derivative of 'haven' (cf. spene, spend; lene, lend). See Dähnert's Lexicon. *s. v.* havenung

Hoving, *sb.* == delay, remaining [hevyng]. Wright's L. P. p. 36

How, *adv.* [hou]. RG. 367; [hu]. O. and N. 728

How, *sb.* == hue, cry. Alys. 5306

Howe, *v. n.* == remove, go away. Wright's L. P. p. 23

Howe, *sb.* == care, anxiety. RG. 461; [hoʒe]. O. and N. 701. AS. hoga

Howsoever, *adv.* 194 B.

Huckster, *sb.* [hokester]. Rel. Ant. ii. p. 176. Dut. hucker

Hue, *sb.* == colour. HD. 2918; [hou]. O. and N. 619; [howe]. O. and N. 577. AS. híw

Hued, *adj.* [ihewed]. 2223 B.

Huene, == wanton girl. St Kath. 97. AS. hunel

Hundred, *adj.* RG. 371. Pol. S. 189

Hunger, *sb.* RG. 404

—— *v. n.* == become hungry. Wright's L. P. p. 37

—— *vb. impers.* 'him hungrede.' HD. 654

Hungred, *sb.* == hunger. HD. 2454

Hunke, *pron. dual.* == to us two. O. and N. 1731

Hunt, *v. a.* RG. 16, 564

Hunter, *sb.* 1099 B.

Hunteth, *sb.* == hunting. RG. 375, 418. AS. huntað

Hunting, *sb.* RG. 564

Hurdice, *sb.* == hurdle. Alys. 2785

Hurdle, *sb.* RG. 232

Hure, *sb.* == a covering for the head. 2111 B. Pol. S. 156. Fr. hure, the head

Hure, *pron. gen. pl.* == of us. O. and N. 185

Hure, 'and hure and hure.' O. and N. 11, 481. This phrase is probably the French 'hure á hure,' or 'téte a téte,' and seems to mean 'in company with, or together.' See Roq. *s. v.*

Hurfte, *sb.* == circumference, circuit. Fragm. Sci. 4. AS. hwearft

Hurl, *v. a.* pret. 'harlede.' RG. 487, 537

Hurne, *sb.* == a corner. RG. 45, 137, 272. AS. hirne

Hurt, *v. a.* Alys. 5814; part. 'y-hurt.' RG. 288

Husband, *sb.* == husbandman. RG. 544

Hwat, *vb.* == quoth. HD. 1878

Hyde. See Hide, *sb.*

Hymn, *sb.* [ympne]. Ps. xcix. 4; cxviii. 171.

116

Hynde, *adj.* == courteous. Alys. 3762. Probably another form of 'hende'

Hynder, *sb.* == an insulter. Fragm. Sci. 282. AS. hynð, or it may mean 'subtle,' as in Laȝ. ii. 12

I.

[For most participles and substantives commencing with 'i' see under the consonant following.]

I, *pron.* [Ich]. O. and N. 1189, et seq.; [Ih]. O. and N. 866

acc. s. 'me.' O. and N. 1182

gen. dual. 'unker.' O. and N. 151

dat. dual. 'hunke.' O. and N. 1731

nom. pl. 'we.' RG. 306. O. and N. 177

gen. pl. 'hure.' O. and N. 185?

acc. pl, 'us.' O. and N. 201

Iambleue, *sb.* == gambolling. Cok. 164

Ibedde, *sb.* == bedfellow, wife. O. and N. 1488

——— == husband. O. and N. 1568

Ibede, *sb.* == command. Fragm. in Warton, H. E. P. vol. i. p. 21

Ibobbed, *part.* == insulted. Fall and P. 59. Fr. bobance

Ice, *sb.* RG. 463

Icholde. See Shall

Icore, == chosen. 718 β

Icund, *adj.* == natural. O. and N. 85

Icunde, *part.* == taught by nature. O. and N. 114

Icundeliche, *adv.* == naturally. O. and N. 1422

Idelgong, *sb.* == idleness. Body and Soul, 50

Idelhede, *sb.* Fragm. in Warton, H. E. P. vol. i. p. 22

Idle, *adj.* == lazy. RG. 195

——— == useless. O. and N. 915; 'on idel' == in vain. O. and N. 918

Idleness, *sb.* RG. 195

Idreiȝt, *part.* == oppressed. St Kath. 45. AS. drécan

Iduȝe, *adj.* == profitable. O. and N. 1580. AS. dugan

If, *adv.* [ȝyf], RG. 405; [ȝef]. RG. 377; [ȝif], O. and N. 902

Ifurn, *part.* == excommunicated? O. and N. 1304. AS. fyrran

Ihende, *adv.* == at hand. O. and N. 1129. AS. gehende

Ildel, == each deal or part HD. 818

Ilete, *sb.* == encumbrance, care. O. and N. 1444

Iliche. See Alike, Like.

Ilithered, == shot out as from a sling. RG. 549. See Luther

Ilk, *adj.* == same. 804 B.

—— == every. Ps. lxxxviii. 14

Ilkan, == each one. Ps. lxi. 12

Ilke, == as, like. Body and Soul, 204; probably a mistake for 'like'

Ill, *adj.* Wright's L. P. p. 61; 'The Ill,' == Devil. O. and N. 421. Cf. the similar phrase 'þe wrse' in La3, *v.* 1140. ON. illr

Illhope, *v. a.* == wish evil to. Ps. lxvii. 17

Illtongued, *adj.* Ps. cxxxix. 12

Illwilland, == ill wisher. Ps. xliii. 6

Ilome, *adv.* == frequently. RG. 378; 'ilomest.' O. and N. 595. AS. gelome

Ilove, *sb.* == lovers. O. and N. 1045

Image, *sb.* RG. 14

Imagour, *sb.* == imagery. Alys. 7689

Imene, *adj.* == common. O. and N. 234. AS. gemǽne

—— *sb.* == a companion. O. and N. 1410

Imone, *adv.* == together, in common. 380 β

Improve, *v. a.* == prove. RG. 466

Imunde, *sb.* == recollection. AS. gemund

In, *prep.* RG. 379, 443

Incarnation, *sb.* RG. 9

Incense, *sb.* [encenz]. Wright's L. P. p. 96

Income, *v. n.* == come in. RG. 48

Incoming, *sb.* Rel. Ant. ii. p. 191

Increeping, *sb.* == piercing. Alys. 2168

Inde, *sb.* == silk of India. Alys. 929

Indrunken, *v. a.* == make drunk. Ps. lxiv. 11

Infat, *v. a.* == make fat, anoint. Ps. cxl. 5

Infight, *v. a.* == fight against; pret. 'infaght.' Ps. cxix. 7; part, 'infightand.' Ps. xxxiv. 1

Infleeing, *sb.* == refuge. Ps. cxliii. 2

Ingang, *sb.* == going in. Ps. cxx. 8

Ingo, *v. n.* == enter; pret. 'inwent,' Ps. xxxvii. 7; 'inyhode.' Ps. xl. 7;

imper. sing, 'inga.' Ps. xlii. 4; pl. 'ingas.' Ps. xcix. 4

Iniquity, *sb.* Alys. 132

Ink, *sb.* [enke]. Marg. 60. Fr. encre. Dut. inkt

Inlie, *v. n.* == lie upon; pret. 'inlai.' Ps. civ. 38

Inlodge, *v. a.* == inhabit, Ps. civ. 19

Inlow, *v. a.* == humiliate; part, 'inlowed.' Ps. lxxii. 21

Inly, *adv.* 1714 B.

Inn, *sb.* 483 B. AS. inn

Innerest, *adj.* == inmost. Ps. lxxxv. 13

Inny, *v. a.* == lodge. RG. 336. AS. innian

Inover, *adv.* == besides. Ps. xv. 7

Inrese, *v. a.* == rush in; pret. 'inrase.' Ps. lxxxv. 14. AS. inræsan

Insend, *v. a.* == send in. Ps. xxxix. 4

Inset, *v. a.* == put in. Ps. lxv. 12

Inshielder, *sb.* == protector. Ps. cxx. 5

Insight, *sb.* RG. 307

Instead, Cf. RG. 214

Instrument, *sb.* 1888 B.

Intent, *sb.* RG. 140

Interdict, *v. a.* RG. 495

—— *sb.* RG. 505

Intermit, *v. a.* == interfere with. Alys. 4025

Inward, *sb.* == stomach. RG. 135; pl. 'inwards' == interior parts. Ps. cviii. 18. AS. innóð

Inwardly, Ps. iv. 2

Inwit, *sb.* == mind, conscience. 561 β. AS. inwit

Inwon, *v. a.* == dwell in. Ps. lxvii. 7

Ioupe, *sb.* == a jacket. HD. 1767. Cf. 'jopen,' in the 'Cambriæ Epitome,' App. to Mapes. p. 350. Fr. jupon

Irain, *sb.* == a spider. Ps. xxxviii. 12. Lat. aranea

Ire, *sb.* == anger. Alys. 906

Irened, *adj.* == made of iron. Ps. ii. 9

Iron, *sb.* RG. 461, 2, 6; [ire]. O. and N. 1028

—— *adj.* [yren]. RG. 399

Is, *vb.* RG. 405; [esse], Ps. xci. 16

—— == art. Ps. l. 6

Ischire, *v. a.* == give, return. O. and N. 1530. AS. scéran

Isle, *sb.* RG. 405; [ydle]. Alys. 4856

Iso, == see. *q. v.*

Isome, *adv.* == together. O. and N. 1733. AS. gesam

—— *adj.* == reconciled, united. Rel. S. v. 254

Ito3en, *part.* == educated. O. and N. 1723. See 'i-teon,' in Gloss, to La3. See Te

Ivored, *adj.* == of ivory. Ps. xliv. 9

Ivory, *sb.* Alys. 7666

Iwarte, Iwarness, == ware, wariness, *q. v.*

Iweived, *part.* == waved or strayed. RG. 526. (Hearne)

Iwis, *adv.* == certainly. RG. 439, 370. AS. gewís

Iwrne, == formerly? O. and N. 637. See 'i-uurn,' in Gloss, to La3.; or perhaps for 'ge-urnen,' part, of 'yrnan,' to run, so that 'i-wrne' would mean 'current'

J.

Jacinth, *sb.* Alys. 5682

Jangler, *sb.* == musician. Alys. 3426

Jasper, *sb.* Wright's L. P. p. 25

Jay, *sb.* Wright's L. P. p. 52

Jealous, *adj.* O. and N. 1075

Jest, *sb.* Alys. 30

Jewel, *sb.* RG. 508

Join, *v. a.* RG. 71

Joliflich, *adj.* == pleasantly. Alys. 4753

Jollity, *sb.* [jolyfté], Wright's L. P. p. 89

Jolly, *adj.* [jolyf]. Wright's L. P. p. 52; [joly]. Alys. 1967, 2467

Journey, *sb.* St Kath. 297. Rel. Ant. ii. p. 178

Joust, *sb.* == encounter in a tournament. RG. 137. Fr. jouste. Lat.

Jouster, *sb.* Alys. 3325

Joustynde, *part.* == jingling, justling. Pol. S. 104

Joy, *sb.* RG. 401; [ʒoe]. RG. 187

—— *v. n.* == rejoice. Wright's L. P. p. 27

Joyful, *adj.* Alys. 30. RG. 53

Joying, *sb.* HD. 2087

Joyous, *adj.* St Swithin, 36

Judge, *v. a.* RG. 345

—— *v. n.* == conceive. RG. 456

Juggler, *sb.* Alys. 159

July,—the month. RG. 395

Juster, *sb.* == a horse. Alys. 1400

Justice, *sb.* == judge. RG. 496, 498, 523

K.

Kaite, *sb.* == a dresser of wool. Rel. Ant. ii. p. 176. (Halliwell)

Kaldhed, *sb.* == coldness. Ps. lxv. 12

Kambe, *sb.* See Comb

Kan, == to know. See Con

Kaske, *adj.* == lively, fierce. HD. 1841. ON. kaskr

Kayn, *sb.* == thane. HD. 31, 1327. Cf. 'cake' and 'cate;' 'wake,' 'watch,' and 'wait'

Keen, *adj.* RG. 496

Keep, *v. n.* == care. RG. 177, 191

—— == take heed [ikeep]. O. and N. 1226

—— *v. a.* == observe, watch for. Wright's L. P. p. 35

—— == receive or get. Body and Soul, 40

—— == protect; part. 'kepande.' Ps. cxlvi. 6

—— *sb.* == heed, caution. Wright's L. P. p. 103. Ps. lxxix. 2

Keft, *part.* == caught. HD. 2005. AS. cépan

Kelyng, *sb.* == a small cod. HD. 757. ON. keila

Keme, *v. a.* == comb. Rel. Ant. ii. p. 176

Ken, *v. a.* == discern. Body and Soul, 54

—— == inform. 31 β

—— == to ask. Marg. 24. AS. cunnan

Ken, *v. a.* == beget. Wright's L. P. p. 36; part. 'kumed' [kunned ?]. Creed of St Athan. 46. AS. cennan

Kete, *adj.* == bright, fierce. Fragm. Sci. 262, used of the sun's rays. ON. katr, glad; cf. the Gr. χαροπός and Χάρων from χαρά

Kettle, *sb.* == pot. Ps. cvii. 10

Kever, *v. a.* == recover. RG. 392

Keverchief, *sb.* Pilate, 126

Kevil, *sb.* == a bit, bridle. Ps. xxxi. 9. AS. cæfli

Key, *sb.* RG. 539, 562. AS. cæg

Kin, *sb.* == relations. RG. 13; [kunne]. RG. 367

Kind, *sb.* == kin. RG. 91

Kind, *sb.* == nature. RG. 45; [icunde]. O. and N. 1381

—— == species [kun]. O. and N. 886

Kindle, *v. a.* == inflame. HD. 915; Ps. xvii. 9. ON. kynda

—— *v. a.* == beget. Alys. 5680

Kindred, *sb.* == affinity. RG. 466. [kemrede]

—— == relations. RG. 15; [cumraden]. Marg. 10

King, *sb.* RG. 371, 372

Kingdom, *sb.* RG. 372, 414

Kingless, *adj.* RG. 105

Kinsman, *sb.* RG. 343

Kippe, *v. a.* == catch up, clutch. RG. 125. HD. 2407. ON. kippa. AS. cépan

Kirk, *sb.* == church, Body and Soul, 46

Kirtle, *sb.* 1167 B. Pol. S. 221

Kiss, *v. a.* [cusse]. 1779 B; pres. 2 and 3 s. 'cust.' RG. 435; pret. 'custe.' RG. 527; 'cussede.' RG. 14

—— *sb.* Wright's L. P. p. 92

Kissing, *sb.* Wright's L. P. p. 70

Kiste, *sb.* == chest. HD. 2018

Kitchen, *sb.* HD. 936

—— == cookery. Alys. 4933

Kite, *sb.* (the bird). Alys. 3048. AS. cyta

Kive, *sb.* == a tub. Rel. Ant. ii. p. 176. In p. 191 it is applied to the pit of hell. AS. cyf

Kiwing, == carving? HD. 1736. Or may it not be 'the chewing' from AS. 'cíwung,' i. e. the meat to be chewed or eaten?

Knarr, *sb.* == a rock? O. and N. 999. Dan. knort, a knur, or knob. ON. gnúpr, mons prominens

Knave, *sb.* == boy. 683 B.

Knee, *sb.* Pol. S. 190

―― == degree. RG. 228

Kneel, *v. n.* RG. 369

Knife, *sb.* RG. 104. AS. cníf

Knight, *sb.* RG. 368, 501; pl. 'knutte.' Alys. 2133. AS. cniht

Knight, *v. a.* K. Horn, 450

Knighthood, *sb.* K. Horn, 492

Knit, *v. a.* pret. 'knutte.' Alys. 2251. AS. cnytan

Knock, *sb.* == a blow. Alys. 1621. AS. cnucian

Knoll, *sb.* == a hill, eminence, rising ground. Ps. lxiv. 13. AS. cnoll

Knot, *sb.* 1479 B.

―― *v. a.* Alys. 4075

Know, *v. a.* RG. 8; pret, 'knew.' 138 B. 'ikneu.' 88 B.; part. 'yknowe.' RG. 432

―― == acknowledge [icnowe]. O. and N. 477

Knowledge, *v. a.* == acknowledge. Body and Soul, 48

Knulled, == heaped. Pol. S. 193. From 'knoll,' a mound

Komelyng, *sb.* == a stranger. RG. 18

Krawkan, == refuse of melted tallow. Ps. ci. 4. See Prompt. Parv. *s. v.* Cracoke, and the note there. ON. krekja, to throw away

Kun, == species. See Kind

Kunde, *adj.* == of kin, lawful or legitimate, as 'kunde,' heir. RG. 370, 371

―― == kinned, related, Fall and P. 49

Kundede, *sb.* == kindness. RG. 452

Kunhede ? RG. 447, should be probably 'onkundhede' == unkindness

Kunrik, *sb.* == mark of royalty. HD. 2143

Kye. See Cow

Kynemerk, *sb.* == a king's mark. HD. 604

Kyneriche, *sb.* == kingdom. Pol. S. 215

Kyneȝerde, *sb.* == king's sceptre. Pol. S. 215

Kythe, *v. a.* == make known. Wright's L. P. p. 91. AS. cýðan

———— *v. n.* == listen? or 'be silent'? Wright's L. P. p. 94, possibly a mistake for 'lythe'

L.

La, *interj.* == lo. O. and N. 1541

Labour, *sb.* 49 B.

Lace, *v. a.* K. Horn, 870

Lack, *sb.* == fault. HD. 190. RG. 389

———— == want, defect. Pol. S. 154. Dut. laecke

———— *v. n.* == be wanting. Pol. S 154

Lad, *sb.* HD. 890. W. llawd

Ladder, *sb.* RG. 148; pl. landren. RG. 410. AS. læedder

Lady, *sb.* RG. 451; [levede], RG. 441, 380. AS. hlæfdige. See on this word the Ormulum, vol. ii. pp. 632-634

Lahte, Laute, Lauthe, *vb.* == received, took. Wright's L. P. p. 46. HD. 744, 1673. AS. læccan

Laite, *v. n.* == look. Ps. 31, 9. AS. wlítan. See Gloss. Rem. to Laȝ. iii. 449

———— *v. a.* == look for, seek. Ps. xxiii. 6

Lake, *sb.* Body and Soul, 160. Rel. Ant. ii. p. 176

Lamb, *sb.* RG. 369

Lame, *adj.* HD. 1938

———— == defective. O. and N. 364

———— *v. a.* HD. 2755

Lammas, *sb.* == Lady-mass. RG. 557

Lamp, *sb.* Alys. 5253

Lamprey, *sb.* RG. 442

Land, *sb*. RG. 377, 494

—— *v. a.* == bring to land. K. Horn, 779

Landfolk, *sb*. O. and N. 1156

Langmode, *adj.* == patient, long-suffering. Ps. cii. 8. AS. langmód

Language, *sb*. RG. 118, 150

Lantern, *sb*. Ps. xvii. 29

Large, *adj.* == big. 1195 B.

—— == liberal. HD. 97

Largely, *adv*. RG. 510, 511, 383

Largeness, *sb*. == liberality. Alys. 6879

Largess, *sb*. RG. 181

Laroun, *sb*. == robber. Alys. 4209. Fr. larron

Las, *sb*. == snare. Alys. 7698. Fr. las. ON. lás

Last, *sb*. == a shoemaker's last. Rel. Ant. ii. p. 175. AS. læst

Last, *sb*. == sin. Wright's L. P. p. 37. ON. löstr. Dan. last

Last, *sb*. == load, burden? Wright's L. P. p. 31. AS. hlæst; or possibly == trace. AS. hlast

Last, *v. n.* == endure, continue. 464 β; pret. 'ylaste.' RG. 263; part, 'ilast,' RG. 509

Last, *adj.* 'atte laste.' RG. 377

Lasteles, *adj.* == faultless. Wright's L. P. p. 52

Late, *adj.* RG. 381; comp. 'later.' RG. 382

—— *adv*. Wright's L. P. p. 99

Lathe, *sb*. == loathing, harm. Alys. 7722. AS. láð

Latter, *adj.* == last. Creed of St Athan. 56

Latymer, *sb*. == latiner, interpreter. Wright's L. P. p. 49. Alys. 7089

Laue, *sb*. == a hill. Alys. 3857. AS. hlǽw. See Lowe

Laugh, *v. n.* [lihe], RG. 93; [lyȝhe], RG. 101; pret. 'louȝ' 710 B.; 'low.' HD. 903

Launch, *v. n.* == shoot into water. Alys. 3746

Laute, Lauthe, == received. See under Lahte

Lave, *vb. a.* == pour out upon. Wright's L. P. p. 72. Rel. Ant. i. 144. AS. lafian

Lavender, *sb*. == launder, washer. Wright's L. P. p. 49

Laveroc, *sb*. == lark. Wright's L. P. pp. 26, 40. AS. lawerc

Law, *sb.* RG. 381; [lay]. 346 B.

Lawfulness, *sb.* == sense of justice. O. and N. 1739

Lax, *sb.* == salmon. HD. 754. AS. leax. ON. lax

Lay, *adj.* == pertaining to the laity, 'lay fee.' RG. 470

Lay, *v. a.* pret. 'leyde.' RG. 393

—— == lay aside. Body and Soul, 166

—— == lay on, attack. Alys. 5832

—— == allay. Ps. lxxxiv. 4

Lay, *sb.* == song. Alys. 5211. Fr. lai. AS. leoð

Lay, *sb.* == religious observance. Alys. 4690. AS. lagu

—— == faith, belief [laȝe]. K. Horn, 69

Layk. See Leyk

Lea, *sb.* == meadow; pl. 'lesen.' RG. 1; 'lese.' RG. 375; AS. læsu

Leach, *sb.* == physician. RG. 380. AS. læce

Leachcraft, *sb.* RG. 141, 150

Lead, *v. a.* RG. 376; pret. 'ladde.' RG. 380

Lead, *sb.* RG. 1

Leader, *sb.* Ps. liv. 14

Leaf, *sb.* 180 B.

Leafworm, *sb.* Ps. lxxvii. 46

Lealté, *sb.* == loyalty. Wright's L. P. p. 53

Lean, *v. n.* RG. 308. AS. hlinian

Lean, *adj.* Pol. S. 150. AS. læne

Leap, *v. n.* pret. 'lepte.' RG. 396; 3 pl. 'lopon.' Alys. 861

—— *v. a.* == forsake (an oath). HD. 2009

Learn, *v. a.* RG. 519; pret. 'lernede.' RG. 434; part, 'ylerned.' RG. 29; 'ylere.' HD. 12

Leasing, == falsehood. See Lesing

Least, *adj.* RG. 37

Leave, *v. a.* 39 B.; [lef]. 136 B.; part. 'ileved.' 616 B.

Leave, *sb.* == permission. 569 B.

Lecche, *v. a.* == comprehend. HD. 252. AS. læccan

Leche, *sb.* == look. O. and N. 1138. See Gloss. Rem. to Laȝ. iii. 454

Lecher, *sb.* == lecherous person. RG. 351. Fr. lecher. AS. liccera

—— == blockhead. Alys. 3916

Lechery, *sb*. RG. 405, 334

Lechure, *sb*. Alys. 6306

Led, *sb*. == song. Fragm. in Warton, H. E. P. vol. i. p. 22. AS. leoð

Led, *sb*. == a cauldron. HD. 924. Rel. S. v. 242. AS. líð, a cup, hollow vessel; or possibly it may be contracted from 'lebet.' Lat. lebes

Ledandlike, *adj*. == ductile. Ps. xcvii. 6

Lede, *sb*. == speech. Body and Soul, 11. AS. leden

Ledron, *sb*. == thief, robber. Alys. 3210. Fr. larron. Lat. latro. Or possibly == leper. Fr. ladre. See Roq. *s. v.* ladrerie, and the Prompt. Parv. *s. v.* Lydron

Leek, *sb*. RG. 341

Lees, *adj*. == bad, wicked. Wright's L. P. pp. 42, 49

—— == false [les]. Pol. S. 214; pl. 'leses,' false persons. Ps. lxxxi. 4. AS. leas

—— *sb*. == falsehood. Alys. 5790

Left, *adj*. (sinister) [lift]. RG. 22

Leg, *sb*. RG. 338

Legate, *sb*. RG. 499, 506

Legh, *sb*. == lying. Ps. lviii. 13

Leik, *sb*. == a body. HD. 2793. AS. líc

Leisure, *sb*. Alys. 234

Leman, *sb*. RG. 496; applied to a man. HD. 1322

Leme, *sb*. == flame. RG. 416, 151, 548. AS. leoma

—— *v. n*. == shine. Wright's L. P. pp. 25, 31

Lenche, *v. n*. == stoop. Rel. Ant. ii. p. 211. In Dutch 'loncken' means to distort the eyes, squint

Lend, *v. a*. 775 B.; [lene]. Wright's L. P. p. 51

Lende, *sb*. == the loins. RG. 377. AS. lendenu

Lene. See Lend

Length, *sb*. RG. 385; [leinþ]. Rel. Ant. ii. p. 217

—— *v. n*. == go a long way off. Ps. liv. 8

Lent, *part*. == gone, departed? Wright's L. P. p. 28. See Gloss. to Orm. *s. v.* 'lendenn'

Lent, *sb*. RG. 495

Leode, *sb.* == people. Wright's L. P. p. 42. AS. leóde

Leofmon, *sb.* == lover. O. and N. 1428

Leopard, *sb.* Ritson's AS. viii. 170

Lepe, *sb.* == basket. RG. 265. O. and N. 359. AS. leap. ON. laupr

Ler, *sb.* == countenance. HD. 2918; [leor]. Wright's L. P. p. 46. AS. hleor

Lere, *v. a.* == teach. Wright's L. P. p. 92. AS. lǽran

Lere, *adj.* == empty. O. and N. 1526; [ilere]. RG. 541. AS. lær, lærnes. Germ, 'leer'

Lere, *sb.* == loss. RG. 526; [leore]. Alys. 1122. AS. lyre

Lered, *sb.* == the learned, i. e. the clergy. Pol. S. 155

Les, *v. a.* == loose. Wright's L. P. p. 29

Lese. See Lose

Leser, *sb.* == looser, liberator. Ps. cxliii. 2

Lesing, *sb.* == falsehood. O. and N. 846. Ps. xvi. 13. AS. leas

Lesing, *sb.* == gleaning. Pol. S. 149. AS. lesan, to gather

Lesness, *sb.* == absolution. RG. 173

Less, *adj.* RG. 379, 558

—— *v. a.* == lessen. Ps. lxxxviii. 46; xi. 2

—— *v. n.* [lasse] == become less. Rel. Ant. ii. p. 211

Lesson, *sb.* Alys. 4823

Lest, *conj.* RG. 506, 563

Lest, *v. a.* == listen to. Alys. 38

Let, *v. a.* == hinder. RG. 380. AS. lettan

Let, *v. a.* == permit, cause a thing to be done. RG. 383; [late]. RG. 445; 'to let blood' == cause blood to flow; part. 'ilate.' RG. 565

—— == let alone. Wright's L. P. p. 49

—— == consider, think. 757 B. Body and Soul, 57. AS. lǽtan

—— *v. n.* == cease. Wright's L. P. p. 29. Pol. S. 201. ON. letta. AS. latian

Let, *adj.* == disturbed, troubled. Ps. vi. 8; xlv. 3 Lit. 'hindered,' from AS. lǽtan, lettan

Lete, *sb.* == countenance. O. and N. 35; [i-lete]. O. and N. 403. AS. wlite. ON. læti. See Gloss. Rem. to La3, iii. 449

Letter, *sb.* == epistle, in pl. RG. 494, 552

129

Lettrure, *sb.* == book, literature. Alys. 3516

Leve, *v. a.* == grant, allow. HD. 334. AS. lefan

—— == believe [ileove]. 2357 B.; pret. 'levede.' RG. 334; 'ilefde.' O. and N. 123; 'leovede.' 687 B.

Leven, *v. a.* == flash out. Ps. cxliii. 6

Levening, *sb.* == lightning. Ps. xvii. 15

Levin, *sb.* == lightning. HD. 2690. W. llafn, a blade, or flake, from the sword-like shape of a flash. Gael, lann, a blade, whence 'lannair,' glitter, or gleaming

Lew, *adj.* == warm. HD. 498. AS. hleow

Lewd, *adj.* == lay. RG. 471. Pol. S. 155. From AS. leóde, leúd, the people

Leyk, *sb.* == play. HD. 1021; [layk], Ritson's AS. viii. 121. AS. lác

Leyken, *v. n.* == to play. HD. 950. AS. lǽcan

Liar, *sb.* Wright's L. P. p. 49

Liard, *sb.* == a grey horse. Pol. S. 71. Fr. liard, from W. llai, raven gray

Libel, *sb.* == a writ of accusation. RG. 498

Lich, *sb.* == body. 259 B. AS. líc

Lichamlic, *adj.* == bodily. M. Ode, st. 190

Lick, *v. a.* Rel. Ant. i. 114. Ps. lxxi. 9

Licome, *sb.* == body. O. and N. 1052; countenance. Ps. xx. 10. AS. lichama

Licoris, *sb.* == liquorice. Alys. 428. Wright's L. P. p. 26. Lat. glycyrrhiza

Licorous, *adj.* == sweet. Wright's L. P. p. 68

Lie, *sb.* == flame. 512 β. AS. lig

Lie, *v. n.* 2s. pres. 'list.' O. and N. 150; 3 s. pres. 'leth.' O. and N. 1492; 2 pl. pres. 'liggeth.' RG. 7; 3 pl. pres. 'ley3en.' Pol. S. 190; pret. 'lay.' RG. 11, 13. AS. licgan

—— == wait, expect. Pol. S. 222

Lie, *v. n.* == speak falsely; part. 'ylow.' RG. 160; 'i-lo3e.' O. and N. 845

—— *sb.* Wright's L. P. p. 100

Lief, *adj.* == dear [leof]. 37 B.; pl. 'leove.' 463 B.; 'lef or loth.' HD. 2379; 'The lef the' == may the right or truth flourish. HD. 2606; comp. 'levere.' RG. 263, 382. AS. leóf

Liefer, *adv.* == rather. RG. 263

Liege, *adj.* RG. 457

Life, *sb.* RG. 301, 376; gen. abs. 'lives' == alive. HD. 1307. O. and N. 1632

—— == position in life. Pol. S. 195

Liflode, *sb.* == sustenance in life. RG. 41, 404. AS. lif-láde, from lád, a way

Lift, *sb.* == air. Fragm. Sci. 204; sky, 200 β, AS. lyft

Light, *sb.* RG. 379, 380

—— *v. a.* == enlighten. Ps. xxxiii. 6

—— == kindle. HD. 585

Light, *adj.* == active. RG. 452

Light, *v. n.* == alight. Cok. 128; part. 'liht.' Wright's L. P. p. 30

Lightly, == easily [liȝtliche]. RG. 515; actively [lyȝtlyche]. RG. 377

Lightness, *sb.* == light. Wright's L. P. p. 96. Ps. cxxxv. 7

Lightning, *sb.* [lyȝtyng]. RG. 378, 415; [leyȝt]. RG. 308

Likand, == similarly, Creed of St Athan. 36

Like, *adj.* [i-liche]. O. and N. 1458; [ilek]. Pilate, 111

Like, *v. a.* == approve of. RG. 92

Like, *v. n.* == take delight in. Ps. xxxvi. 4; please, be pleasing. O. and N. 342; *impers.* 'hym likede.' RG. 21

Likeful, *adj.* == pleasant. Cok. 70

Likeness, *sb.* == similitude. RG. 463

Liking, *sb.* == pleasure. Wright's L. P. p. 23

Lily, *sb.* Wright's L. P. p. 44

Lilywhite, *adj.* Wright's L. P. p. 30

Limb, *sb.* [lyme]. RG. 278, 411

Limbmeal, *adv.* 1815 B.

Lime, *sb.* == calx. St Swithin, 54

Lime, *sb.* == birdlime. O. and N. 1054

Limed, *part.* == caught. Alys. 5701

Lin, *sb.* == linen. Wright's L. P. p. 46. AS. lín

—— *v. n.* == cease, for 'blin.' Wright's L. P. p. 103. AS. linnan

Linde, *sb.* == tree. Wright's L. P. p. 45. Alys. 2489. AS. lind

Line, *sb.* == cord. HD. 539; net. K. Horn, 701. AS. líne

—— == course of proceeding. Alys. 7266

Linen, *sb.* RG. 405

Ling, *sb.* == a fish. HD. 833

Lion, *sb.* RG. 457

Lip, *sb.* Wright's L. P. p. 34

Lisse, *sb.* == comfort. Wright's L. P. p. 57. M. Ode, 119. AS. liss

List, *sb.* == craft. O. and N. 172. AS. list

List, *v. a.* == listen to [lest]. Alys. 38; imper. 'lust.' O. and N. 263

Listen, *v. n.* Wright's L. P. p. 24

Listening, *sb.* == attention. Alys. 4798

Litany, *sb.* 1084 B.

Lited, *part.* == stained. Ps. lxvii. 17. ON. lita

Litelhede, *sb.* == smallness. Ps. lvii. 4

Lith, *sb.* == body. Body and Soul, 39 AS. líð

Lith, *sb.* == people, possessions. HD. 2515. AS. leode. Germ. leute

Lith, *sb.* == comfort. HD. 1338; [lythe]. Ib. 147. AS. liðs

—— *v. a.* == to comfort, give ease. Alys. 433

Lith, *v. n.* == listen. Ps. xxx. 3. Ritson's AS. viii. 187. ON. hlyða

—— *adj.* == fallow. Pol. S. 152. Probably from AS. liðs, rest

Lithe, *adj.* == gentle. Ps. cvi. 29. AS. líðe

Lither, *v. n.* == do harm. Ps. civ. 15. See Luther

—— == act wickedly. Ps. xxxvi. 9

Litherand, *adj.* == wicked. Ps. xxv. 5

Littene, *part.* == cut up? HD. 2701

Little, *adj.* [lytul], RG. 19; [lute]. RG. 378; [lutel]. RG. 376

—— *v. a.* == make little. Ps. viii. 6; lxxiv. 9; [lutli]. O. and N. 540

—— *v. n.* == become little. Rel. Ant. ii. p. 211

Littleless, == almost. Ps. xciii. 17

Live, *v. n.* RG. 381

Liver, *sb.* (part of the body). Alys. 2156

Liver, *v. a.* == deliver. RG. 39

Liverede, *adj.* == red. RG. 39

Livering, *sb.* == delivering of provisions. Alys. 7171

Liversoon, *sb.* == sustenance. Alys. 1011. Fr. livraison

Lo! 1769 B. AS. lá

Load, *sb.* Body and Soul, 238

Loaf, *sb.* 278 β; pl. 'loves.' 293 β; 'laves.' Ps. xli. 4

Loath, *adj.* == hateful. RG. 40; [yladh]. O. and N. 1605; [lath], Ps. xvii. 8

———— *v. n.* == be angry, displeased. RG. 32

Loathly, *adj.* Body and Soul, 56; [lolich]. Pol. S. 203

Loc, *sb.* == gift. M. Ode, 37. AS. lác

Lock, *v. a.* == enclose. O. and N. 56. AS. lúcan

———— == lock, fasten, as a door. RG. 495; pret. 'lek.' Body and Soul, 236; part. 'iloke.' 824 B.

———— *sb.* == lock of a door. Ps. cxlvii. 13. O. and N. 1555

Lock, *sb.* == a tress of hair. Wright's L. P. p. 34. AS. locc

Locket, *sb.* Pol. S. 154

Lodge, *v. a.* Alys. 3132. AS. logian

———— *v. n.* Alys. 4098

———— *sb.* Alys. 4295

Lofe, *sb.* == praise. Ps. xxi. 26; [loof]. Ib. 4

Loft, *sb.* == air. RG. 7; 'upo lofte' == aloft. Pol. S. 154

Loftsang, *sb.* == song of praise. Ps. lxiv. 2. Germ. lob-gesang

Logede, == lewd, lay? Fragm. in Warton, H. E. P. vol. i. p. 21

Loin, *sb.* Pol. S. 191

Loke, *v. a.* == decide. RG. 53; part. 'iloked.' RG. 534

———— == guard. Pilate, 69; [loki], O. and N. 604

Loking, *sb.* == decision. RG. 506

Loking, *sb.* == care. K. Horn, 350

Lome, *adv.* == frequently. Pol. S. 197

Lome, *sb.* == spade, or mattock. Wright's L. P. p. 41. AS. lóma, gelóma

———— == instrument, tool. Ps. vii. 14

———— == vessel. Ps. xxxii. 7

Londisse, *adj.* == of the country. K. Horn 648

Lone ? Wright's L. P. p. 26

Long, *adj.* RG. 376, 410; 'longer.' RG. 377

—— *adv.* == for a long time. O. and N. 466

—— *v. n.* == become long. Alys. 139

Long, *v. n.* == desire. RG. 176. AS. langian

Longing, *sb.* Wright's L. P. p. 29

Look, *v. n.* RG. 14

Loose, *v. a.* [louse]. Pol. S. 239; part. 'losed.' Wright's L. P. p. 99

Lopered, == coagulated, clotted. Ps. cxviii. 70; lxvii. 17. Dan. löbe, runnet, from löbe, to run, run together, hence to coagulate. Sw. löpa i hop, to curdle

Lord, *sb.* RG. 432

Lording, *sb.* RG. 431, 524

Lordless, *adj.* RG. 142

Lordswike, == traitor. Pol. S. 220. RG. 313. See 'laverdswike' in La3, ii. 506

Lore, *sb.* 'a lore.' M. Ode, st. 1, either means 'in learning,' or should be written 'alore,' otherwise, in other respects. Fr. allors

—— *sb.* == learning, teaching. 2065 B.

Lore, *sb.* == loss. Alys. 7247

Loreless, *adj.* == without learning. Cok. fin.

Loren, *part.* == lost. See Lose

Loreyns, *sb.* == reins. 190 B. Fr. lorain. Lat. lorum

Los, *sb.* == fame. RG. 180, 330, 137. Fr. los

Lose, *v. a.* [lese]. RG. 436; 2 s. pres. 'lust.' 859 B.; pret. 'las.' Body and Soul, 123; part. 'y-lore.' RG. 160; 'loren.' RG. 39

Lot, *sb.* RG. 111. Ps. xxi. 18

—— == deceit? Wright's L. P. p. 31. AS. lot

Lote, *sb.* == play, sport. Wright's L. P. p. 49. ON. lota

Loting, *part.* == struggling? Alys. 6203. Fr. lutter

Loud, *adj.* RG. 140. HD. 2079; comp. 'louder.' 450 β

Lour, *v. n.* [lure]. K. Horn, 276; part. 'luring.' O. and N. 423. Lat. luror

Louring, *adj.* Alys. 526

Louse, *sb.* Pol. S. 238

Lout, *v. n.* == go low. Body and Soul, 80; crouch, lie hid. O. and N. 373. AS. lútan

Love, *v. a.* [luvie]. Rel. S. v. 262; pret. 'lovede.' RG. 370, 375. AS. lufian

—— *sb.* RG. 18. 39 B.

Love, *v. a.* == praise. Ps. cl. 2, sing. Ps. cv. 12; [loove]. AS. lófian

—— *adj.* == agreeable. O. and N. 1033

Loveing, *sb.* == praise. Ps. ix. 15

Lovely, *adj.* K. Horn, 464

Lovesome, *adj.* [lossom], Wright's L. P. p. 26; comp. 'lussomore.' Ib. p. 51

Lovesong, *sb.* Wright's L. P. p. 74

Low, *adj.* == humble, 'high and low.' RG. 514; [loȝe]. Wright's L. P. p. 73; sup. 'lowest.' 1187 B.

—— == soft (of sound). HD. 2079

—— *v. n.* == become low, sink. Alys. 5746

Lowe, *sb.* == flame. Body and Soul, 216. ON. log

Lowe, *sb.* == hill. Alys. 4348. AS. hlǽw

Lud, *sb.* == voice. Wright's L. P. p. 27. ON. hljoð

Lugge, *sb.* == log, rod. O. and N. 1607. Dut. blok. Cf. 'lin' and 'blin,' 'liss' and 'bliss'

Lugre, *sb.* == a precious stone. Cok. 89. The ligure of our version of the Bible. Ex. xxviii. 19. Gr. λυγκουρίον

Lumbar, *sb.* == a ship of burthen. Alys. 6063

Lung, *sb.* Alys. 2156

Lure, *sb.* == loss. RG. 181. O. and N. 1151. AS. lor, lyre

Lurk, *v. n.* HD. 68. Sw. lura

Lust, *sb.* == sensuality. Wright's L. P. p. 25

—— *vb. impers.* 'him luste.' RG. 472; 'me lust.' O. and N. 39, 287

Luther, *adj.* == wicked. RG. 389, 524. AS. lýðer

Luther, *sb.* == leather, a sling. RG. 394

Lutherhood, *sb.* == wickedness. RG. 454

Lutherness, *sb.* == wickedness. RG. 389, 465

Ly, *sb.* == voice. St Andrew, 84. AS. hlýd

135

Lye, *sb.* == moisture, [leȝe]. Pol. S. 154. AS. leah
Lyen, *sb.* == reward. M. Ode, 32. AS. leán
Lying, *sb.* Ps. iv. 3

M.

Ma, == more. Ritson's AS. viii. 246
Ma, == make. Ps. liii. 5
———— == made. Ps. xxxii. 6

In the majority of passages where this word occurs in the Surtees Psalter, it seems to be a mere expletive, introduced for the sake of the rhyme. Cf. Ps. xv. 3; xvii. 34; xxi. 2; xxvii. 4; lxxxviii. 6; xcv. 5; xcviii. 7; &c. &c.

Ma, == May? Ritson's AS. viii. 146

Mace, *sb.* == club. RG. 207. Fr. massue

Mace, *sb.* == spice. Cok. 73. Fr. macis

Mace, *sb.* == masonry. Alys. 6258. Fr. maçonnerie

Mackarel, *sb.* HD. 758. Fr. maquereau

Mad, *adj.* Wright's L. P. p. 29

Maid, *sb.* RG. 431

Maiden, *sb.* RG. 435

Maidenclean, *adj.* HD. 995; and see Wright's L. P. p. 82

Maidenhead, *sb.* == virginity. RG. 95

Maim, *v. a.* part. 'ymaimed.' RG. 288. Fr. mahaigner, mahain

Main, *sb.* == power. RG. 564

—— == host or army. RG. 436. AS. mægen

Mainhede, *sb.* == multitude. Ps. xxx. 20

Maintain, *v. a.* RG. 407

Maintenant, *adv.* == at once, immediately. Alys. 5302

Maistrie, *sb.* == craft, science. Alys. 43, 5591. Fr. maistrie. Lat. magister

—— == mastery, *q. v.*

Make, *v. a.* RG. 376; 3s. pres. 'mas.' Ps. xxviii. 10; pret. 'made.' RG. 279, 372; part, 'ymaked.' Wright's L. P. p. 111

Make, *sb.* == mate. Wright's L. P. p. 28

Making, *sb.* == creation. Ps. cxlii. 5

Malapert, *adj.* Alys. 3259

Male, *sb.* == bag, satchel. HD. 48. Fr. malle. OHG. malaha

Malese, *sb.* == discomfort. Alys. 7366; written 'male ese.' Alys. 1351

Malison, *sb.* == curse. HD. 426

Mallock, *sb.* == cursing. Ps. ix. 28; xiii. 3

Maltalent, *sb.* == ill-will. Alys. 906

Man, *sb.* RG. 89, 377, 454

Manacle, *v. a.* part. 'mankled.' Pol. S. 218

Mandeflanc, *sb.* 893 B. probably a mistake for 'mau-de-flanc,' a pain

137

in the side

Mandment, *sb.* == commandment. RG. 194, 201

Mandrake, *sb.* Wright's L. P. p. 26

Manging, *sb.* == mongering, changing. Ps. xliii. 13. AS. mangian

Mangle, *sb.* == confusion; 'in mangle' == entangled. Alys. 7412

Mangonel, *sb.* [magnale]. RG. 394, 549. Fr. mangonne. Gr. μάγγανον

Manhood, *sb.* == humanity, as opposed to Godhead or Divinity. RG. 131

—— == manliness. RG. 101

—— == homage. RG. 421, 259

Manifold, *adj.* RG. 378

Manihede, *sb.* == multitude, number. Ps. cl. 2

Manke, *sb.* == plenty. M. Ode, 35. AS. menigeo

Mankind, *sb.* Wright's L. P. p. 70

Manliched, *sb.* == mercy. Fragm. in Warton, H. E. P. vol. i. p. 22

Manlike, *adv.* == manlily. Ps. xxx. 25

Manly, *adj.* 149 B.

Manna, *sb.* Ps. lxxvii. 24

Manner, *sb.* RG. 381

Manor, *sb.* RG. 497

Manqualm, *sb.* == slaughter of men. RG. 416

Manqueller, *sb.* RG. 455. Judas, 140

Manrede, *sb.* == homage. HD. 484. AS. man-ræden

Mansing, *sb.* == cursing. RG. 472, 504. AS. a-mánsumian

Manslaughter, *sb.* [mansla3t.] RG. 394

Manslayer, *sb.* Ps. lviii. 3

Manticore, *sb.* == a kind of serpent. Alys. 7094; the 'mantichora' of Pliny, H. N. viii. 30, 45. See also the Anturs of Arthur, st. 43, and Skelton's Phyllyp Sparowe, v. 294

Mantle, *sb.* RG. 539, 435

Mantleless, *adj.* Alys. 204

Many, *adj.* RG. 370, 504

—— == much or very, as 'many wroth.' RG. 496

—— *sb.* See Meyné

Mar, *v. a.* Wright's L. P. p. 29. AS. myrran, to hinder

Marblestone, *sb.* RG. 476

March, *sb.* == kingdom, territory. Alys. 3019. AS. meare

—— == The Marches (in England). RG. 537, 538

Mare, *sb.* HD. 2449; [mere], Ps. cxlvi. 9; [more ?] Wright's L. P. p. 36. AS. mære

Margarite, *sb.* == pearl. Alys. 5683. Wright's L. P. p. 26. Gr. μαργαρίτης

Mark, *sb.* == the coin so called. RG. 390. AS. marc, manca

Mark, *v. a.* RG. 116.

Marreys, == marsh, *q. v.*

Marriage, *sb.* RG. 532.

Marrowed, *adj.* [merghed], Ps. lxv. 15. AS. mearh

Marry, *v. a.* RG. 434

Marsh, *sb.* O. and N. 304; [marreys]. Alys. 6540. AS. mersc

Marshal, *sb.* RG. 491, 510

Martinape, *sb.* Alys. 6464

Martre, *sb.* == a martin. M. Ode, 182

Martyr, *sb.* 651 B.

—— *v. a.* part. 'ymartred.' RG. 441, 476

Martyrdom, *sb.* RG. 81, 407, 477

Marvel, *sb.* Alys. 5268

Marvelling, *sb.* == marvel. Alys. 5572

Marvellous, *adj.* Alys. 7152

Mas, == makes. See Make

Mash, *v. a.* == beat, tear to pieces. O. and N. 84. Connected with 'smash.' Fr. macher. Sw. mäska

Mask, *v. a.* == bewilder; part. 'maskede.' 115 β. Fr. masque. Lat. masca. See Burguy, *s. v.* 'masquer'

Mason, *sb.* Alys. 2370. Fr. maçon

Mass, *sb.* == church service. RG. 369, 405; pl. 'masson.' RG. 545

Massbook, *sb.* HD. 186

Massday, *sb.* Ps. lxxv. 11; lxxiii. 8

Massecos, *sb.* == masskiss. 1771 B.

Massgear, *sb.* == apparatus of the mass; [messe-gere], HD. 188

Mast, *sb.* (of a ship). HD. 709

Master, *sb.* RG. 397; [mesteir]. Alys. 7480

―― == master town, or metropolis. Alys. 6112

―― *adj.* == crafty. RG. 454

Masterling, *sb.* Alys. 400

Mastery, *sb.* == superiority; [maistrie]. RG. 395, 558

Masthede, *sb.* == might. Ps. xxviii. 3

Mastlyng, *sb.* == a kind of brass. RG. 87. AS. mæslen. See Hearne's Gloss, to RG. *s. v.*

Mate, *sb.* == companion. RG. 536

Matins, *sb.* RG. 369

Matresche, *sb.* == elegant, well-dressed. RG. 344. Fr. maistrie

Matyng, *sb.* == a dream. See Meting

Maugre, *adj.* == in spite of; 'magrei ys nose.' RG. 94

Maundy, *sb.* == duty, commandment; [mandé]. 359 β. Lat. mandatum

Maveis, *adj.* == bad. RG. 537. Fr. mauvais

Maw, *sb.* == stomach. RG. 311; [mahe]. Rel. S. v. 171

Mawmet, *sb.* == idol. RG. 14. Probably the word originally meant a scare-crow, a bundle of clouts or rags, from the verb 'maim.' See Prof. Key's remarks on this word, Phil. Soc. Trans. 1856, p. 245.

May, *sb.* == maiden. Wright's L. P. p. 26, 28. AS. mæg.

May, *vb.* O. and N. 1622; [mowe]. RG. 454; [muhe]. O. and N. 1579; [muȝe]. O. and N. 62. 3 pl. pres. 'mahen.' Rel. S. iv. 74. pret. 'myȝte.' RG. 377

May, *sb.* (the month) [ma ?] Ritson's AS. viii. 146; [me ?] Wright's L. P. p. 61

Maynage, *sb.* == suite, attendants. RG. 183

Mayor, *sb.* [mor]. RG. 542

Maze, *sb.* == folly. RG. 322, 498

Mazed, *adj.* == drunk. Ps. lxxxvii. 65

Me, == May? Wright's L. P. p. 61

Me, with verbs,—as 'me ne dorste,' they did not dare. RG. 367, et passim

Me. See I

Mead, *sb.* == meadow. RG. 496; [maied]. Alys. 7323. AS. mǽd

140

Meal, *sb.* == ground corn. HD. 780. AS. melu

Meal, *sb.* == repast. RG. 496; pl. 'meals.' Rel. Ant. i. p. 111. AS. mǽl

Mean, *v. a.* == signify. HD. 597. AS. mænan

—— *v. n.* == intend, part. 'yment.' Alys. 4570

Measurable, *adj.* == just. Alys. 7050

Meat, *sb.* RG. 389. AS. mete

Meatless, *adj.* RG. 252

Medicine, *sb.* Wright's L. P. p. 88

Meding, *sb.* == reward, meed. Alys. 5533

Medlay, *sb.* == tumult, conflict. Alys. 4612. Fr. medlée; from medler, to mix

Meed, *sb.* RG. 437, 503. AS. méd

Meek, *adj.* RG. 435

—— *v. a.* == make meek. Ps. ix. 31

Meekhede, *sb.* RG. 389

Meekly, *adj.* Cok. 142. Ps. cxxx. 2

Meekness. Ps. ix. 14

Meet, *adj.* == fit, proper. Wright's L. P. p. 36. AS. gemét

Meet, *v. a.* == HD. 1810; [imete]. Rel. S. v. 205. AS. métan

—— *v. n.* == with reflexive dat. of pron. 'to gadere hem sone mette.' RG. 400

Meeting, *sb.* == encounter. Alys. 2697, 6747

Mei, *sb.* == male relation. Rel. S. v. 162. M. Ode, st. 15. AS. mæg. See Gloss. Rem. to Laȝ, iii. 441

Mein, *v. a.* == mingle. O. and N. 943. part. 'meind.' O. and N. 131. 'imeind.' O. and N. 18. AS. mengian, pret. 'meinde'

Meld, *v. a.* == make mild. Rel. Ant. ii. p. 210

Mele, *v. n.* == speak. HD. 2059. AS. mǽlan. ON. mæla

Mell, *v. a.* == mix, mingle, part. 'imelled.' 276 β Fr. medler

Melody, *sb.* 381 β

Member, *sb.* RG. 560

Menage, *sb.* == family. Alys. 2087. Fr. manage, from 'manoir,' to remain

Mend, *v. a.* == amend. Marg. 24; [mand]. Wright's L. P. p. 44

Mending, *sb.* == remedy. Alys. 5206

Menge. See Ming

Menison, *sb.* == dysentery. RG. 568. Fr. menison, menoison

Menske, *adj.* == gracious. RG. 33. From AS. mennisc, human; cf. our double sense of 'humanity'

—— *sb.* == grace, civility. Wright's L. P. p. 37

—— *v. a.* == treat graciously. Ritson's AS. viii. 83

Menskful, *adj.* == gracious. Wright's L. P. p. 51

Merchandise, *sb.* RG. 99

Merchant, *sb.* Alys. 704

Merciful, *adj.* Ps. cxliv. 8

Mercy, *sb.* RG. 370; to 'do into mercy' == force a man to beg his life. RG. 539

Mere, *adj.* [mire]. O. and N. 1739

—— *adv.* == merely, entirely. O. and N. 496

Mere, *sb.* == a boundary. Ps. ii. 8. AS. ge-mære

Mere, *adj.* == famous, beautiful, noble. Wright's L. P. p. 26. M. Ode, 196. AS. mæra

Merksoot, *sb.* == distance between two limits. Ritson's AS. viii. 31. See Wyntoun, ix. 47

Merrily, *adv.* [murdly]. Body and Soul, 17

Merry, *adj.* 141 β; [miri]. Ritson's AS. viii. 118; comp. 'murgore.' RG. 190, 281; sup. 'murgost.' RG. 349. AS. mergð

—— *v. n.* == to be merry, 3 s. pres. 'murgeth.' Wright's L. P. p. 45

—— *v. a.* == make merry. Wright's L. P. p. 44

Mes, *sb.* == meal, mess. Body and Soul, 137, Sermon 6. AS. mesan, to eat

Message, *sb.* 2020 B.

Messegere, *sb.* == apparatus of the Mass. See Massgear

Messenger, *sb.* RG. 475, 505

Mestere, *sb.* == craft. K. Horn, 235. Fr. maistrie. Lat. magister

Mestere, *sb.* == trade, profession. Alys. 6719. Fr. métier. Lat. ministerium. 'Of all mestere men' == of all sorts of men. Rel. Ant. i. 115.

Mestre—'with the mestre' == with need, or with craft. Alys. 5466

Metal, *sb.* RG. 6; [matel]. Alys. 6242

Mete, *v. n.* == dream. K. Horn, 1458. pret. 'mette.' Judas 8. AS. mætan

Meth, *sb.* == respect. Wright's L. P. p. 103. AS. mæð

Meth, *sb.* == measure. Ps. lxxix. 6. AS. ge-mete

Methful, *adj.* == kind. Wright's L. P. p. 32. AS. mæd-full

Methful, *adj.* == weary. Ps. iii. 6. AS. méðe

Methfullike, *adj.* == moderate, short? Ps. xxxviii. 6. AS. mæte. The V. L. has 'metlic'

Meting, *sb.* == a dream. 1576 B. Alys. 327; [matyng]. Alys. 261. AS. mætan

Meyné, *sb.* == company. 144, 1582 B.; [maigné]. Alys. 1119. Fr. maignée, from manoir. See Burguy, *s. v.* 'manoir'

Mid, *prep.* == with. RG. 371. AS. mid.

—— *adv.* == together. O. and N. 136

Midday, *sb.* Wright's L. P. p. 41

Middelerd, *sb.* == the world. RG. 560. AS. middan-geard

Middle, *sb.* == waist. RG. 435

—— *adj.* [myldel]. RG. 437

Midmost, *adj.* == middle. RG. 29

Midnight, *sb.* RG. 202

Midovernoon, == 3 P. M. Alys. 5216. Ps. xxxvi. 6

Midst, [myddes]—'in the myddes.' RG. 61

Midsummer, *sb.* RG. 499

Midwinter, *sb.* RG. 367, 408

Might, *sb.* See May

—— *sb.* RG. 23. HD. 35. AS. miht

Mightand, *sb.* == powerful man. Ps. lxxxix. 10

Mightful, *adj.* RG. 253

Mighthede, *sb.* Ps. cxliv. 7

Mighting, *sb.* == might. Ps. lxiv. 7

—— == mighty act. Ps. cv. 2

Mightsome, *v. n.* == be powerful. pret. 'mightsomed.' Ps. lxxvii. 38. part. 'mightsomand.' Ps. lxxii. 12

Mightsomeness, *sb.* Ps. xxix. 7

143

Mighty, *adj.* 341 β

Mikel, *adj.* == great, incomprehensible. Creed of St Athan. 25; [mochel]. 305 B. AS. mycel

—— *v. a.* == magnify. Ps. xi. 5; xvii. 51; lxxi. 17

Mikelhed, *sb.* == greatness. Ps. cv. 45

Mikelnes, *sb.* Ps. xxxvi. 11

Milce, *sb.* == mercy. RG. 388. A substantive formed from 'mild.' AS. milts

Mild, *adj.* RG. 246, 374

Milderthede, *sb.* == mildness, mercy. Ps. lxxvii. 38. For milderhede, the 't' inserted euphonically, as in 'are-t-hede,' honour

Mildheartness, *sb.* Ps. xci. 3

Mildly, *adv.* [milthely]. 52 β

Mildness, *sb.* Wright's L. P. p. 73

Mile, *sb.* == a measure of distance. RG. 375. AS. mîl

Mile, *sb.* == a girl? Wright's L. P. p. 44. AS. meowle

Milful, *adj.* == merciful. RG. 435

Milk, *sb.* RG. 43

Mill, *sb.* [mulen]. O. and N. 86. AS. mylen

Millhouse, *sb.* [milnehus]. HD. 1967

Millpost, *sb.* [mulnepost]. Pol. S. 70

Millstone, *sb.* Fragm. Sci. 185

Millward, *sb.* Pilate 4

Milt, *sb.* == the spleen. Rel. S. v. 171. AS. milt

Milth, *sb.* == mildness. Ps. xxiv. 6

—— *v. n.* == be mild. Ps. xxiv. 11; lxvi. 2

Mind, *sb.* [mund]. Signa ante Jud. 78

Mind, *sb.* [munde]. == memory. RG. 392, 527. AS. myne

Mine, *adj.* == my, before a consonant. RG. 214, 215

Mine, *sb.* == an unknown game. HD. 2326. Roquefort *s. v.* says of it, 'Il étoit trés-dangereux, et on pouvoit s'y ruiner en peu de temps'

Mine, *v. a.* == remember. Ps. viii. 5. part. 'mined' == mindful. Ps. vi. 6. See Minne

Mine, *v. a.* == dig up. RG. 518. Fr. mine. See Burguy, *s. v.*

—— *v. n.* == dig. Alys. 1216

Miner, *sb.* Alys. 1218

Ming, *v. a.* == mingle. RG. 42; [menge] 1995; pret. 'monge.' RG. 239; part. 'ymenged.' RG. 48, 'minging.' RG. 95. AS. mengian

Minister, *sb.* Pol. S. 195

Miniver, *sb.* Alys. 5474. Fr. menu vair

Minne, *adj.* == less. Creed of St Athan. 56. ON. minni

Minne, *v. a.* == remember. Wright's L. P. 37; [munne]. Ibid. p. 112. imper. 'munt'? Ibid. p. 37. AS. mynan

Minor, *sb.* == Minorite. RG. 498

Minster, *sb.* RG. 518

Minstrel, *sb.* [menstral]. RG. 53; [menestral]. RG. 272

Miracle, *sb.* RG. 73, 121

Mirk, *adj.* Ps. xvii. 12. AS. mirc

Mirkness, *sb.* Ps. x. 3

Mirror, *sb.* Pol. S. 213

Mirth, *sb.* O and N. 341

—— *v. n.* == be joyful. Ps. xxxi. 11

Mirthing, *sb.* Ps. lxxxviii. 16

Misadventure, *sb.* == written divisim, 'mys aventure.' RG. 205; [misauntre]. RG. 375, 529

Misbear, *v. a.* == misbehave, part. 'misbore.' 1248 B.

Misbegotten, *adj.* RG. 42

Misbelief, *sb.* RG. 121

Misbelieved, *adj.* == infidel. RG. 239

Mischance, *sb.* RG. 137, 380

Mischief, *sb.* Alys. 3784; 'with mischief' == hardly. Alys. 3775

Misclaiming, *part.* RG. 375

Misdeed, *sb.* RG. 279

Misdo, *v. a.* RG. 381. pret. 'mysdude.' RG. 429, 34

Misease, *sb.* RG. 34, 450, 490

—— *adj.* 520 β

Miseislich, *adj.* == miserable. Rel. Ant. ii. p. 217

Misfaring, *adj.* == of evil shape and condition. Alys. 6470

Misfonge, *v. a.* == take amiss, misunderstand. O. and N. 1372

Misgo, *v. n.* HD. 2707

Misliche, *adv.* == erroneously, unfairly. O. and N. 1771

Mislike, *v. a.* 536 B.

—— *v. n.* O. and N. 344

Misliking, *sb.* Ps. lxxvii. 49. Wright's L. P. p. 72

Mismotynde, *part.* == arguing wrongly. Pol. S. 157

Misnime, *v. a.* == mistake, part. 'misnume.' O. and N. 1512

Misniming, *sb.* == wrongful taking. RG. 508

Mispay, *v. a.* == displease. 2046 B.

Misrede, *v. a.* == misadvise. O. and N. 160, 1061

Misreke, *v. n.* == misreckon. O. and N. 490, 675

Misrempe, *v. n.* == misstate or misstrive in an argument. O. and N. 1785. ON. remba, niti

Miss, *v. a.* 50 B. AS. missian

—— *v. n.* == fail of. O. and N. 823

Missay, *v. a.* HD. 49

Misstart, *v. n.* O. and N. 675

Misstep, *v. n.* O. and N. 1351

Mist, *sb.* 684 B

Misthink, *v. a.* [think mis]. Ps. ix. 23

Mistide, *v. n.* == happen unfortunately. O. and N. 1499

Mistread, *v. a.* == tread awry. Rel. Ant. ii. 175

Misunderstand, *v. a.* RG. 42

Miswend, *part.* == gone in the wrong way. RG. 351

Misȝenge, *sb.* == failure. O. and N. 1227

Mithe, *v. a.* == conceal. HD. 652. AS. míðan

Mitten, *sb.* == might. Marg. 44

Mixed, *adj.* == foul. HD. 2533. AS. mix

Mo, == more. RG. 369

Moan, *v. n.* [mene]. 1284 B. AS. mǽnan

—— *sb.* Wright's L. P. p. 23

Mock, *v. a.* Pol S. 238

Mody, *adj.* == proud. Body and Soul 3. AS. módig

Molest, *sb.* == sorrow. Alys. 5443, 5811

Mon, == shall, as 'mon grinde.' Ps. xxviii. 6; [mone]. Ps. lxviii. 37.

ON. mun

Mon, *indef. pron.* == 'one;' as the Germ. 'man.' O. and N. 455

Monday. RG. 495

Mone, *sb.* See Mon

Mone, *sb.* == companion. K. Horn, 540. AS. gemána

Mone, == share, portion. K. Horn, 1147. AS. gemæne

Mone, *sb.* == saying, proverb. Alys. 1281. ON. munnr

—— == opinion. HD. 816. AS. monian, mánian

Mone, *sb.* == wrong, harm? RG. 315. AS. mán

Mone, *v. a.* == tell, repeat. Wright's L. P. p. 92. AS. mænan?

Mones, == many? Ps. lxv. 5

Monk, *sb.* RG. 105, 369

Monoceros, *sb.* == an animal with one horn. Alys. 5721, 6539

Monscip, *sb.* == mercy. Marg. 69; or possibly 'honour.' See Gloss. Rem. to La3. iii. 439

Month, *sb.* RG. 44, 399, 435

Mood, *sb.* == temper. RG. 15; disposition. RG. 61; [med]. RG. 157

Moodiness, *sb.* O. and N. 1403

Moody, *adj.* O. and N. 500. Wright's L. P. p. 44

Moor, *sb.* Pol. S. 216

Moorhen, *sb.* Pol. S. 158

Mopish, *adj.* == foolish, silly. 78 B.

Mor. See Mayor

More, *sb.* == root. RG. 39, 352. 'Moren' is used by La3amon, but the etymology is uncertain

—— *v. a.* == root up. RG. 499

More, *adj.* == greater. RG. 421

—— == more (of quantity). 814 B.

—— *adv.* == rather. RG. 453

Moretide, *sb.* == morrow tide. Alys. 4106. AS. morgentíd

More3eiing. See Morning

Morheden, *vb.* 3 pl. pret. == murmured. Ps. cv. 25. AS. murcnian. Dut. morren

Morning, *sb.* [morweninge]. RG. 558; [more3eiing]. O. and N. 1716

Morrow, *sb.* [morwe]. RG. 382; [marewe]. Wright's L. P. p. 41. AS. morgen

Morsel, *sb.* RG. 342

Morselmeal, *adv.* == in pieces, or morsels. St Kath. 250

Mortar, *sb.* == cement, RG. 128

Mortar, *sb.* == an instrument in which substances are pounded. Alys. 332

Mose, *sb.* == hedgesparrow. O. and N. 69. Cf. AS. máse, a titmouse, and ON. músa-rindill, passer troglodytes

Most, *adj.* == greatest. 184, 123 B.

Mostdel, == most part. RG. 287

Mot, *sb.* == dispute, moot. O. and N. 468.

Mot, *adj.* == mute? Wright's L. P. p. 31. Fr. mut, muet

Mote, *vb. pres.* == may. RG. 508.

—— == must, 826 B. pret. 'moste' == must, should. RG. 53, 367; 2 s. pret. 'mostest.' 1214 B.

Mother, *sb.* RG. 465

Mould, *sb.* == earth, 'on molde.' Wright's L. P. pp. 29, 31

Mound, *sb.* == helmet. Alys. 2277. AS. mond == a basket

Mound, *sb.* == power, value. Alys. 2655, 2207

—— == size, hence a crowd of people. Pol. S. 189. Pr. mont, munt

Mouns, *sb.* == mountains. RG. 220, 392

Mount, *v. n.* == ascend. 184 B.

Mountain, *sb.* 27 β

Mountance, *sb.* == duration. Alys. 6211. Fr. montance

Mourn, *v. n.* Wright's L. P. p. 34. AS. murnan

Mourning, *sb.* 23 B.

Mouse, *sb.* Wright's L. P. p. 111. AS. mús

Mouth, *sb.* HD. 1256. 868 B.

Mouthed, *adj.* Alys. 6125

Move, *v. a.* RG. 453

Mow, *v. a.* RG. 496, strike hard. HD. 1852. AS. máwan

—— *sb.* == crop. O. and N. 1038

Mowe, *sb.* == a female relation. Rel. S. v. 162. M. Ode, st. 15. RG.

316. AS. mage. See Gloss. Rem. to Laʒ. iii. 441

Much, *adj.* RG. 372. 19 B.

Muchdel, == great part, RG. 376

Muchehed, *sb.* == greatness, size. Alys. 7352

Muchel. See Mikel

Muck, *sb.* Fr. on the Seven Sins, 29

Muge, *sb.* == mugwort. Wright's L. P. p. 26. AS. mug-wyrt

Mulberry, *sb.* Ps. lxxvii. 47. Germ. maulbeere. Lat. morus

Mule, *sb.* RG. 189

Mumble, *v. n.* Pol. S. 238. ON. mumla. Dut. mommelen

Munne, *v. n.* == remember. Wright's L. P. p. 112. imper. 'munt.' Ibid. p. 37

Munning, *sb.* == remembrance, remorse? Wright's L. P. p. 37. AS. munan

Munten, *v. a.* == measure out; hence, give, pay. Pol. S. 151. Rel. Ant. ii. p. 216. Fr. munter

Muray, *sb.* == wall. Alys. 6244. Fr. murail

Murder, *sb.* RG. 559

—— *v. a.* pret. 'morthrede.' RG. 263. part. 'ymorthred.' RG. 110. AS. myrðrian

Murgost, Murgore, Murge. See under Merry

Murne, *adj.* == sorrowful. K. Horn, 724

Muthe, *sb.* == army, 1638. Fr. muete

Mutton, *sb.* == the meat so called. Pol. S. 198

My, *adj.* RG. 443

Mynde, *adj.* == merciful, kind. Wright's L. P. p. 82. The word occurs in the Manuel d. Pecches, v. 727,

'And y am euere so mynde
For to pray for al mankynde.'

AS. myn

Myrrh, *sb.* Wright's L. P. p. 96. Body and Soul, 118

Mysel, *sb.* == leper. RG. 435. Fr. mesel. Lat. misellus

N.

Nail, *sb.* == clavus. HD. 712. AS. nægel

—— == unguis. K. Horn, 238

—— *v. a.* Wright's L. P. p. 84. part. 'ynailed.' 93 β

Naked, *adj.* RG. 458, 557. AS. nacod. This word is a participle of a verb, of which the root is *nag* (cf. ON. gnaga), meaning to gnaw, strip off bark or covering from anything

Nakedhed, *sb.* Alys. 7056

Nakins, == no kind. Ps. xxxii. 16

Name, *sb.* RG. 367

—— *v. a.* pret. 'nempnede.' RG. 28

Namely, *adv.* RG. 381, 537

Nanmon, == no more. RG. 291

Nap, *sb.* == napkin. Rel. S. v. 107. Fr. nape. Lat. mappa

Nap, *v. n.* == sleep. Ps. lxxv. 7. Rel. Ant. ii. 211. AS. hnæppian

Nape, *sb.* == back of neck. Alys. 1347. Swed. nakke

Napping, *sb.* == sleep. Ps. lxxv. 6. AS. hnæppung

Nare, == narrow, *q. v.*

—— *v. a.* == oppress. Ps. xxxiv. 5

Narrow, *adj.* RG. 401; [nare]. Fr. Sci. 318. AS. nearo

—— *adv.* == narrowly, closely. O. and N. 68

Natheless, == nevertheless. RG. 375

Navel, *sb.* Alys. 493. AS. nafela

Nawighte, *adv.* == not at all, not a bit. Ps. lxxvi. 3

Nay, *adv.* Wright's L. P. p. 32

Ne, == not. O. and N. 48. RG. 470

—— == nor. O. and N. 905, 906. RG. 470

In composition. A. With the verb To Be

pres. sing. 1. 'nam.' Wright's L. P. p. 42. 2. 'nart.' O. and N. 407. 3. 'nis.' RG. 454

pret. sing. 3. 'nes.' Wright's L. P. p. 52. 'nas.' RG. 372

pl. 'nere.' RG. 376

pret. conj. 'nere.' O. and N. 22

B. With the verb To Have

pret. sing. 1. 'navy.' Wright's L. P. p. 37. 2. 'nast.' Ibid p. 102, 103. 3.

150

'nath.' Wright's L. P. p. 42. 'nafdh.' Rel. S. v. 80

pl. 3. 'nabbeth.' O. and N. 253

pret. sing. 2. 'naddest.' O. and N. 1509

pl. 'nadde.' RG. 19

pres. conj. 3. 'nabbe.' Rel. S. v. 41

C. With the verb To Will

pres. sing. 1. 'nul.' Wright's L. P. p. 32, 'nullyt.' Id. ibid.

2. 'nyltu.' RG. 13. 'nultu.' O. and N. 903

3. 'nele.' O. and N. 1480.

pl. 3. 'nolle.' RG. 265. 'nulleth.' O. and N. 1762

pret. 'nolde.' RG. 508. 'noldestu.' Rel. S. v. 167

D. With the verb To Wit

pres. sing. 1. 'not.' O. and N. 1619. 3. 'not.' RG. 518

pl. 2. 'nuȝte.' O. and N. 1749. 3. 'nute.' O. and N. 1008. neotith. Alys.

3767

pret. sing. 3. 'nuste.' RG. 13

Neat, *sb.* == cattle. RG. 404, 518. AS. nýten, neát

Neb, *sb.* == face. Fragm. in Warton, H. E. P. vol. i. p. 24. AS. neb

Neck, *sb.* RG. 539, 375. AS. hnecca

Necromancy, *sb.* Alys. 137

Nedre, *sb.* == adder. RG. 43. AS. næddre

Need, *sb.* == necessary duty. RG. 527

—— == service, help. RG. 403. O. and N. 388

—— *v. n.* 976 B. RG. 370

Need, *v. n.* == dare. Alys. 6525, AS. néðan

Needful, *adj.* == needy. Ps. cviii. 22. Sermon, 17

Needing, *sb.* == need. Ps. ix. 10

Needle, *sb.* RG. 99

Needless, *adj.* 1664 B.

Needy, *adj.* RG. 330

Neeres, *sb.* == reins, kidneys. Ps. xxx. 3. ON. nyra. Dut. nier. Cf. 'kydneer,' the form found in Wiclif, Ex. xxix. 13

Neghtsom, *adj.* == propitious. Ps. lxiv. 4; lxxvii. 38. AS. hnǽgan

Neigh, *v. n.* RG. 459. part. 'neyghynge.' Alys. 1872. AS. hnǽegan

Neighbour, *sb.* RG. 538

151

Neighing, *sb.* Alys. 2091

Neither, *pron.* [nother]. RG. 421; *conj.* [nother]. O. and N. 465; [nouther]. Wright's L. P. p. 102

Neld, *sb.* == needle. Sermon, 22

Nende, *sb.* == end. RG. 153, 297

Nephew, *sb.* RG. 325, 393

Nere, *sb.* == ear. Ps. xxx. 3

Nese, *v. n.* == sneeze. Rel. Ant. ii. 211. AS. niesan

Nesh, *adj.* == soft, tender. 1623 B. O. and N. 1385; [neys]. HD. 217. AS. hnesc

—— *v. a.* == make soft. part. 'nesched.' Ps. liv. 22

Neshly, *adv.* == softly. [nessely]. RG. 435

Nest, *sb.* O. and N. 282

Nestle, *v. n.* Ps. ciii. 17

Net, *sb.* HD. 752

Nether, [nyther] == lower. 522 β. sup. 'netherest.' Ps. cxxxviii. 15. 'nythemeste.' Fr. Sci. 331

Netherward, *adv.* [notherward]. O. and N. 144

Nettle, *sb.* O. and N. 593

Neve, *sb.* == fist, neif. HD. 1917. ON. hnefi

Never, *adv.* RG. 13; [newe]. RG. 468

Nevereft. 946 B.

Neverthelater, *adv.* RG. 11

New, *adj.* [nywe]. RG. 375; [nowe]. O. and N. 1127

—— *sb.* == infant. Ps. xviii. 8

—— *v. a.* == renew. Ps. xxxviii. 3

Newe, == never. *q. v.*

Next. See Nigh

Nice, *adj.* == silly, foolish. RG. 109, 106. Fr. niais

Nifle, *v. n.* == talk folly, drivel. Rel. Ant. ii. p. 211

Nigh, *adj.* [neȝ]. 94, 208 B.; [neh]. Wright's L. P. p. 34. sup. 'next.' RG. 11; [nest]. Wright's L. P. p. 59

Nigh, *v. n.* == draw near to. Wright's L. P. p. 84. Alys. 781

Night, *sb.* RG. 383. gen. absol. 'nightes' == in the night-time, or 'by night.' O. and N. 238

Nightingale, *sb.* O. and N. 4, 13. AS. nightgale, from 'galan,' to sing

Nighwhat, == almost. RG. 81, 398

Nime, *v. a.* == take. 822 B.; pret. 'nome.' RG. 367; 'nam.' 285 B.; 'neme.' 254 B.; part. 'ynome.' RG. 3; part. 'niming' == taking prisoners. Alys. 1614. AS. niman

Nine. RG. 382, 393

Nineteen. RG. 517

Nineteenth, *adj.* RG. 421

Ninety. RG. 485

Ninth, *adj.* RG. 473

Nithe, *v. a.* == lower, bend. Marg. 17

Nithe, *sb.* == hatred, envy. Wright's L. P. p. 49. AS. níð

—— *v. n.* == strive, emulate. Ps. xxxvi. 8

Nitheful, *adj.* == malicious. M. Ode, 138

Nithemest, *adj.* == nethermost, lowest. Fragm. Sci. 331

Nithing, *sb.* == villain. K. Horn, 202. AS. níðing

No, *adv.* 'no shaltow' == shalt thou not. Alys. 6925

No, *adj.* == none. 24 B.

Noble, *adj.* RG. 367

Nobleman, *sb.* RG. 393

Nobleye, *sb.* == nobility. RG. 376, 420

Nobly, *adv.* RG. 367; [noblelike]. HD. 2640

Noise, *sb.* RG. 151, 396. Fr. noise. Prov. nausa. Lat. nausea

Noll, *sb.* == head. Pol. S. 157. AS. cnoll, hnol

Nomore, *adv.* [namore]. RG. 384

None, *adj.* before a consonant. RG. 369, 370; [nond]. Ritson's AS. xvii. 35.

—— == no one. RG. 468

Nook, *sb.* == 'note' or value? 'not a far-things nook.' HD. 820

Nook, *sb.* == corner, nook. Ps. cxvii. 22. ON. hnocki, a hook; hence an angle or corner

Noon, *sb.* RG. 398

North. RG. 14

Northern, *adj.* Wright's L. P. p. 51

Northward, *adv.* 1127 B.

Norye, *sb.* == a foster-child. Alys. 4730

Nose, *sb.* RG. 94

Not, *adv.* [noȝt]. 102 B.

Note, *sb.* (in music). St Dunstan, 165

Note, *sb.* == use, power, possession. O. and N. 51. AS. notu. The Jesus Coll. MS. however reads 'vote,' i. e. 'foot'

—— *v. a.* == employ. O. and N. 1031

Notheles, *adv.* 'notheles A' == without the aid of A. Alys. 3658

Nother, *conj.* == nor. RG. 421

Nothfulhede, *sb.* == use, advantage. Ps. xxix. 10

Nothing. RG. 367

Nought, == nothing; [naȝt]. RG. 403; [noȝt]. 1094 B.

Nourish, *v. a.* [norysy]. RG. 434, [norischi]. 1876 B.

Nourishing, *sb.* == nourishment. Fragm. Sci. 382

Now, *adv.* [nou]. RG. 368; [nouthe]. RG. 458

Nowe, *sb.* == cattle. Body and Soul, 73. Yorksh. 'nowie.' ON. naut

Nowhere, *adv.* RG. 428

Nowhither, *adv.* Body and Soul, 179

Noy, *v. a.* == annoy. 198 B.

Nughtsom, *v. n.* == abound. Ps. lxiv. 14. AS. genihtsumian

—— *v. a.* == make to abound. Ps. xlix. 19

Number, *sb.* RG. 396

Numbering, *sb.* RG. 61

Nun, *sb.* RG. 370. Fr. nonne

Nunnery, *sb.* RG. 369

Nut, *sb.* HD. 419. Alys. 5193. AS. hnut

Nutmeg, *sb.* Alys. 6792. Fr. muguette, noix muscade

Nycke, *v.* == 'to nycke nay.' Wright's L. P. p. 32

Nyte, *v. a.* == use, enjoy. HD. 941. AS. neotan. ON. nyta

Nythemest, == lowest. See Nether

O.

O, == one. RG. 430, 454

O, == ever. O. and N. 1474. See Oo

Oak, *sb.* RG. 22. AS. ǽc

Oaken, *adj.* Alys. 6415

Oar, *sb.* HD. 711. AS. ár

Oath, *sb.* RG. 383, 506. AS. áð

Obedience, *sb.* 921 B.

Obeysant, *adj.* == obedient. RG. 503

Obligation, *sb.* RG. 391

Oblige, *v. a.* RG. 12. part. 'y-obliged.' RG. 389

Obok, == on the book. HD. 2311

Obon, == on, or in body. HD. 2505. See numerous other exx. of this form in Sir F. Madden's Gloss. to Havelok under this word

Observe, *v. a.* Legend of St Cuthbert in Warton, H. E. P. vol. i. p. 15, *n.*

Ocean, *sb.* RG. 40

Ocquerne, *sb.* == dog-leather well dressed. M. Ode, st. 183. Fr. ocaigne

Odame, *sb.* == brother-in-law. Alys. 2081. See v. 2349. AS. áðum. N. H. G. eidam

Odwite, *sb.* == reproach. O. and N. 1231. AS. edwít, oðwítan

Of. O. and N. 9, 11

—— == on account of. O. and N. 40

Ofbore, *v. n.* == forbear. O. and N. 408

Ofchamed, *part.* == ashamed. O. and N. 932. AS. of-sceamian

Ofdawen, *v. n.* == recover one's senses. Alys. 2265

Ofdrad, *part.* == afraid. O. and N. 1141

Oferen, *v. a.* == terrify. O. and N. 976. part. 'oferd.' O. and N. 399. AS. offǽred, affrighted

Off, *adv.* [of.] Pol. S. 188

Offer, *v. a.* RG. 545

Offering, *sb.* == donation. RG. 545; oblation. Alys. 6163

Office, *sb.* == duty. RG. 468

Offspring, *sb.* RG. 9

Ofgo, *v. a.* == overtake. 52 B.

Ofgrede, *v. a.* == call to. Alys. 581

Ofken, *v. a.* == bring forth (a child). Rel. S. iv. 42

Ofligge, *v. n.* == lie by, or on. O. and N. 1503

Oflonged, *part.* == oppressed with longing. O. and N. 1585

Ofscape, *v. a.* == escape. RG. 398

—— *v. n.* == escape. RG. 570

Ofsee, *v. a.* == see. pret. 'of-sygh.' Alys. 6060. AS. of-seón

Ofseek, *v. a.* == seek out. Miracles, 87

Ofsend, *v. a.* == send for. Alys. 1006, 1912

Ofserve, *v. a.* == observe. RG. 265

Ofslahe, *part.* == slain. O. and N. 1609

Ofspeak, *v. a.* == speak of, part. 'ofspoke.' Alys. 6518

Ofswink, *v. a.* == fatigue. RG. 40

Oft, *adj.* == frequent. RG. 264; comp. oter. RG. ibid.

—— *adv.* RG. 443

Oftake, *v. a.* == overtake. 53 B. 409 β

Ofthink, *v. a.* used impersonally == to repent of. 'hem of-thouȝte here prute.' RG. 163. AS. of-þincan

—— *v. a.* == think of, consider. Rel. S. v. 2

Oftoned, *part.* == made angry. O. and N. 254. AS. teonan

Ogaine, == again. For words compounded with 'ogaine,' see under Again

Oh, Ohen. See Owe

Oil, *sb.* RG. 13; [oli]. Ps. xxii. 5; [ely]. Marg. 60

Ointment, *sb.* Judas 126

Ok, == eke, also. HD. 1081

Ok. See Ache

Ok, == ac, but. Pol. S. 205

Okir, *sb.* == usury. Ps. xiv. 5. ON. okr. from auka, to increase

Oknes, == on knees. HD. 2252

Old, *adj.* RG. 474

Oli. See Oil

Olifaunt. See Elephant

Olive, *sb.* RG. 193

Olive, *adv.* == on, or in life, alive. HD. 2865. RG. 81

Oliver, *sb.* == olive. Alys. 5785

Oloft, *adv.* == aloft; lit. in the air. Ps. lxxiv. 8

On. See Owe

On, *prep.* Wright's L. P. pp. 22, 38

Onan, *adv.* == anon. Ps. civ. 11

Onde, *sb.* == spite. RG. 40. AS. anda

Onde, *sb.* == breath. Alys. 3501. ON. anda

Ondi ? Body and Soul, 103

One, == the numeral. RG. 523. acc. s. 'anne.' O. and N. 792

—— == a certain person. RG. 289

—— == alone, single. Wright's L. P. p. 81

Onelote, *sb.* == offering, or sacrifice. Ps. xxxix. 7; l. 21. Probably a corruption of AS. 'of-lete'

Oneness, *sb.* == unity. Creed of St Athan. 11

Ones, *adv.* == of one kind. O. and N. 1393

Onfang, *v. a.* == conceive (of a woman); pret. 'onfogh.' Ps. l. 7. part. 'onfanged.' Id. ibid.

Onfrest, *v. a.* == delay. HD. 1337. AS. fyrst

Ongrede, *v. a.* == lament. O. and N. 1586

Onhede, *sb.* == unity. Creed of St Athan. 72

Oning, *sb.* == a darling, only child. Ps. xxi. 21

Onith, *adv.* == by night. HD. 1251

Onlepi. See Anilepi

Onlight, *v. a.* == illuminate. Ps. cxviii. 135

Onrese, *v. n.* == rush upon. Ps. lviii. 4

Onsene, *sb.* == countenance. O. and N. 1704. AS. on-syn

Onsprute, *sb.* == a sprouting forth. Ps. xvii. 16

Onwar, *adj.* == ware, aware. Wright's L. P. p. 46

Onycle, *sb.* == onyx. Wright's L. P. p. 25

Onyx, *sb.* Cok. 90

Oo, *adv.* == aye, ever. Wright's L. P. pp. 43, 99

Ope, *adj.* == open. O. and N. 168. AS. open. ON. opinn, from 'op,' ostium, foramen. Lat. ap-erio

Open, *v. a.* Wright's L. P. p. 71

—— *v. n.* 2209 B.

Openheaded, *adj.* == bareheaded. RG. 530

Openly, *adv.* Alys. 4003; [opeliche]. O. and N. 851

Orchard, *sb.* Alys. 1684. AS. orcerd

Ordain, *v. a.* (a clerk). 276 B.

—— == set in array. RG. 452, 456

Ordainer, *sb.* == tutor. RG. 469

—— == a setter in order. St Dunstan, 45

Orde, *sb.* == a point. K. Horn, 638. Alys. 1838

—— == beginning. O. and N. 1783. AS. órd.

Order, *sb.* == disposition, arrangement. Ritson's AS. xvii. 100

Order, *sb.* (of friars). RG. 492

—— == holy orders. RG. 106; an order in the church, as the priesthood. St Swithin, 17

Ore, *sb.* == beginning. M. Ode, st. 91. AS. ór

Ore, *adj.* == one, an. O. and N. 17, 1748, 1752

Ore, *sb.* == grace, mercy. RG. 1, 8, 381. ON. eira, to spare

Oreless, *adj.* == merciless. M. Ode, st. 109

Orf, *sb.* == sheep. RG. 6, 378; [oreve]. O. and N. 1155. AS. yrfe

Orfreys, *sb.* == embroidery. Alys. 179. Fr. orfrais, vid. Roq. *s. v.*

Organ, *sb.* == musical instrument. Ps. cxxxvi. 2

Orgle, *sb.* == organ. Alys. 191. Germ. orgel

Orgulous, *adj.* == proud. Alys. 2006. AS. orgel. Fr. orgueil

Orison, *sb.* == prayer. RG. 435, 475

Orn. See Wine

Orpedship, *sb.* == valour. Alys. 1413. Orpinn is the partic. of 'verpa,' to 'warp,' or 'throw,' in O. Norse. Hence 'orped' comes to signify 'headlong,' 'daring,' or 'valorous'

Osier, *sb.* [oyser]. Alys. 6186. Fr. osier

Ostede, == in the place. HD. 2549

Oth, *adv.* == out of. O. and N. 359

Oth, == other? O. and N. 115

Other, *adj.* RG. 375

Other, == or. RG. 376; 'other—other' == either—or. 638 β

Otherluker, *adv.* == otherwise. M. Ode, st. 76

Othom, *sb.* == uncle. RG. 182, 440. Germ. oheim. Dut. oom.

Ought, *vb.* See Owe

Ought, == anything. 765 B.

Oule, *sb.* == firehook. 478 β. Body and Soul, 207. AS. awel, ǽl

Ounce, *sb.* == the animal. Alys. 5228. Fr. once. Span. onza

Our, *adj.* 428 B.

Our, *adj.* == your? RG. 455

Out, *adv.* RG. 546

—— *prep.* 'out of.' RG. 547

Outbear, *v. a.* == bear out. Ps. lxxvii. 52. part. 'outborn.' Ps. ix. 26

Outbishett, *part.* == shut out. Alys. 25

Outcast, *v. a.* part. 'outcasten.' Ps. lxxxiii. 11

Outcasting, *sb.* == an outcast. Ps. xxi. 7

Outdraw, *v. a.* pret. 'outdroghe.' Ps. xxi. 10

Outdrive, *v. a.* Ps. xliii. 3

Outelyng, *adj.* == external, beyond others. Alys. 4914

Outen, *adj.* == foreign. Ps. xvii. 46

Outend, *v. a.* == exterminate. Ps. lxxix. 14

Outerly, *adv.* 'al outerliche' == intently. Alys. 220

Outgang, *sb.* Ps. xxx. 23

Outgate, *sb.* == going out. Ps. cxiii. 1

Outgo, *v. n.* Ps. xliii. 10. pret. 'outyhode.' Ps. xviii. 5

Outgoing, *sb.* Rel. Ant. ii. p. 191

Outlaw, *sb.* HD. 41

Outlead, *v. a.* Ps. lxvii. 7

Outlet, *sb.* [utlete]. O. and N. 1752

Outloted, *part.* == overthrown? Ps. cxl. 6. AS. lútan. part. 'loten'

Outly, *adv.* RG. 66, 239

Outmost, *adj.* RG. 549

Output, *v. a.* Ps. v. 11

Outrage, *sb.* RG. 136; 'said none outrage' == spoke truly. RG. 432

Outseek, *v. a.* RG. 435

Outsend, *v. a.* Ps. ciii. 30

Outsheath, *v. a.* Ps. xxxvi. 14

Outshun, *v. a.* == make to avoid. Ps. xxiv. 15; to pluck up? Ps.

cxxviii. 6

Outspit, *v. a.* part. 'outspat.' Alys. 1628

Outspring, *v. n.* pret. 'outsprang.' Alys. 493

Outsterandness, *sb.* == excuse. Probably for 'outscerandness.' Ps. cxl. 4. See the V. L. AS. scíran

Outstere, *sb.* == excuse. Probably for 'outscere.' Ps. cxl. 4. See the V. L. So 'stakered' is written for 'skatered' in v. 7

Outtake, *v. a.* == take out. Ps. vi. 5. part. 'outane.' Ps. cxxiii. 7

Outthrow, *v. a.* Ps. lxxii. 18

Outward, *adv.* 2208 B.

Outwending, *sb.* == departure. Wright's L. P. p. 75

Outweringnes, *sb.* == vexation, weariness. Ps. xxx. 19

Outwryghe, *v. a.* == discover. Alys. 6483. AS. wreon

Ovemest, *adj.* == highest, upmost. Fragm. Sci. 24

Oven, *sb.* O. and N. 292 (in dat. 'ofne'). AS. ofen

Ovenon, *adv.* 'on ovenon' == above, upon. Alys. 2234. S. S. anovenan. See La3. iii. 34

Over, *prep.* == 'across.' Pol. S. 70

—— == superior to, beyond. Ps. cxviii. 103

Overal, *adv.* RG. 375

Overcast, *adj.* (of the sky). 1415 B.

Overcome, *v. a.* RG. 401, 454, 548

Overdear, *adj.* == very costly. RG. 389

Overdeed, *sb.* == a doing too much, surfeit. O. and N. 352

Overest, *sb.* == highest part. Ps. ciii. 3

Overfall, *v. a.* == fall upon. Ps. lvii. 9

Overfare, *v. n.* == pass away. HD. 2163

—— *v. a.* == pass over. O. and N. 387. pret. 'overfore.' Ps. cxxiii. 5. part. 'overfaren.' Ps. cxxiii. 5

Overgilt, *part.* == gilt. St Kath. 158

Overgo, *v. n.* [over-gan]. O. and N. 950

Overhead, *sb.* == blow on the head. Alys. 7396

Overheave, *v. a.* part. 'overhoven.' Ps. lxxi. 16

Overhele, *v. a.* == conceal. Ps. xliii. 16

160

Overhohe, *v. a.* == despise. O. and N. 1404. AS. ofer-hogian

Overhope, *v. n.* == hope constantly. Ps. cxviii. 43

Overmirth, *v. n.* == insult. Ps. xxxiv. 19

Overmost, *adj.* == highest. Ps. ciii. 13

Overnoon, *sb.* == midday. Ps. xxxvi. 6

Overquatie, *v. a.* == overfill. O. and N. 353. Halliwell gives 'Quatted' == full, satiated. Probably from the ON. kvett, meat; another form of kjöt

Oversee, *v. a.* == look over (lit.). O. and N. 30

Overshun, *v. a.* == swallow up? Ps. cxxiii. 4

Oversid. O. and N. 1436; either == oversees, looks after, from AS. ofer-seon; or == regards, takes charge of, from AS. ofer-sittan

Oversore, *adj.* RG. 280

Overspread, *v. a.* RG. 380

Overstie, *v. a.* == go over, surpass. Rel. S. iii. 1

Overswallow, *v. a.* [oure-swelyhe]. Ps. lxxviii. 16

Overtake, *v. a.* HD. 1816. Ps. vi. 2

Overthwart, *adv.* HD. 2822

Overward, *adv.* RG. 531

Overwerp, *v. n.* == lit. to throw over; hence neut. to overflow, boil over. Wright's L. P. p. 83

Overwin, *v. a.* Ps. cviii. 3

Owe, *v. a.* == own or have. pres. 'owe.' RG. 432. pret. 'ow.' Pol. S. 204

—— *v. a.* == owe a person a thing, pres. 'on.' (*s. q.* if not 'ou.') RG. 311

—— *v. n.* == be obliged; have to do a thing. pres. 'oh.' Wright's L. P. p. 70. pl. 'ohen.' Rel. S. v. 2; pret. 'aute.' RG. 452; 'aȝte.' RG. 202

Own, *adj.* [owe]. RG. 372, 437; [oȝe]. O. and N. 1648; [onne]. Wright's L. P. p. 104

Ox, *sb.* 133 β

Oȝer, *adj.* == great, dreadful. O. and N. 118. AS. óga

Oȝyrt, == other. RG. 192

P.

Pace, *sb.* == step. RG. 387, 513

Pack, *sb.* == bundle, burden. Ritson's AS. viii. 248

Paddock, *sb.* == toad. Alys. 6126. ON. padda

Pae, *sb.* == peacock. Ritson's AS. viii. 20. AS. pawa

Page, *sb.* == a lackey. Pol. S. 237. Fr. page. Vid. Roq. *s. v.*

Pain, *sb.* == penalty. 481 B. RG. 377

—— == anguish, [pyne]. Alys. 5059; [peyne]. Ibid. 5060

Paint, *v. a.* part. 'ypeynt.' RG. 174

Pair, *sb.* RG. 390

Palace, *sb.* RG. 190

Palfreiour, *sb.* == palfrey-keeper. Pol. S. 237

Palfrey, *sb.* RG. 490. Fr. palefroi. Lat. paraveredus

Pall, *sb.* == coverlet. Alys. 7733. Body and Soul, 15. Lat. palla

Pall, *v. n.* == grow pale. Rel. Ant. ii. 211

Pallion, *sb.* == pall. 248 B.

Palmer, *sb.* Alys. 4981

Palter, == bough. Ps. lxxix. 12; *s. q.* if 'paltres' be not == 'palm-trees.' Lat. palmites. See the V. L.

Pan, *sb.* == dish. Alys. 4939. AS. panne

Pan, *sb.* See Penny

Pannier, *sb.* HD. 760

Pans, *sb.* == furs. Alys. 1572. Fr. pane

Pans, *sb.* == pence. See Penny

Panter, *sb.* == panterer. RG. 187; [pantrer]. RG. 438. Fr. panetier

Panther, *sb.* Alys. 6352

Pap, *sb.* == woman's teat. HD. 2132. Ps. xxi. 10. Ital. poppa. Lat. papilla

Papejay, *sb.* == parrot. Wright's L. P. p. 26. Fr. papegai

Paradise, *sb.* Alys. 5685; [parays]. 353 β

Parage, *sb.* == rank. Alys. 2953. Fr. parage

Paramours, *adv.* = with love, tenderly. Wright's L. P. p. 91

Parchment, *sb.* [parchemyn]. Pol. S. 156. Fr. parcamin

Pard, *sb.* == leopard. Alys. 6709

Pardie, *interj.* == by God. 2082 B. Fr. par Dieu

Pardon, *sb.* 2458 B.

Pare, *v. a.* Pilate, 234. Fr. parer

Parish, *sb.* 1881 B.

Park, *sb.* RG. 1. AS. pearroc. W. parc

Parliament, *sb.* RG. 449

Parred, *part.* == locked up. HD. 2439. ON. sperra

Parson, *sb.* RG. 471, 496

Part, *sb.* Pol. S. 193

—— *v. a.* == separate. RG. 436

Parting, *sb.* == departure. Alys. 2906

Partner, *sb.* RG. 309

Party, *sb.* == part. RG. 394, 400

Parvenke, *sb.* == periwinkle. Wright's L. P. p. 26. Pol. S. 218. AS. pervence

—— == the flower, excellence of a thing. Ritson's AS. xvii. 42

Pasken, *v. n.* == push, strike? 'to pasken in the watere,' St Andrew 8, seems to mean to beat the water by throwing in the net. Swed. piska. O. Engl. 'pash.' Cf. our phrase of 'whipping a stream.'

Pass, *v. a.* == surpass. 1031 B.

—— == pass over. RG. 436. Alys. 5580

—— *v. n.* == go through, pass by. RG. 556

Passage, *sb.* 676 B.

Passion, *sb.* == the suffering of our Saviour. RG. 495

Pasty, *sb.* HD. 644. Cok. 52. Dut. pastei. Fr. pâte

Pate, *sb.* == head Pol. S. 237. Judas, 83

Paten, *sb.* HD. 188. Lat. patina

Path, *sb.* HD. 2390. O. and N. 380

Patriarch, *sb.* RG. 479

Patron, *sb.* RG. 470

Paune, *sb.* == head. See Poune

Pautener, *sb.* == rascal. Alys. 1737. Fr. pautonier. Ital. paltone. Vid. Roq. and Burguy, *s. v.*

Paved, *adj.* Pol. S. 190

Pavement, *sb.* RG. 476

Pavilion, *sb.* [pavelon]. RG. 48, 569; [payloun]. Alys. 5067

—— *v. a.* == to lodge under tents. part. 'ypavylounded.' Alys. 2038. Fr. pavillon. Lat. papilio

Pay, *v. a.* (money); pret. 'payde.' RG. 374, 498. part. 'ipaiid.' Pol. S. 204

—— *v. a.* == please, appease. RG. 314. part. 'ypaid.' RG. 391; 'ipaised' == restored to peace. RG. 570. Fr. paier. Lat. pacare

Pay, *sb.* == peace. RG. 125. Fr. paix

Payloun. See Pavilion

Paynim, *sb.* == heathen, pagans. RG. 395

Pays, == pitch, *q. v.*

Pea. See Pese

Peace, *sb.* RG. 491, 500

Peaceful, *adj.* Ps. cxix 7

Peacefully, *adv.* Ps. xxxiv. 20

Peacock, *sb.* Alys. 5410

Peak, *sb.* == The Peak of Derbyshire. RG. 7

Pear, *sb.* 1203 B.

Peer, *sb.* == equal. RG. 17

Peer, *v. n.* == look into. [pure]. K. Horn, 1124; [pouren]. Alys. 5799

Pelican, *sb.* Ps. ci. 7

Pell, *sb.* == fur, skin. Alys. 6697. Lat. pellis

Pelle, *v. n.* == drive, go? HD. 810. Lat. pello

Pelure, *sb.* == a furred robe. Alys. 4129. Fr. pel

Penance, *sb.* RG. 255

Pencel, *sb.* == pennon, banner. Alys. 2688. Fr. pencel. Lat. penna

Penny, *sb.* RG. 404, 493; [pan]. Pol. S. 204. pl. 'panes.' RG. 473; 'pans.' 530 β

Pepper, *sb.* Alys. 7032

Perauntre, *adv.* == peradventure. RG. 375

Perch, *sb.* == the fish. Alys. 5446. Fr. perche. Lat. perca

Perche, *v. a.* == prick, spur. Alys. 2460. Fr. percer

Perforce, *adv.* Alys. 4577

Peril, *sb.* RG. 452

Pers, *sb.* == a cloth or stuff. Alys. 4987; usually of a blue colour. Fr. pers. Vid. Roq.

Pervink. See Parvenke

Pese, *sb.* == a pea. Alys. 5959. AS. pise

Pesens, *sb.* == neck-armour covering the breast. Alys. 3697; same as 'pesane' in the later Romances. Fr. pis, piz, the breast

Pett, *sb.* == pit. Alys. 5764

Pett, for pight? == made. Alys. 7495

Peys, == pitch, *q. v.*

Phantom, *sb.* == vanity. Ps. iv. 3. Fr. fantosme

Philosophy, *sb.* RG. 130

Physic, *sb.* RG. 151

Physician, *sb.* RG. 68

Pick, *v. a.* Pol. S. p. 150. part. 'pycchynde.' Wright's L. P. p. 110

Piece, *sb.* == a portion, bit. RG. 555. St Kath. 229

—— == a man. RG. 355

Piecemeal, *adv.* RG. 278

Pierce, *v. a.* RG. 437

Piete, *sb.* == pity. Pol S. 213

Pike, *sb.* == sharp stake. RG. 51

—— *v. a.* == pierce. RG. 51

Pile, *sb.* == hair. Body and Soul, 38

Pilgrim, *sb.* 2360 B.

Pilgrimage, *sb.* 5 B.

Pilkoc, *sb.* == the penis. Rel. Ant. ii. 211

Pill, *v. a.* == rob. Pol. S. 150. Fr. piller

Pillar, *sb.* Alys. 6242. Fr. pilier. Lat. pila

Pillory, *sb.* Rel. Ant. ii. p. 176

Piment, *sb.* == a kind of wine. HD. 1728. Alys. 4178. See the recipe for making it in Halliwell, *s. v.*

Pin, *sb.* == pinnacle. Cok. 57

—— == pin (in the modern sense). Alys. 6146

Pinch, *v. n.* Rel. Ant. ii. p. 176

Pine, *sb.* == pain. RG 326

—— *v. a.* == make to pine. Ps. xxxvi. 28. part. 'ypyned.' RG. 449

Pink, *v. n.* == prick or stab. Pol. S. 156. AS. pyngan

Pinnuc, *sb.* == hedge-sparrow. O. and N. 1128. See Wright's Vocabularies, p. 177, where 'lirifa' is translated 'pynok'

Pinse, *v. a.* == pinch, torture, part. 'ipinsed.' Fall and P. 89. Dut. pinssen. Fr. pincer

Pipe, *sb.* == musical instrument. Alys. 7769. AS. píp

—— *v. n.* Alys. 1012. Pol. S. 216

Pirate, *sb.* == a kind of ship. Alys. 6182

Pircle, *v. n.* == slobber at the mouth. Rel. Ant. ii. 211

Pirope, *sb.* == a precious stone. Alys. 5682. Gr. πυρωπός

Piss, *v. n.* Rel. Ant. ii. 211

Pit, *sb.* RG. 409, 540; [pett]. Alys. 5764

Pitch, *sb.* RG. 410; [peys]. Alys. 1620; [pays]. Alys. 1630

—— *v. a.* == smear with pitch. HD. 707. part. 'ipiched' 94 β

Pitch, *v. a.* == fix. pret. 'pight.' RG. 51, 29. part. 'ypiʒt.' RG. 48

Piteous, *adj.* RG. 491, 548

Piteously, *adv.* RG. 449, 508

Pitfall, *sb.* Pol. S. 193

Pith, *sb.* [pid]. Body and Soul, 38. AS. piða

Pity, *sb.* == pitiful state. Alys. 7269. RG. 532, 537

Place, *sb.* RG. 6, 14, 397

Plaice, *sb.* == the fish. HD. 896

Plaid, **Plait**, *sb.* == pleading. O. and N. 1735, 5

Plain, *sb.* RG. 7

Plain, *v. n.* == complain. RG. 533

Plaining, *sb.* RG. 473

Plaint, *sb.* Alys. 7488. HD. 2961

Planet, *sb.* RG. 112

Plant, *v. a.* Ps. lxxix. 10

Plaster, *sb.* == remedy, 'plaster of penance.' Wright's L. P. p. 89

Plate, *adj.* == flat. Alys. 2001. Fr. plat. Germ. platt

Plate, *sb.* == a piece of silver. Rel. Ant. i. 144. Span. plata

Plattinde, *part.* == journeying. See Plette and Strike

Play, *sb.* RG. 272; [ple]. RG. 266; [plawe]. RG. 291. AS. plega

—— *v. n.* [plawe]. Wright's L. P. p. 45; pret. 'pleide.' RG. 507

—— *v. a.*—'to play hands' == clap hands. Ps. xcvii. 8

Playing, *sb.* Wright's L. P. p. 88

Plea, *sb.* RG 471, 473

Plead, *v. n.* Pol. S. 159

Pleading, *sb.* RG. 471, 473

Plenar, *adj.* == full. 1537 B.

Plenarly, *adv.* 1538 B.

Plenteous, *adj.* RG. 23

Plenty, *sb.* RG. 1

Plette, *v. a.* == strike. HD. 2444; pret. 'plat.' HD. 2755; 'plette.' HD. 2626. part. 'plattinde' == journeying. HD. 2282. Compare the double sense of 'strike,' *q. v.* AS. plættian

Plight, *v. a.* == pluck, pull. Alys. 5831, 5859

Plight, *sb.* == harm, danger. HD. 1370, 2002. AS. pliht

—— == condition. Body and Soul, 184

Plight, *v. a.* == pledge. RG. 357; part. 'yplyȝt.' RG. 388. AS. plihtan

Plot, *sb.* (of ground). RG. 536. Fr. plat

Plough, *sb.* [ploth]. Rel. Ant. i. p. 111. ON. plógr

Ploughfere, *sb.* Wright's L. P. p. 49

Ploughland, *sb.* RG. 374

Ploughstave, *sb.* RG. 99

Plump, *v. n.* == fall heavily. Alys. 5776. Dan. plumpe

Po, *sb.* == peacock. Pol. S. 159. AS. pawa

Point, *sb.* == sharp end. RG. 395

—— == opportunity. Pilate, 17

—— == particular. St Andrew, 36

Phrases—'upon the *point* to smite.' RG. 543

'in such *point*' == in such case. RG. 391

Pointed, *adj.* [yponyted]. RG. 310

Poison, *sb.* RG. 122, 151

—— *v. a.* Alys. 600

Poke, *sb.* == bag, pouch. HD. 555. AS. pocca

Poke, *v. n.* == stoop in walking. Rel. Ant. ii. 211

Polk, *sb.* == pool. HD. 2685, the Norfolk 'pulk.'

Polk, *v. a.* == put. Pol. S. 157

Poll, *sb.* == head. Pol. S. 237. Dut. bol, whence our 'bolster.' Germ. polster

Polled, *sb.* == shaven. Alys. 216

Pomon, *sb.* == lungs. Alys. 4374. Fr. poumon. Lat. pulmo

Pomple, *v. n.* stumble. Rel. Ant. ii. 211. ON. pompa

Pool, *sb.* RG. 131. AS. pól

Poor, *adj.* [povere]. RG. 376; comp. 'poverore.' RG. 370

Poorly, *adv.* [pourelike]. HD. 323

Pope, *sb.* RG. 502

Porch, *sb.* Ps. xcix. 4. Lat. porticus

Pore, *v. n.* See Peer

Port, *sb.* == gate. RG. 51

Porter, *sb.* RG. 539, 544

Portere ? *sb.* deportment. St Swithin, 25. Fr. portée

Portereve, *sb.* == 'head magistrate of a town.' Hall. RG. 541

Portray, *v. a.* Alys. 1520

Posse, *v. n.* == push, drive. K. Horn, 1041

Postern, *sb.* RG. 19. Alys. 4593

Pot, *sb.* Ps. xxi. 16. ON. pottr

Pot, *v. n.* == go, tramp. Pol. S. 71. AS. pæðan

Potion, *sb.* Alys. 3509

Pottage, *sb.* RG. 404

Potter, *sb.* Rel. Ant. ii. p. 176

Pottle, *sb.* Rel. Ant, ii. p. 176

Poudré, *sb.* == dust. Alys. 2180

Pound, *sb.* (of money). RG. 59, 383

Poune, *sb.* == the head. Alys. 2770. 'paunes.' Ibid. 2800. Another form is 'pan.' W. pen

Pouraille, *sb.* == the poor. Pol. S. 223. Alys. 1229

Pouren, see Peer, *vb.*

Pousté, *sb.* == power. Alys. 7879

Pout, *v. n.* Rel. Ant. ii. 211

Poveral, *sb.* == poor persons. RG. 254

Powder, *sb.* == dust. RG. 345

Powdered, *adj.* [pudrid]. Cok. 108

Powe, *v. n.* == be poor? RG. 313

Power, *sb.* RG. 370, 371

Praer, *sb.* == meadow. Cok. 69. Cf. Fr. praiau—prairie

Praise, *v. a.* RG. 57. 1362 B.

Prangle, *v. a.* == compress. HD. 639. Dut. prangen

Prasiune, *sb.* == chrysoprase. Cok. 89. Gr. πράσος, a leek

Pray, *sb.* == crowd, press. Alys. 1991, 2595

Pray, *v. a.* Wright's L. P. p. 58

——— *v. n.* [prye]. Pol. S. 222

Prayer, *sb.* 1089 B.

Preach, *v. a.* RG. 392

——— == exhort. Alys. 2042

Preacher, *sb.* RG. 392, 492

Preaching, *sb.* RG. 173

Precious, *adj.* 42 β

Predication, *sb.* 1969 B.

Preit, *v. a.* == pray, beseech. Marg. 1. Fr. prier

Prejudice, *sb.* 1735 B.

Prelate, *sb.* RG. 472

Preone, *v. a.* == sew up. Rel. S. v. 68. AS. preon, a needle. ON. prióna, to sew

Preovest, *adj.* == proofest, most approved. Alys. 6891

Presence, *sb.* == bearing, dignity, [presauns]. RG. 485

Present, *sb.* == gift. RG. 485

—— *v. a.* == give. Wright's L. P. p. 96

—— == introduce a person to another. part. 'ipresented.' 231 B.

Press, *sb.* == throng. 2469 B.

—— *v. a.* part, 'ypreost.' Alys. 2342

Prest, *adj.* == ready. RG. 485. Ital. presto

Prey, *sb.* RG. 15, 376

Price, *sb.* 150 B.; 'to have the price' == to be highly esteemed. Pol. S. 153

Prick, *v. n.* hasten. RG. 459

—— *v. a.* == spur, pierce (as a horse). RG. 553. AS. priccian

—— == adorn. Body and Soul, 12. ON. prýda, to adorn

Pricker, *sb.* == rider. Pol. S. 150

Pride, *sb.* RG. 376. AS. prýt

Priest, *sb.* 364 B.; [prost]. O. and N. 733

Priesthood, *sb.* 1032 B.

Priestless, *adj.* RG. 544

Prime, *sb.* == the first hour of prayer, or 6 A. M. 219 B. Ritson's AS. viii. 196

Primerole, *sb.* == primrose. Wright's L. P. p. 26

Prince, *sb.* RG. 367, 402. In Alys. 4727 Weber suggests that 'prynces' is a mistake for 'traitors,' but may it not be another form of 'prenches' == stratagems, tricks? see 'at-prenche,' supra

Principal, *adj.* RG. 446

Prior, *sb.* == head of a priory. 2462 B.

Priory, *sb.* RG. 369, 370

Pris, *sb.* == a note of a horn blown on the death of the deer. Body and Soul, 214. Fr. pris, from prendre

Prison, *sb.* RG. 376

—— == prisoner. RG. 550

Privilege, *sb.* Pol. S. 157

Privily, *adv.* RG. 518. Alys. 3765

Privity, *sb.* RG. 468

Privy, *adj.* RG. 435

Procession, *sb.* (of friars). RG. 405, 530

170

Procurator, *sb.* 352 β

Procure, *v. a.* RG. 551

Professe, *sb.* == a professed person. RG. 434

Profession, *sb.* == a professing. 1407 B.

Proffer, *v. a.* Alys. 3539

Proper, *adj.* == suitable, fit. 934 B.

Prophecy, *sb.* RG. 132

Prophet, *sb.* RG. 38

Prou, *sb.* == advantage. Ritson's AS. viii. 88. Fr. prod

Proud, *adj.* RG. 377, 465

Proudly, *adv.* Alys. 3413

Prove, *v. n.* == turn out, result. 2400 B.

—— *v. a.* == try; part, 'yproved.' RG. 457

—— == confirm, prove. Ritson's AS. xviii. 30

Provender, *sb.* Pol. S. 239

Prow, *sb.* == prowess. RG. 65

Prowess, *sb.* RG. 462, 453

Psalm, *sb.* Ps. lxv. 4

—— *v. n.* == sing psalms. Ps. vii. 18

Psaltery, *sb.* Ps. xxxii. 2

Pudding, *sb.* Cok. 57. Dan. budding. Fr. boudin

Puff, *v. n.* [pofte]. Rel. Ant. ii. 211

Pulte, *v. a.* == push. RG. 376; put. RG. 459. 1316 B.

Pulting, *sb.* == pushing. RG. 212

Punge, *sb.* == purse. Alys. 1728. AS. pung. ON. pung, our Engl. 'bung'

Puppet, *sb.* == small figure. Alys. 77

Purblind, *adj.* RG. 376, written divisim == entirely blind; not as in the modern sense == one whose sight is impaired. Probably therefore from 'pure' == entire, and blind. Cf. 'purewhite.' RG. 8. In Wiclif, Ex. xxi. 26, it means, 'blind of one eye,' and is still written divisim; the later version gives 'oon iȝed'

Purchase, *v. a.* == procure. RG. 472, 499; to procure food. Alys. 5197. Fr. pourchacer. Ital. procacciare

Purchase, *sb.* RG. 381, 516

Pure, *adj.* == entire, complete. RG. 546

—— == rightful, legitimate. RG. 106

—— *adv.* == entirely, very. RG. 397

Purely, *adv.* == entirely, completely. RG. 66, 173

Purewhite, *adj.* RG. 8

Purgatory, *sb.* 622 β

Purge, *v. a.* 371 B.

Purpose, *sb.* RG. 558

Purse, *sb.* Alys. 1798. AS. púse

Pursue, *v. a.* 937 B.

Purvey, *v. a.* RG. 289; part. 'ypurveyed.' Alys. 6212

Purveyance, *sb.* RG. 533, 535

Puste, *vb.* == pushed? St Andrew, 70

Put, *v. a.* == throw (a stone). HD. 1023, 1044

—— *sb.* == a cast or throw. HD. 1055

—— *v. a.* place, lay before. Wright's L. P. p. 53. See Pulte. Dan. putte

Putting, *sb.* == throwing. HD. 1042

Pykeys, *sb.* == pick-axe. Manuel d. Pecches, 940

Pyne, *sb.* == pain, *q. v.*

—— *v. a.* == trouble. Alys. 5914

Pypyn, *sb.* == windpipe. Alys. 3256

Q.

Quaint, *adj.* RG. 408, 412, 566; [koweynte]. Body and Soul, 10. Fr.
coint

Quaintance, *sb.* == acquaintance. Alys. 6173

Quaintise, *sb.* == device. RG. 19

Quaintly, *adv.* RG. 28

Quake, *v. n.* RG. 132, 336; pret. 'qwoke.' Ps. xiii. 5

Quaking, *sb.* == fear. RG. 336. Ps. ii. 11

Qual, == whale, *q. v.*

Qualm, *sb.* == destruction. RG. 378. AS. cwealm

—— *v. a.* == annoy. Ps. xxxvi. 14

Quarrel, *sb.* == arrow. RG. 491, 537. Fr. quarel

Quarry, *adj.* == square. RG. 412. Fr. carré

Quarry, *sb.* == a place whence stone is excavated. RG. 412. Fr. carriere

Quart, *sb.* == a measure. Rel. Ant. ii. p. 176

Quarter, *sb.* (of a man's body). Pol. S. 213

Quash, *v. a.* [cwesse]. O. and N. 1386. Fr. quasser. AS. cwysan

Queche, *v. n.* == make a disturbance. Alys. 4747. See the Prompt. Parv. *s. v.* Qvycchyn. AS. cwecian

Qued, *adj.* == wicked. Alys. 5619. Dut. kwaad

—— *sb.* == the devil. RG. 314. Rel. S. v. 225

—— == evil. Alys. 4237. Body and Soul, 243

Quede, *sb.* == bequest. Alys. 8020

Quednes, *sb.* == wickedness. Ps. c. 7

Queen, *sb.* RG. 368

Quell, *v. a.* RG. 38, 499. AS. cwellan

Queller, *sb.* St Kath. 247

Quelling, *sb.* == destruction. RG. 296

Queme, *adj.* == agreeable. HD. 130. AS. cweman

—— *v. a.* == please. Wright's L. P. p. 25. O. and N. 209

—— *v. n.* [icweme] == be pleased, satisfied. K. Horn, 497

Queming, *sb.* == pleasure. Ps. cxlvi. 10

Quenching, *sb.* Fragm. Sci. 164.

Quern, *sb.* == a mill. Pilate, 5. AS. cwéorn

Quert, *adj.* == joyful. Ps. vii. 11. Fr. cœur, queor. Cf. our own 'hearty' and 'in good heart'

—— *sb.* == joy. Ps. lxiii. 11; lxxxviii. 27

Quethe, *v. n.* == speak, say. [iquethe]. O. and N. 502. 3 s. pres. 'quath.' RG. 435; part. 'icwede.' O. and N. 1651. AS. cwéðan

Quibibe, *sb.* == cubeb. Wright's L. P. p. 27. Alys. 6796

Quick, *adj.* == swift. RG. 369, 387. AS. cwic

—— == alive. RG. 289

Quicken, *v. a.* Ps. lxxxiv. 7

Quickly, *adv.* RG. 383

Quide, *sb.* == a saying. O. and N. 685. AS. cwide

Quilt, *sb.* [cowlte]. Body and Soul, 15

Quinre, *sb.* == an unknown animal. Alys. 5609

Quire, *sb.* (of a church). RG. 534

Quiste, *sb.* == bequest. HD. 219

Quistron, *sb.* == scullion. Alys. 2511. Fr. questron, quistoun

Quit, *adj.* == free from, released. RG. 392, 522

—— *v. a.* == leave. Rel. S. vii. 75

Quite, *v. a.* == pay, requite. Pol. S. 71

Quithe, *v. a.* == promise, grant? Marg. 72. AS. cwéðan?

Quiture, *sb.* == care, release. RG. 435

R.

Rabbe, *sb.* == turnip. Alys. 4983. Dut. raap.

Race, *sb.* == course. Wright's L. P. p. 100. AS. ræs

—— == speed, hence a short time [res]. Pol. S. 200; [ras]. Alys. 7830

Rache, *sb.* == hound, brach. Body and Soul, 214. AS. ræcc

Rack, *sb.* == torture. Body and Soul, 66. Swed. räcka, to stretch

Rade, *adj.* == ready. O. and N. 423; [rath]. HD. 75. AS. rád

Radely, *adv.* == readily, swiftly. Ps. vi. 11

Radness, *sb.* == terror, horror. Ps. liv. 5. AS. hréð

Rag, *sb.* Pol. S. 150. AS. hrac? implied in 'hracod'

Rage, *sb.* == haste? Alys. 980; rashness. Alys. 4336

Ragged, *adj.* Body and Soul, 185. AS. hracod

Ragged, *adj.* == raged, raging. Alys. 4471

Rail, *v. a.* == put on as a garment. Wright's L. P. p. 43. AS. hrægl.

Rain, *sb.* RG. 416, 560

—— *v. n.* [ryne]. Fr. Sci. 212. Alys. 6450

—— *v. a.* Ps. lxxvii. 27

Rainbow, *sb.* Signa ante Jud. 170

Raise, *v. a.* Wright's L. P. p. 100. Ps. cxii. 7

Rake, *v. n.* == depart, go away from. Rel. Ant. ii. p. 193. ON. reka

Rake, *v. n.* == hawk, spit. Rel. Ant. ii. p. 211. AS. hracan

Rake, *sb.* == the common instrument so called. Rel. S. v. 214. AS.

ráce

Raisin, *sb.* Alys. 5193

Raketyne, *sb.* == chain. RG. 142. AS. raccenta

Ram, *sb.* == the animal. Alys. 388

Randon, *sb.* == haste, eagerness. Alys. 2484; 'into randon.' Cok. 130. AS. randún. Probably from the ON. rönd. Germ. rant, the border or edge of a thing. In Provençal we have the phrase 'a randa,' on the edge or border, hence close or pressing. From this comes the Fr. verb, 'randir,' to approach, rush towards a thing, and 'randon,' lit. rushing, and generally 'haste, violence.' See Burguy's Grammaire, vol. ii. p. 323, whence the above is derived

Rank, *adj.* Ps. lxxvii. 44. AS. ranc

Ransack, *v. a.* Ps. vii. 10; lxiii. 7. ON. ransaka

Ransacking, *sb.* Ps. lxiii. 7

Ransom, *sb.* RG. 374, 433. Fr. rançon

Rap, *sb.* == blow? Body and Soul, 66. Sw. rapp

Rape, *sb.* == haste. K. Horn, 566; [rap]. Rel. Ant. i. 115. ON. rápa, cursitare

Rath, *adj.* soon, early. HD. 2391. Pol. S. 195. comp. 'rather' == sooner. O. and N. 1240; former. RG. 285. AS. hræð

Rather, *adv.* RG. 459, 397

Raught. See Reek

Raven, *sb.* Fragm. Sci. 63. AS. hræfen

Ravish, *v. a.* == rob, despoil a person of. RG. 194. Fr. ravir

Raw, *adj.* Pol. S. 237. AS. hreáw

Ray, *sb.* == striped cloth. Rel. Ant. ii. p. 192

Rayme, *v. n.* == rule, lord it. Pol. S. 150

Razor, *sb.* Ps. li. 4

Reach, *v. a.* == tell. O. and N. 1447; part. 'raht.' Wright's L. P. p. 42. AS. recan

Reach, *v. a.* == hold out to a person, as we say, 'to reach one a thing.' Pol. S. 157. AS. ræcan

Read, *v. a.* HD. 2327. AS. rædan

Reader, *sb.* 1068 B.

Readily, *adv.* O. and N. 1279

Ready, *adj.* [iredi]. 766 B.

Realm, *sb.* 948 B.

Reap, *v. a.* Pol. S. 152

Rear, *v. a.* == raise up. RG. 369; part. 'yrerd.' RG. 214

Rearmain, *sb.* == a backhanded blow. Alys. 7395

Rearward, *sb.* == the rear. Alys. 7787

Reason, *sb.* RG. 459

Reave, *v. a.* == carry away, despoil of. HD. 2590; pret. 'rafte.' Wright's L. P. p. 31. 'rewede.' RG. 171, AS. reáfian

Rebel, *adj.* RG. 72

Recet, *sb.* == place of refuge. RG. 98, 406; [resset]. Alys. 603

—— *v. a.* == receive into a refuge. RG. 214

Reck, *v. n.* == care. O. and N. 533, 3 s. pres. 'rehth.' O. and N. 1401, pret. 'rauȝte.' RG. 390; 'roȝte.' RG. 216. AS. récan

Reckless, *adj.* RG. 287

Reckon, *v. a.* Wright's L. P. p. 68. AS. recnan

Reckoning, *sb.* == account. Sermon 23

Red, *adj.* RG. 383. AS. read

—— *v. n.* == become red. Wright's L. P. p. 34

Red, *sb.* == counsel. RG. 556, 566; [rade]. Alys. 6165. AS. réd

Rede, *v. a.* == counsel. RG. 98, 214. AS. rǽdan

Redless, *adj.* == without counsel. O. and N. 691

Reed, *sb.* RG. 540. Alys. 5064; [reod]. Alys. 6433

Reedpipe, *sb.* == pen. Ps. xliv. 2

Reek, *sb.* == smoke. Ps. xvii. 9. AS. reác

—— *v. n.* == to smoke. Ps. cxliii. 5

Reeve, *sb.* See Reve

Refuse, *v. a.* Ritson's AS. xvii. v. 122

Rehearse, *v. a.* == tell. Alys. 1664

Reign, *v. n.* RG. 29

Reinable, *adj.* == reasonable. RG. 414. Fr. raisnable.

Reioshe, *v. a.* == enjoy? Manuel d. Pecches, 2036. Fr. réjoyer

Rekles, *sb.* == incense. Ps. cxl. 2. AS. recels

Reken, *adj.* == wise, prudent, excellent. Wright's L. P. p. 27. Ritson's AS. viii. 156. AS. recan, to order or direct; part. 'recen'

Reken, *adv.* == quickly. 2103 B. AS. recene

Release, *v. a.* RG. 500

Relics, *sb.* == remains. Ps. xxxvi. 37; in the ecclesiastical sense, as the 'relics of saints.' RG. 177, 255

Relieve, *v. a.* Ritson's AS. xviii. 38

Rem, *sb.* == cream. Marg. 32. AS. ream. Germ. rahm

Rem, *sb.* == sorrow, injury. O. and N. 1214. Cf. AS. reomig, sad

Reme, *v. n.* == call out, cry. Rel. S. iv. 22. AS. hreman. Another form of 'scream'

Reme, *v. a.* == leave, evacuate. K. Horn, 1312. AS. rúmian

—— == make room, clear a passage. Alys. 3347. AS. rýman

Remnant, *sb.* Alys. 5707

Remove, *v. a.* RG. 533; part. 'iremewed.' RG. 550

—— *v. n.* Alys. 7238

Removing, *sb.* Alys. 7821

Rent, *sb.* RG. 370. Fr. rente. Lat. reditus

Rent, *sb.* == stream, course. Cok. 83, AS. rent

Repent, *v. n.* 101 β. RG. 350

Repentant, *adj.* RG. 291

Reprove, *v. a.* Ritson's AS. xviii. 46

Respite, *sb.* 637 B. Fr. respit. Lat. respectare

Response, *sb.* 825 B.

Resset. See Recet

Rest, *sb.* 1130 B.

—— *v. a.* Wright's L. P. p. 52

Resting, *sb.* Wright's L. P. p. 29. Alys. 2807

Restore, *v. a.* RG. 319, 500

Resurrection, *sb.* 363 β

Rette, *v. a.* == impute, reckon. Alys. 7247. ON. retta

Reume, *v. a.* == speak. Alys. 4237. See Reme, *vb.*

Reure, *sb.* == a robber, reaver. HD. 2104

Reve, *v. n.* == swear? K. Horn. 1368. ON. rifja, recitare?

Reve, *sb.* == sheriff or reeve. HD. 1627. M. Ode, st. 129. AS. geréfa

Reve, *sb.* == depredation, spoiling. O. and N. 458. AS. reáf

Rever, *sb.* == robber. AS. reáfere

Reverence, *sb.* 115 B. Alys. 793

Reverye, *sb.* == robbery. RG. 193

Revest, *v. a.* == put on. RG. 537; part. 'irevested.' St Swithin, 139

Reving, *sb.* == robbery. Ps. xvi. 12. M. Ode, st. 128

Rewe, *sb.* == streak. 2218 B. Probably the same as 'row'

—— *v. n.* == show a streak? 'Ere the dai *rewe*.' Pol. S. 239

Reynes, *sb.* == realms. Wright's L. P. p. 31

Reʒel, *sb.* == dress. O. and N. 562. AS. hrægl. Cf. O. Eng. 'night-rail,' for a night-dress

Rhinoceros, [rinocertis]. Alys. 6529

Rhyme, *sb.* HD. 21

Rib, *sb.* RG. 22

Ribald, *sb.* Pol. S. 155, 237. Fr. ribald; from OHG. hrûpa, a prostitute. See Burguy on this word

Ribaldry, *sb.* [ribaudye] == a ribald story. Alys. 21

Rich, *adj.* RG. 377; [ruche]. RG. 13

Riche, *sb.* == kingdom. Wright's L. P. p. 94. O. and N. 357

Richesse, *sb.* RG. 433

Richly, *adv.* RG. 377

Ride, *v. n.* RG. 463; pret. 'rode.' RG. 375; part. 'riding.' RG. 377

Rife, *adj.* == frequent. RG. 4, 252; comp. 'rifer.' RG. 260. AS. ryf

Right, *sb.* == redress for an injury. RG. 374

—— == in plur. 'rights,' 'to maintain their rights.' 171 B.

Right, *adj.* == dexter. Wright's L. P. p. 25

—— == good, excellent. Wright's L. P. p. 25

Right, *adv.* == just, exactly. RG. 8

—— == rightly. Wright's L. P. p. 30

—— *v. a.* == to set right. Ps. xvii. 36

Righteous, *adj.* [ryhtwise]. Wright's L. P. p. 25

Righteousness, *sb.* Ps. iv. 2

Rightful, *adj.* RG. 501; comp. 'rightfuller.' RG. 266

Rightfulness, *sb.* Wright's L. P. p. 53

Righting, *sb.* == a setting right. Ps. xcvi. 2

Rightness, *sb.* 1629 B.

Rightwished, *sb.* Ps. xviii. 10

Rimefrost, [ren-forst]. *sb.* Fr. Sci. 232. AS. hrím

Rind, *sb.* Alys. 6187. AS. rind

Rine, *sb.* == a course, hence a course of years, life; 'for to rine' == for ever? Ps. xliv. 11. AS. ryne

Ring, *v. a.* RG. 509

—— *v. n.* == resound. Wright's L. P. p. 43

Ring, *sb.* RG. 489

Ringing, *sb.* St Swithin, 45

Ripe, *adj.* == applied to young birds. RG. 177. AS. ríp, harvest. *adj.* rípe

Ripeness, *sb.* == the ripeness of the day, i. e. full day. Ps. cxviii. 147

Rippe, *sb.* == a fish-basket. HD. 893. ON. hrip

Ris, *sb.* == a branch. Wright's L. P. pp. 26, 30. Pol. S. 149. Dan. riis

Rise, *v. n.* == arise. Pol. S. 149

—— *v. a.* == raise. 1082 B.

Ritte, *v. a.* == rip. HD. 2495. ON. rista

Rivage, *sb.* == river bank. Alys. 6079

Rive, *v. n.* == arrive. RG. 14, 16

Rive, *v. a.* == split, snap. Rel. S. i. 14

Rive, *sb.* == bank. Alys. 4090

Rivel, *v. n.* == become wrinkled. Rel. Ant. ii. 211

River, *sb.* RG. 1

Rivering, *sb.* == hawking by a river's side. Alys. 678

Rixe, *v. a.* == rule. Moral Ode, st. 190. AS. ricsian

Ro, *sb.* == rest. Wright's L. P. p. 37; [roo]. Ibid. p. 32. AS. row. ON. ró

Road, *sb.* Body and Soul, 209; [rude]. Wright's L. P. p. 32. AS. rád

Roam, *v. a.* HD. 64

—— *v. n.* == dwell. Alys. 7207, 7625. The older and newer senses of this word are analogous to the double meaning of the Lat. 'versor'

Roar, *v. n.* HD. 2438; part. 'rorand.' Ps. xxi. 14

Roast, *v. a.* RG. 207; part, 'yrosted.' RG. 244

Rob, *v. a.* RG. 377, 385

Robber, *sb.* RG. 389

Robbery, *sb.* RG. 16, 550

Robe, *sb.* RG. 180

Rocher, *sb.* == rocks, rocky place. Alys. 7090

Rock, *sb.* RG. 22. Fr. roche, connected with 'crag,' and W. rhwg

Rode, *sb.* == complexion. Wright's L. P. p. 30; [rody]. Alys. 164; [rude]. O. and N. 443. ON. rodi

Roe, *sb.* == the animal. Wright's L. P. p. 29. AS. rá

Roil, *v. a.* == rove about. Rel. Ant. ii. 175. ON. hrolla

Rokke, *v. a.* == drive. RG. 98. ON. reka

Roll, *sb.* (of parchment). Pol. S. 157

Romance, *sb.* RG. 487

Rome, *v. n.* == roar. Ps. ciii. 21. AS. hreman

Rone, *v. a.* == comfort. Ps. lxx. 21; cxviii. 76, 82; part. 'roned.' Ps. lxxvi. 3. Perhaps from ON. rúni, amicus, colloquiorum socius

Roning, *sb.* == comfort. Ps. xciii. 19

Rood, *sb.* == cross. RG. 532. AS. ród

Roof, *sb.* RG. 404, 416; [rove]. Alys. 513. AS. hróf

Rook, *sb.* O. and N. 1128. AS. róc

Rooles, *adj.* == restless. Wright's L. P. p. 42

Room, *v. a.* == clear (a way). RG. 536. AS. rýman. See Reme

Room, *adj.* == empty. RG. 303

———— == broad, spacious. O. and N. 643. Ps. ciii. 25

Roomhouse, *sb.* == privy. O. and N. 592

Roomlyke, *adv.* == abundantly. Ps. xxx. 24

Root, *sb.* RG. 404

Rope, *sb.* RG. 448, 509; 'in his rope' == in his noose, or power. Alys. 6298. AS. ræp

Rorde, *sb.* == voice. O. and N. 311. AS. reord

Rose, *sb.* RG. 331

Roser, *sb.* == rosebush. HD. 2919

Rot, *v. n.* RG. 411. AS. rotian

Roter, *sb.* == rooter, eradicator. RG. 297

Rothe, *v. a.* == rathe or advise. HD. 2817

Rother, *sb.* == cattle. RG. 52. Pol. S. 220. AS. hryðer

Rotle, *v. b.* == rustle, *q. v.*

Rotted, *adj.* == rotten. Pol. S. 152

Rotten, *adj.* Body and Soul, 37

Rough, *adj.* comp. 'rughher.' Alys. 5956

Roun, *sb.* == a song; [ron]. Wright's L. P. p. 43

Roun, *v. n.* == whisper, round. 1200 B. AS. rúnian

Round, *adj.* Fr. Sci. 121. Alys. 594

Rout, *sb.* == company. RG. 371, 428, 546

Rout, *v. a.* == disturb, confound. Serm. 30

Route, *v. n.* == roar. HD. 1911. Fr. router. ON. rauta

Rovertid, *part.* == recovered from, i. e. left off (crying). Alys. 7895

Row, *sb.* == array, order. Wright's L. P. pp. 25, 35. AS. rawa. See
Rewe

Row, *v. n.* pret. 'rewe.' 1159 B.

Rowe, *adj.* == rough. RG. 25, 507; [ruʒe]. O. and N. 104

Roxle, *v. n.* == grunt. Rel. Ant. ii. 211. Dut. rotelen

Ruby, *sb.* Wright's L. P. p. 25

Rudder, *sb.* [rother]. K. Horn, 194. AS. róðer

Rude. See Road

Rue, *v. a.* == pity. Wright's L. P. p. 29

——— *v. n.* == have compassion on. RG. 449

Rue, *v. n.* == grieve for, repent of; 'that was to rewe sore.' RG. 493.
AS. reówan

——— *sb.* == pity. 1051 B; [reowe]. O. and N. 1443

Rueful, *adj.* == sad. RG. 327

Ruely, *adj.* == sad. Body and Soul, 171

——— *adv.* == ruefully. RG. 126, 263

Rueness, *sb.* == compassion. HD. 2227

Ruer, *sb.* == a compassionate person. Ps. lxxxv. 15

Rugge, *sb.* == back. RG. 525, 460. AS. hrycg

Rule, *sb.* == regulation. St Dunstan, 46

Ruls, *adj.* == overripe, said of corn. Pol. S. 152. See Halliwell, *s. v.*
Rule. ON. rusill, qui effundit—rusla, prodigere

Run, *v. n.* pret. 'ronne.' Wright's L. P. p. 68; part. 'rennyng' (of water).
RG. 80. See Urne

Runci, *sb.* == a nag. HD. 2569. Fr. roncin

Rundel, *sb.* == circle. Fragm. Sci. 62

Rune, *sb.* == conversation. O. and N. 1154. AS. rún

Rure, *sb.* == full. O. and N. 1152. AS. hrýre

Russin, *sb.* == meal between dinner and supper. Cok. 20. ON. rúss, temulentia

Rustle, *v. n.* [rotle]. Alys. 930. ON. rosta, a tumult

Ruwet, *sb.* == bugle-horn. Alys. 3699. Fr. ruet, rouette. Lat. rota. See Wright's Vocab. p. 104, where 'litui' is translated by 'ruez.' The name is derived from the circular flexures of the instrument

Rye, *sb.* [ruȝe]. Pol. S. 152. AS. rige

Ryme, *v. a.* == cry out, tell; Ritson's AS. viii. 99, 137. AS. hryman

S.

Sabeline, *sb.* == sable. M. Ode, st. 182

Sack, *sb.* HD. 2019. AS. sacc

Sacre, *v. a.* == consecrate. RG. 445, 522

Sacred, *adj.* Alys. 6777

Sacrificing, *sb.* Alys. 272

Sacring, *sb.* == consecration. RG. 446

Sad, *adj.* == sorrowful. Wright's L. P. p. 29

—— == heavy. Alys. 5587. AS. sæd

Saddle, *sb.* RG. 401

Safe, *adj.* Pol. S. 198; [saufe]. Creed of St Athan. 102

Safely, *adv.* RG. 239

Sage, *adj.* == wise. RG. 198. Fr. sage. Ital. saggio. Lat. sapiens

Sage, *sb.* == a plant, the 'Salvia pratensis' of botanists. Wright's L. P. p. 26. Fr. sauge

Saht, *adj.* == reconciled. Wright's L. P. pp. 46, 47. AS. saht

Sail, *sb.* RG. 47

Saine, *v. a.* == bless. Ps. lxii. 5. AS. senian. Germ. segnen

Saint, as an appellative, 'Seint Thomas.' 1878 B. 'Seyn Poule.' RG.

—— *sb.* [sonte]. Wright's L. P. p. 96; [seynte]. Alys. 6763

Sake, *sb.* == contention. O. and N. 1158. AS. sacu

Sake, *sb.* == matter, thing. Wright's L. P. p. 23. Dut. zaak

—— == cause; 'for thine sake.' Wright's L. P. p. 28

Saken, *v. a.* == fight against, kill. Alys. 1884. AS. sacan

Sale, *sb.* == hall. Wright's L. P. p. 26. AS. sal

Salmon, *sb.* Alys. 5446

Salt, *adj.* RG. 1

Saltmarsh, *sb.* Ps. cvi. 34

Salve, *sb.* HD. 1835

Samded, *adj.* == half dead. RG. 163. AS. sám, Lat. semi, with 'dead'

Samen, *adv.* == together. HD. 2251. ON. saman

—— *v. a.* == collect together; pret. 'samened.' Ps. xlvi. 10; part. 'samenand.' Ps. xxxii. 7; 'samened.' HD. 2890

Samfayle, == without fail. RG. 405. Fr. sans faille

Samyte, *sb.* == a kind of silk. Alys. 1027; a robe of silk. Alys. 2095. Fr. sami, samit

Sand, *sb.* HD. 708

Sanglic, *adj.* == fit for song. Ps. cxviii. 54

Sanne, *sb.* == sun? Wright's L. P. p. 26

Sans, *prep.* == without. Pol. S. 215. Fr. sans

Sapphire, *sb.* Wright's L. P. p. 25

Saturday. 807 B.

Saturnight. RG. 557

Sauf, *adv.* == save. *q. v.*

Saufe. See Safe

Sauhting, *sb.* == peace, reconciliation? Wright's L. P. p. 23

Saut, *sb.* == leap. RG. 564. Fr. sault, saillir

Savage, *adj.* Alys. 2088. Fr. sauvage. Ital. selvaggio. Lat. silva

Save, *adv.* [sauvé, sauf]. 434, 435 B.

—— *v. a.* RG. 449, 519, 550

Savour, *sb.* Wright's L. P. p. 87

Saw, *sb.* == saying, opinion. Wright's L. P. pp. 31, 47; [saye]. O. and N. 1036

Sax, *sb.* == short sword. RG. 125. AS. seax

Say, *sb.* == silk. RG. 390. Fr. saie. Lat. sagum

Say, *v. a.* pres. 'segge.' RG. 501; plur. 'segeth.' RG. 502; pret. 'seyde.' RG. 390; 'sede.' RG. 418; part, 'ysaid.' RG. 11; 'ysed.' RG. 420

Saygyng, *sb.* == omens as to land, air, &c. Alys. 61

Saylyng, *sb.* == assailing. Alys. 7392, 676

Scab, *sb.* [shabbe]. Pol. S. 239. AS. sceabb

Scabbard, [scaubert]. RG. 273. ON. skálpr. Dut. schabbe, Kil. Connected with 'sheath,' and the AS. scǽð, scádan

Scabbed, *adj.* HD. 2449

Scald, *v. a.* Marg. 59. Ps. cxx. 6

Scaldand, *sb.* == a torrent. Ps. cxxv. 4; cxxiii. 5. Probably formed in imitation of 'torrent,' from 'torreo,' and AS. 'byrna,' a burn, or brook, from 'byrnan'

Scalding, *adj.* == hot. Ps. lxxxii. 10

Scalp, *sb.* Ps. vii. 17. ON. skálpr, a sheath

Scape, *v. n.* == escape. Pol. S. 152

Scarce, *adj.* RG. 334. Fr. escars. Lat. excarpere

Scarcely, *adv.* == in small quantities. Alys. 1012

Scarcity, *sb.* Alys. 5495

Scarlet, *sb.* Alys. 6376

Scathe, *sb.* == harm. HD. 1352. AS. sceáðan

Scathing, *sb.* Ps. cv. 30

Scatter, *v. a.* Ps. xvii. 15; xxxiv. 16; part. 'stakered,' by a metathesis in Ps. cxl. 7. AS. scateran

Scenche, *sb.* == a cup. M. Ode, st. 167. AS. scenc

Sceptre, *sb.* Alys. 6716

Schamel, *sb.* == footstool. Ps. xcviii. 5. AS. scamel. Lat. scamnum

Schamil, == shambles, *q. v.*

Schare, *sb.* == penis. Fr. Sci. 322. AS. scaru. 'Schere' is given as the translation of 'pubes' in Wright's Vocabb. p. 246

Schede, *vb.* == separate. O. and N. 197. AS. sceádan

Schef, *sb.* == creature. Rel. Ant. ii. p. 177

Schenche, *v. a.* == destroy. Alys. 4482. AS. scénan

184

Schenche, *v. a.* == pour out. Alys. 7581. Rel. Ant. i. 113. AS. scencan

Schenlon, *sb.* == rascal, vile person. Rel. Ant. ii. p. 211. Probably a corruption of Dut. schelm

Schille. See Shrill

Schinde, *sb.* == shingle, rafter. Rel. Ant. ii. p. 176. Dutch schindel

Schoningnes, *sb.* == awe. Ps. xxxiv. 26. Formed from 'shun'

School, *sb.* 152 B.

Schulle, *sb.* == some fish, resembling a sole in flavour, according to Sir T. Browne. See N. and Q., 2nd ser. vi. 382; vii. p. 79, 135. It may be derived from the Swed. skolla, a plaice, ON. skolli, a fox. Cf. Gr. ἀλωπεκίας, and Lat. vulpes marina, and Sylvester's Sea-Fox, p. 97. In Wright's Vocabb., p. 254, among the Nomina Piscium Marinorum we find the entries 'Hec solia, a sole,' and 'Hec testa, a schylle;' showing clearly that the 'schylle' was not the same as the sole, and that it was some sort of flatfish, probably the plaice

Scion, *sb.* == stem, stock. Cok. 72. Fr. cion

Sclavyne, *sb.* == a palmer's robe. K. Horn, 1086. It is given as the translation of 'Sarabarda' in Wright's Vocabb. p. 259

Scoff, *sb.* Alys. 667

Scomfit, *sb.* == discomfiture. Alys. 959

Scoppe, *sb.* == a leap, skip. Alys. 5777. Swed. skutta, to leap

Score, *sb.* RG. 20, 519

Scorn, *v. a.* Ps. ii. 4. 80 B. OHG. skernon. Fr. escharnir. SS. scarn, scare. Ital. scorno

Scornly, *adv.* 710 B.

Scorpion, *sb.* Alys. 5263

Scot, *sb.* == payment, contribution, shot. Pol. S. 71. AS. scot

Scour, *v. n.* == rush quickly. Alys. 3722. Ital. scorrere. Fr. escourre
—— *sb.* == haste, 'good scour.' Alys. 4276

Scourge, *v. a.* RG. 263; part. 'iscourged.' St Kath. 118
—— *sb.* Wright's L. P. p. 84

Scrape, *v. a.* [shrape]. Pol. S. 239. AS. screopan

Scream, *v. n.* Pol. S. 157. AS. hreman

Screnche, *v. a.* == withdraw. M. Ode, st. 167. AS. screncan

Scrip, *sb.* K. Horn, 1093. ON. skreppa

Scrub, *v. a.* [scrobbe]. Alys. 4310. Swed. skrubba

Sculde, *v. a.* == defend. M. Ode, st. 167. AS. scyldan

Scythe, *sb.* HD. 2553. Alys. 5722. AS. siðe

Se, == the. HD. 534. This is, however, probably an error

—— == thee. O. and N. 62

Sea, *sb.* RG. 436, 443

Seal, *sb.* == the fish. HD. 755. AS. seol

Seal, *sb.* RG. 77. Fr. seau

—— *v. a.* part. 'ysealed.' RG. 446

Seam, *sb.* (of a garment). Rel. Ant. ii. 176. AS. seám

Season, *sb.* == time. Alys. 5251

Seat, *sb.* == sitting down. Ps. cxxxviii. 2

Second, *adj.* RG. 414

Secular, *adj.* 918 B.

Seculars, *sb.* == an order of monks. RG. 282

Sedewale, *sb.* == the herb valerian, or setwell. Wright's L. P. p. 27. AS. sydewale

Sedge, *sb.* [segge]. O. and N. 18. AS. secg

See, *sb.* == throne. Pol. S. 215, 773 B. Fr. siége

—— == a bishop's see. 567 B.

See, *v. a.* [ysey]. RG. 369; [iso]. O. and N. 327, 370; [iseo]. 125 B.; [so]. O. and N. 34; [y-seen]. Alys. 5524; pret. 'sey.' RG. 418; 'ysey.' RG. 367; 'isey.' 38 B.; 'seye.' 39 β; 'iseye.' 171 B.; 'isay.' 772 B.; 'say.' Alys. 4352; 'sygh.' Alys. 6913; part. 'iseʒe.' 281 B.; 'isene.' 1305 B.; 'yseye.' RG. 418

Seed, *sb.* Pol. S. 152. AS. séd

Seek, *v. a.* [siche]. 60 B.; [i-seche]. O. and N. 74; part. 'isoʒt.' 68 B. AS. sécan.

Seem, *v. n.* == appear. Wright's L. P. p. 23. AS. seman

Seem, *v. a.* == become, beseem. Wright's L. P. p. 44

Seemly, *adj.* Wright's L. P. p. 26; sup. 'seemlokest,' ibid. p. 27

Seeth, *v. a.* RG. 404, 408; part. 'ysode.' RG. 446. AS. seóðan

Segge, *sb.* == cuttlefish. HD. 896. Fr. seche

Seignours, *sb.* == lord, master. Alys. 1458

Seisin, *sb.* RG. 314, 382; [sesyng]. Alys. 8014

Seize, *v. a.* RG. 436

—— == (in law) to give a person possession of a thing. HD. 2513

Selcouth, *adj.* == strange. HD. 124. AS. seld-cuð

—— *sb.* == a marvel. HD. 1059

—— *v. a.* == show wonderfully. Ps. xv. 3

Selcouthly, *adv.* Ps. xliv. 5

Seldom, *adv.* [seld]. RG. 416. The dat. pl. of the AS. adj. 'seld'

Sele, *adj.* == glad, content. Alys. 7430. AS. sǽl

Sele, *sb.* == a short time. O. and N. 951. AS. sǽl

Self [sulve], *adj.* == same. RG. 373, 263

Himself. RG. 377; [him silve]. 274 B.; [him sulfne]. M. Ode, st. 7

Myself [my sulf]. RG. 405

Thyself. Wright's L. P. p. 26

Selfwilly, *adv.* == without a cause. Ps. cviii. 3; cxviii. 161

Selike, *sb.* == willow. Ps. cxxxvi. 2. Fr. saulx. Lat. salix

Sell, *v. a.* RG. 223, 397; pret, 'solde.' 530 β; part. 'isold.' St Lucy, 77

Selthe, *sb.* == advantage. HD. 1338. AS. sélð

Semblant, *sb.* == countenance, appearance. RG. 157

Semble, *sb.* == assembly. RG. 125

Seme, *sb.* == burden. O. and N. 773. AS. seam

Seme, *v. a.* == arbitrate, judge. O. and N. 187. AS. seman

Semee, *adj.* == seemly. 116 B.

Senator, *sb.* RG. 193, 219

Send, *v. a.* RG. 383; part. 'ysend.' RG. 398

Sendal, *sb.* == a fine silk stuff. Body and Soul, 15. Fr. cendal. See Roq. *s. v.*

Sene, *sb.* == sight, power of vision. O. and N. 368. AS. sýn

Sengellic, *adj.* == eternal. Creed of St Athan. 41. AS. singallíc

Sentence, *sb.* 924 B.

Seollic, *adj.* == marvellous. O. and N. 1297. AS. séllíc

Sepulture, *sb.* RG. 186

Seraph, *sb.* Marg. 75

Sere, *v. a.* == dry, burn. Alys. 796; [serie]. K. Horn, 1435. AS. searian

Serfborow, *sb.* == surety. HD. 1667

Sergeant, *sb.* HD. 1929. 681 B.

Serie. See Sere

Serk, *sb.* == a shirt. HD. 603. AS. syrce

Sermon, *sb.* Rel. S. vii. 4

Serne, *sb.* == equipment. Ps. xliv. 10. AS. searo

Serpent, *sb.* Cok. 31

Servage, *sb.* RG. 11, 284

Serve, *v. a.* RG. 390, 404

—— == worship. Ps. xxi. 31

—— == serve out, reward; part. 'yserved.' RG. 26

—— == observe. RG. 507

Service, *sb.* RG. 412, 501

Serving, *sb.* Wright's L. P. p. 69

Set, *v. a.* == place, appoint. RG. 501; pret. 'sed.' RG. 470; part. 'yset.' RG. 394; 'set.' 1084 B. AS. settan. ON. setja

—— *v. n.* == sink (of the sun). HD. 2671. ON. setja

Sete, *adj.* == pleasant, at ease. Body and Soul, 123. Wright's L. P. pp. 89, 114. Probably from ON. sætr, dulcis, jucundus. AS. swét, our 'sweet'

Setelgang, *sb.* == sunset. Ps. xlix. 1

Settle, *v. n.* (of a bird). Alys. 484

—— *sb.* == seat. O. and N. 594. AS. setl

Seu, *sb.* == suit or contention? KG. 470

Seven. KG. 440, 491

Sevenight, *sb.* 1149 B. Alys. 7045

Seventeen. RG. 515, 499

Seventh, *adj.* [senethe]. RG. 372

Seventy. RG. 373

Sew, *v. a.* [suve] == follow. RG. 42

Sew, *v. a.* == stitch. Lat. suere; part. 'isowed.' 1840 B.

Seyned ? Body and Soul, 101

Shade, *sb.* == shadow. RG. 108

Shadow, *v. n.* Ps. cxxxix. 8

—— *sb.* Alys. 2628

Shaft, *sb.* (of an arrow). RG. 419. AS. sceaft, from scafan

Shaft, *sb.* == a creature. O. and N. 786. AS. sceaft, from scapan

Shake, *v. a.* RG. 24, 218; pret. 'ssoc.' RG. 186

Shake, *v. n.* == tremble. Wright's L. P. p. 110; pret. 'ssok.' RG. 208

—— == go hastily. Alys. 4255. AS. scacan

—— *sb.* == haste. Alys. 232

Shall, *vb.* RG. 3; 2 s. 'schaltu' == shalt thou. O. and N. 209; 3 pl. 'schul.' RG. 147; pret. 'scholde.' RG. 146; 'icholde.' RG. 539

Shambles [shamil], *sb.* Rel. Ant. ii. p. 176

Shame, *sb.* RG. 376, 532 [same]. HD. 1941

—— == shameful deed. RG. 85

—— *v. n.* == be ashamed. Pol. S. 157

—— *v. a.* == fear. RG. 361

Shameless, *adj.* Cok. ult.

Shamely, *adv.* == shamefully. Rel. S. vii. 9. HD. 2462

Shank, *sb.* == legs. HD. 1903. AS. scanca

Shape, *sb.* == creature. Body and Soul, 222

—— *v. a.* part. 'yshope.' RG. 215

Shaping, *sb.* [shupping] == shape? Wright's L. P. p. 38

Share. See Schare

Share, *sb.* == ploughshare. RG. 335

Sharp, *adj.* RG. 395

—— *v. a.* == sharpen. Ps. lxiii. 4

Shaw, *sb.* == wood. Alys. 6109. ON. skógr

Shawel, *sb.* == scarecrow. O. and N. 1646

Sheaf, *sb.* O. and N. 455. AS. sceaf

Shear, *v. a.* == cut. HD. 1413. AS. scéran

Shears, *sb.* HD. 857. AS. sceare

Sheath, *sb.* O. and N. 135. AS. scæð

Shed, *v. a.* RG. 57; pret. 'schedde.' Wright's L. P. p. 58; 'chadde.' O. and N. 1614; part, 'y-schad.' Alys. 2772. AS. scedan

Shedding, *sb.* RG. 388

Sheen, *adj.* == bright. Wright's L. P. p. 58; [scene]. M. Ode, st. 171. AS. scíne

Sheep. RG. 6, 458

Sheet, *sb.* RG. 435; [scete]. M. Ode, st. 174. AS. scyte

Shell, *sb.* Alys. 571

Shend, *v. a.* == injure. RG. 379, 506; part. 'ischend' == corrupt. Pol. S. 197; 'yssend.' RG. 212. AS. scendan

Shendfully, *adv.* RG. 310, Miracles, 84

Shendness, *sb.* RG. 342, 525; [shendisse]. 1304 B.

Shepe, *sb.* == skip; 'at on shepe' == at once. Alys. 3577

Shepherd, *sb.* RG. 351

Sheriff, *sb.* RG. 535, 536; [scirreve]. M. Ode, st. 25. AS. scír-geréfa

Shew, *v. a.* RG. 416, 563

Shewer, *sb.* == a mirror. Alys. 18

Shide, *sb.* == a piece of wood. HD. 917. Alys. 6421. AS. scíd

Shield, *sb.* RG. 435; [chelde]. O. and N. 1711

—— *v. a.* RG. 386, 525; [i-shilde]. O. and N. 779

Shielder, *sb.* Ps. xxx. 5

Shilling, *sb.* RG. 383. AS. scill, scylling

Shin, *sb.* O. and N. 1058. Ps. cxlvi. 10. AS. scina

Shine, *v. n.* 1411 B. AS. scínan

Shingle, *sb.* == a rafter, roof. Alys. 2210. Germ. schindel

Shining, *sb.* Ps. cix. 3

Ship, *sb.* RG. 466

—— *v. a.* == furnish, store. RG. 538

—— == cause to embark in a ship. Alys. 6062

—— *v. n.* == sail in a ship. Alys. 1495

Shipful, *sb.* RG. 265; 'ssypvolmen' == shipfuls of men. RG. 371

Shipping, *sb.* == ships. Alys. 990

Shipwright, *sb.* Alys. 3665

Shir, *adj.* == bright. HD. 587. AS. scír

Shire, *sb.* RG. 3. 374. AS. scíre

Shireness, *sb.* == purity. Ps. cxviii. 130

Shirt, *sb.* 260 B.

Shit, *adj.* == obscene. O. and N. 286

—— *v. a.* Alys. 5670. AS. scitan

Shiver, *v. n.* Rel. S. v. 142

Shoe, *sb.* HD. 860. AS. sceó

—— *v. a.* HD. 1138; pres. 'shoyeth.' Pol. S. 238; part. 'ischud.' O. and N. 1527

Shonde, *sb.* == injury. RG. 65. AS. sceond

Shoot, *v. n.* [ssete]. RG. 377; [scheote]. Alys. 6347; 3 s. pres. 'schit.' Fr. Sci. 138

—— *v. a.* pret. 'sset.' RG. 419; part. 'yssote.' RG. 419, 377. AS. scítan

Shooting, *sb.* [ssetinge]. RG. 543

Shop, *sb.* RG. 541. Fr. eschope

Shore, *sb.* HD. 321. AS. score, from 'scéran,' to divide

Shoren, for 'sholen' == shall. HD. 1640

Short, *adj.* RG. 412

Shortly, *adv.* RG. 181, 446

Shotship, *sb.* == a party paying scot and lot. HD. 2099. AS. scot

Shoulder, *v. a.* HD. 1056

Shoulderblade, *sb.* HD. 2644

Shouldered, *adj.* == having shoulders. Alys. 4968

Shoulders, *sb.* RG. 377, 401

Shove, *v. n.* RG. 148; pret. 'schef.' 408 β

—— *v. a.* Ps. lxi. 5. AS. scúfan

Shovel, *sb.* RG. 99. AS. scofl

Shoving, *sb.* RG. 212

Shower, *sb.* Wright's L. P. p. 89. AS. scúr

Shrede, *sb.* == clothing. HD. 99

Shrenke, *v. a.* == blast, wither, make to shrink up. Fr. Sci. 194. AS. screncan. Swed. skrynka

Shrew, *adj.* == wicked. RG. 383, 419

—— *sb.* == enemy. RG. 407

Shreward, *sb.* == shrew, used always of men. RG. 268

Shrewd, *adj.* [schrewede] == cursed, wicked. RG. 164

Shrewhede, *sb.* == wickedness. RG. 280

Shride, *v. a.* == shroud or clothe oneself. HD. 963; pret. 'shred.' K. Horn, 868. Ps. xcii. 1; part. 'y-shred.' Alys. 6819. AS. scrýdan

Shriek, *v. n.* Pol. S. 157; [schirche]. O. and N. 223. pret. 'shrighte.' Alys. 5738. ON. skríkja

Shrift, *sb.* RG. 419; [schifte]. HD. 1829. AS. scrift

Shriftfather, *sb.* == confessor. Miracles, 69

Shrill, *adj.* [schille]. O. and N. 142

—— *v. n.* == sound. Alys. 777

Shrine, *sb.* RG. 478, 518. AS. scrin

—— *v. a.* == enshrine. RG. 469

Shrink, *v. n.* [scrynke]. Pol. S. 157. AS. scrincan

Shrive, *v. a.* RG. 392, 544

—— == confess. Ps. vii. 18; lxxxviii. 6

Shroud, *sb.* == clothing. HD. 303. AS. scrúd

Shudder, *v. n.* Wright's L. P. p. 110

Shueles, *adj.* == soulless. O. and N. 1126. AS. sáwl-leas

Shun, *v. a.* == avoid. Body and Soul, 105. AS. scunian

——— == make to shun, repel. Ps. cxviii. 10; bring to nought, quash. Ps. xxxii. 10; xxxix. 15

Shunt, *v. a.* == shun. O. and N. 236

Shut, *v. a.* pret. 'shytt.' Alys. 5137. 3 pl. 'schutten.' Ibid. 2640. part. 'y-scheot.' Alys. 6185; 'y-shote.' Alys. 5953. AS. scittan

Sib, *adj.* == akin. RG. 346, 446; [ysyb]. RG. 315. AS. gesib

——— *sb.* == peace, concord. O. and N. 1003. AS. sib

Sibrede, *sb.* == kinship. RG. 492. AS. sibrǽden

Sick, *adj.* RG. 564

——— *v. n.* == sicken, become sick. 506 B.

Sickle, *sb.* Fr. Sci. 62. AS. sicel

Sickness, *sb.* RG. 378, 251

Side, *sb.* RG. 553

Side, *sb.* == time. *v.* Sithe

Side, *adj.* == wide, ample. RG. 117. Wright's L. P. p. 37. AS. síd

Siedh, *sb.* == sinks. Rel. S. iii. 5; 3 s. pres. síhð. AS. sígan

Siege, *sb.* == seat, RG. 132

——— *v. a.* == besiege. Alys. 2672

Sigh, *sb.* [syke]. Wright's L. P. pp. 40, 90

——— *v. n.* [syke]. Wright's L. P. p. 85; part. 'sykynde.' RG. 323. AS. sýcan

Sighing, *sb.* [siking]. 9 β. Wright's L. P. p. 53

Sighingness, *sb.* Ps. ci. 6

Sight, *sb.* == appearance. RG. 6

——— == a spectacle. RG. 539

——— == view, prospect. Cok. 46

Sign, *sb.* RG. 180, 193

Signifiance, *sb.* == meaning. Alys. 583

Signify, *v. a.* RG. 345

Signiory, *sb.* RG. 440

Siker, *adj.* == secure. RG. 430, 503

Sikerhede, *sb.* O. and N. 1263

Sikerlich, *adv.* == certainly. O. and N. 1137. HD. 422

Sikerness, *sb*. RG. 434. HD. 2856

Silence, *sb*. 319 β

Silk, *sb*. Wright's L. P. p. 36. AS. seolc

Silken, *adj*. Alys. 278

Silly, *adj*. RG. 428. Literally, happy, then innocent, foolish, from AS. sælig

Silver, *sb*. RG. 379

—— *adj*. 'silver ore.' RG. 1

Simnel, *sb*. == a biscuit. HD. 779. Lat. 'siminellus,' from 'simila.' Sw. semla

Simple, *adj*. RG. 97

Simply, *adv*. RG. 125

Sin, *sb*. RG. 195, 405

Sinew, *sb*. 2429 B

Sinful, *adj*. RG. 173, 405

Sinfully, *adv*. RG. 445

Sing, *v. a*. RG. 508. Alys. 1044

—— *v. n*. Wright's L. P. p. 26

Singing, *sb*. Alys. 6745

Sink, *v. n*. Wright's L. P. p. 37. AS sincan

—— *v. a*. == make to sink. pret. 'sanke.' Ps. lxviii. 3. AS. sencan

Sir, as a title, 'Syre Geffray.' RG. 440. 'Sir King.' RG. 501

Sire, *sb*. == an appellative. RG. 500, 501

—— == a lord. RG. 321

Sise, *sb*. == assize. Body and Soul, 143

Sisour, *sb*. == a person deputed to hold assizes. Manuel d. Pecches, 2638

Sister, *sb*. RG. 453

Sit, *v. n*. RG. 535

—— == fit (as a dress). Body and Soul, 199

—— *v. a*. == oppose, for 'at-sitte.' HD. 2567

Sithe, *sb*. == time. 'at the first sithe' HD. 1052. RG. 264; [side]. O. and N. 299. AS. sið

Sithen, *adv*. == afterwards. HD. 2251

Siththe, *adv*. == since (of time). 1864 B.; afterwards. RG. 266;

[suththe]. RG. 368, 378. AS. síðða

    Six. RG. 428, 395

    Sixteen. RG. 474

    Sixth, *adj.* RG. 416

    Sixty. RG. 368

    Skeet, *adj.* == swift. Alys. 5637. ON. skjóttr

    Skekking, *sb.* == battle. Alys. 3563. ON. skekja, to shake

    Skente, *v. a.* == amuse, delight. O. and N. 449. ON. skemta

    Skenting, *sb.* == a merry song. O. and N. 446

    Skere, *adj.* == clear, pure. Pol. S. 155. AS. scír

    ——— *v. a.* == purify, justify. RG. 334, 335

    Skere, *adj.* == divided from. Rel. S. iv. 78

    Sket, *adv.* == quickly. HD. 1926. Alys. 974; [skit]. Alys. 6029. ON. skjótt

    Skewe, == sky. *q. v.*

    Skilful, *adj.* == reasonable. Creed of St Athan. 76

    Skill, *sb.* == intelligence. Body and Soul, 25; reason. Pol. S. 198. Alys. 3372

    ——— == cause. Ps. xlii. 1. ON. skil, skilning

    Skin, *sb.* Alys. 6807

    Skinner, *sb.* Rel. Ant. ii. p. 176

    Skip, *v. n.* [schippe]. Alys. 1108

    Skirm, *v. n.* == skirmish. Alys. 197, 1046. HD. 2323; 'skirmen' is used in Laȝamon in the sense of 'skirmish.' Dan. skjerm, a defence

    Skit. See Sket

    Skruke, *v. n.* == shrink, wither. Wright's L. P. p. 87. Cf. ON. skrucka, 'anus rugosa,' skrucklegr, 'deformis,' and Eng. 'shrug'

    Skulk, *v. n.* Ps. xxxviii. 12; 'skulded.' Ps. cxviii. 158. Sw. skolka

    Skulking, *sb.* RG. 256

    Skull, *sb.* RG. 16

    Sky, *sb.* Alys. 479, 561; [skewe]. Ps. xvii. 12. ON. ský, a cloud

    Skyke, *v. n.* == fight. Alys. 6077. ON. skekja. See Skekking

    Skymyng, probably for 'skyrming' == fighting. Alys. 1615

    Slab, *sb.* Fr. Sci. 141. AS. slífan

    Slack, *adj.* Alys. 1252. AS. sleac. Dan. slap

—— *v. a.* == slacken. Ps. lxxxviii. 10

—— *v. n.* == become slack, remiss, [slake]. Wright's L. P. p. 54

Slade [slede], *sb.* == a green plain. RG. 447. AS. slǽd

Slake. See Slack

Slander [sclaundre], *sb.* RG. 333, 354

—— == fame, report. Alys. 4797

Slating, == slaying. Alys. 200

Slave, *sb.* Body and Soul, 100

Slay, *v. a.* [sle]. 1128 B.; pret. 'slowe.' RG. 528; 'slou.' RG. 376; 'slouȝ.' 2373 B.; 2. pl. imper. 'sleth.' RG. 236; part. 'yslawe.' RG. 9

Slaȝt, *sb.* == slaughter. RG. 493, 379

Sledde, *sb.* == an old blind person. Rel. Ant. ii. 211. Dut. sladde. ON. slæfr, 'hebes,' 'ignavus,' slitti, 'res flaccida'

Slede. See Slade

Sleech, *adj.* == sly. Ritson's AS. viii. 147. Rel. Ant. ii. 175. ON. slægr

Sleep, *sb.* RG. 429

—— *v. n.* Pol. S. 152

Sleeper, *sb.* Fr. Sci. 278

Sleeping, *sb.* == sleep. 1576 B.

Sleet, *sb.* Cok. 39

Sleeve, *sb.* HD. 1957. AS. sléf

Sleight, *sb.* Ps. civ. 22

Sleme, *sb.* == weariness. Ps. cxviii. 28. AS. sluma. ON. slæmi

Sletten, *vb.* == slid, fell. See Slide

Slice, *sb.* Alys. 3833. AS. slican, to strike

Slide, *v. n.* Wright's L. P. p. 110. 3 pl. pret. 'sletten.' Alys. 2262; part. 'islide.' O. and N. 686

—— *v. a.* == make to slide. Ps. lxxxviii. 24. AS. slídan

Slider, *adj.* == slippery. O. and N. 954

Sliding, *sb.* Ps. cxiv. 8; lv. 13

Slike, *v. a.* == make smooth, comfortable. Rel. S. i. 43. part. 'isliked.' O. and N. 841. ON. slikja

Sling, *sb.* Alys. 3223. AS. slingan

—— *v. a.* pret. 'slonge.' RG. 362; pret. 'slongen.' Body and Soul, 233

—— *v. n.* == leap, fling oneself, pret. 'slang.' Alys. 5538

Slit, *v. a.* Ps. xxix. 12; part. 'slat.' Pol. S. 154

—— *sb.* == pocket. O. and N. 1116

Sloe, *sb.* HD. 849. Alys. 4983. AS. slá

Slot, *sb.* == bar. Ps. cvi. 16. Dut. slot

Sloth, *sb.* RG. 195. AS. slæwð

Slough, *sb.* == bog. Alys. 6075; [slo]. O. and N. 1392. AS. slog

Slow, *adj.* RG. 455. AS. sláw

Sly, *adj.* == cunning. Ps. viii. 4. RG. 350. ON. slægr. Dan. slu

Slyly, *adv.* Cok. 156. Rel. Ant. ii. p. 176

Smack, *sb.* == scent. O. and N. 821. AS. smæc

Small, *adj.* 2218 B.

—— *sb.* == infant, Ps. xvi. 13

Smaragde, *sb.* == emerald. Alys. 5683. Lat. smaragdus

Smart, *adj.* == sharp, 'a smart yard.' Rel. Ant. i. 115; pert. Alys. 4160

—— *v. a.* == to give pain to, torment. Wright's L. P. p. 70

—— *v. n.* == to ache, feel pain. pret. 'smourte.' RG. 322. 3 pl. 'smerten.' Alys. 5845. AS. smeortan

Smear, *v. a.* == anoint [smyrie]. St Kath. 183; part. 'ysmered.' RG. 457. AS. smérian

Smell, *sb.* == odour. RG. 43. Body and Soul, 219

—— == scent (of a dog). O. and N. 820

—— *v. n.* Wright's L. P. p. 88. Body and Soul, 22. The ON. smella, 'crepere, tinnire,' is probably the origin of our 'smell;' words relating to the senses are frequently shifted from one to the other in different languages

Smerle, *sb.* == ointment. Ps. cxxxii. 2. AS. smérels

Smile, *sb.* 80 β. Swed. smila

Smite, *v. a.* 1579 B.; pret. 'smite.' RG. 397; part. 'ismyte.' 2155 B.; 'to smite a battle.' RG. 55

—— *v. n.* == go, pass. St Dunst. 74

—— (with 'out') == to burst out of a place. RG. 564. Alys. 494

Smith, *sb.* HD. 1876

—— *v. a.* Ps. cxxviii. 3

Smithy, *sb.* St Dunstan, 60

Smock, *sb.* Wright's L. P. p. 40. AS. smoc

Smoke, *sb.* RG. 437, 493. AS. sméc

—— *v. n.* 485 β

Smoky, *adj.* 466 β

Smooth, *adj.* [smethe]. RG. 424. AS. sméðe

Smother, *sb.* == smoke, fumes. Body and Soul, 218. AS. smorian

Snache, *v. a.* == pierce? Alys. 6559. AS. snás, a spear, or spit

Snail, *sb.* O. and N. 87. AS. snægel

Snake, *sb.* Alys. 5972. AS. snácu

Snare, *sb.* Pol. S. 197. AS. sneáre

Sneer, *v. n.* Ps. ii. 4. Lat. 'nares,' the nostrils. Cf. Gr. μυϰτηϱίζειν, and Engl. 'sneeze,' from AS. næs. Lat. nasus

—— *v. a.* == scorn. Ps. lxxix. 7

Sneering, *sb.* Ps. lxxviii. 4

Sneipe, *v. n.* == blow the nose. Rel. Ant. ii. 211. Cf. Snyte

Snell, *adj.* == swift. K. Horn, 1517. AS. snel

Snellich, *adv.* == quickly. Cok. 161

Snepe, *adj.* == foolish. O. and N. 225. ON. snápr

Snivelling, *part.* Fr. Sci. 279. AS. snofel

Snobbe, *v. n.* == sob? Rel. Ant. ii. 211. Dut. snof == singultus, Kil.

Snode, *sb.* == a morsel. Ps. cxlvii. 17. AS. snid

Snout, *sb.* K. Horn, 1114. Alys. 6534. ON. snúdr

Snow, *sb.* RG. 463

—— *v. n.* Alys. 6450. 3 s. pres. 'snuith.' O. and N. 620

Snub, *v. a.* [snibbe]. Ps. ix. 6. ON. snubba

Snubbing, *sb.* == rebuke. Ps. xvii. 16

Snurpe, *v. n.* == become shrivelled. Rel. Ant. ii. 211. Sw. snörpa

Snyte, *v. a.* == blow the nose. St Dunstan, 85; part, 'ysnyt.' Ib. 91. ON. snýta

So, *adv.* with adj. 'a so gret best.' 674 β. 'of so noble fame.' RG. 367 with adv. 'so that.' 643 β. 651 β. 'so soon' == as soon as. 635 β

—— == as if. HD. 594

—— == in such manner. RG. 369

—— == as. Wright's L. P. p. 28, 'wery so water in wore'

—— == how [sa]. Ps. xxxiii. 9

So. See See

So, *sb.* == a pail. HD. 933. ON. sár. Dan. saa. Fr. seau

Soap, *sb.* RG. 6

Sobbing, *sb.* HD. 234

Socket, *sb.* == blade. Alys. 4415. Fr. soc, a ploughshare

Soffid, *part.* == sought? Ritson's AS. viii. 209

Soft, *adj.* RG. 475, 557; merciful. Ps. xxxiii. 9

—— *adv.* == softly. 2128 B.

Soil, *v. a.* RG. 469. AS. sol

—— *v. n.* == become soiled. O. and N. 1274

Sojourn, *sb.* 1585 B.

—— *v. n.* RG. 469

Sojourning, *sb.* Alys. 5209

Solace, *sb.* RG. 442

—— *v. a.* RG. 552

Solacing, *sb.* Alys. 6746

Soldan, *sb.* Alys. 1781

Solement, *adv.* == solely. 197 β

Solemnity, *sb.* 2237 B. Ps. lxxiii. 4

Solsecle, *sb.* == the herb solsequium, or heliotrope. Wright's L. P. pp. 26, 53

Somdele, *adv.* RG. 545

Some, *adj.* 'sum holi childe.' 104 B.; used absolutely, 'somme' == some persons. RG. 396, 459

Somer, *sb.* == bedstead. Body and Soul, 18. Fr. somier

Somer, *sb.* == sumpter horse. Alys. 827. Fr. sommier

Somer, *sb.* == burden, luggage. Alys. 5109. AS. seman. Fr. some

Something. RG. 368

Sometime. RG. 377

Somewanne, *adv.* == at some time. RG. 260

Son, *sb.* RG. 370

Sonde, *sb.* == a messenger. RG. 383. AS. sand, sond

—— == a message. Alys. 2893

Sondres. See Sunder

Song, *sb.* 1888 B.

Sonte, *sb.* == saint, *q. v.*

Soon, *adv.* RG. 367

Soot, *sb.* Pol. S. 195. Alys. 6636. AS. sót

Sooth, *adj.* == true. 1201 B. AS. sóð

—— *sb.* == truth, in the phrase 'to sooth,' i. e. 'in truth.' 1023, 2118

B.

Soothfastness, *sb.* Ps. xci. 3

Soothful, *adj.* Fragment in Warton, H. E. P. vol. i. p. 21

Soothly, *adv.* Ps. xxxvi. 33

Soothness, *sb.* RG. 457

Sorcery, *sb.* Alys. 478. Fr. sort. Lat. sors

Sore, *adj.* RG. 435

—— *sb.* 130 B.

Sorefully, *adv.* Body and Soul, 6

Soreness, *sb.* RG. 131

Sorimod, *adj.* == sorrowful. O. and N. 1216

Soriness, *sb.* K. Horn, 950

Sorrow, *sb.* RG. 374, 378; [seorhe]. O. and N. 1597. AS. sorh

—— *v. n.* Wright's L. P. p. 50

Sorrowful, *adj.* HD. 1248

Sorrowing, *sb.* Wright's L. P. p. 53

Sorry, *adj.* == sorrowful. RG. 52

—— == bad or sad, 'a sori chirchegon.' RG. 379

Sortes, a misprint for 'sottes.' O. and N. 1469

Sot, *adj.* == sottish. O. and N. 1433. Rel. S. ii. 37. AS. sot

—— *sb.* O. and N. 297

Sothede, *sb.* O. and N. 1372

Sotoned, *adj.* == made like a long cassock. Alys. 5150. Fr. soutane

Sotter, *sb.* == a cobler. Rel. Ant. ii. 175. Lat. sutor

Soul, *sb.* RG. 383, 526

Soulneed, *sb.* Body and Soul, 49

Sound, *sb.* (sonus). RG. 283; [sone]. Alys. 1183

Sound, *adj.* RG. 402; [isunde]. O. and N. 1100

Soundeful, *v. n.* == prosper. Ps. i. 3. AS. sundfullian

—— *adj.* == prosperous. Ps. xliv. 5

200

Sour, *adj.* Wright's L. P. p. 114. AS. súr

—— *v. n.* == become sour. Alys. 7002

Sourmouncie, *sb.* == lordship. Alys. 595. Fr. surmonter

Sousprior, == subprior, *q. v.*

South. Wright's L. P. p. 53

Southeast. Alys. 5225

Southern, *adj.* 463 β

Southward. 513 β

Southwest [southerwest]. Ritson's AS. viii. 155

Sove, == seven. Fr. Sci. 29

Sovereign, *sb.* RG. 15

Sow, *v. a.* RG. 499; 'to sow of one's land.' RG. 496; pret. 'sewe.' RG. 29; part. 'isowe.' O. and N. 1127

Sowel, *sb.* == anything eaten with bread; sauce, meat, &c. HD. 767. Dan. suul

Spade, *sb.* RG. 99. AS. spád

Spakely, *adv.* == surely, certainly. Wright's L. P. p. 37. ON. spakligr. 'spakky' in Rel. Ant. ii. 212, is a mistake for 'spakly'

Spale, *sb.* == rest? O. and N. 258. Sw. 'spel,' game or play

Span, *sb.* Wright's L. P. p. 35. AS. span

—— *v. a.* == allure. O. and N. 1488. AS. spanan

Spannew, *adj.* Alys. 4055. HD. 968; lit. 'as new as a chip,' from AS. spón, a chip; cf. Swed. 'spillerny' == span-new, with Sw. spiltra, a splinter, and Engl. 'spill'

Sparc, *sb.* == park. RG. 439

Spare, *v. a.* RG. 428, 429

Spark, *sb.* HD. 91

—— *v. n.* == sparkle. HD. 2144

Sparkle, *sb.* Body and Soul, 208

Sparrow, *sb.* 1098 B.

Spatle, *v. n.* == slobber in speaking. Rel. Ant. ii. 211

Speak. RG. 497; pret. 'speke.' RG. 419; part. 'ispeke.' 936 B.

Spear, *sb.* RG. 48, 564. AS. spére

Spearman, *sb.* RG. 378

Special, *adj.* RG. 422

201

—— *sb.* == a particular friend. Alys. 3288. St Dunstan, 194

Specially, *adv.* RG. 497

Speech, *sb.* RG. 412, 419

Speed, *v. n.* == succeed. pret. 'spedde.' RG. 303, 396; part, 'isped.' 1487 B. AS. spédan

Spell, *sb.* == tale. HD. 338, 2530. AS. spell

—— *v. n.* == tell, relate. HD. 15

Spelling, *sb.* == tale. Ps. lxxii. 28

Spence, *sb.* == expenses. RG. 167; money to defray expenses. RG. 275; [spounse]. 1566 B.

Spend, *v. a.* RG. 528; pret. 'spende.' RG. 390

Spending, *sb.* [spenynge]. RG. 389

Sperd, *part.* == barred, locked up. HD. 448. ON. sperra

Sperver, *sb.* == sparrowhawk. Alys. 183. Fr. espervier

Spew, *v. n.* Pol. S. 240. AS. spíwan

Spice, *sb.* Wright's L. P. p. 34

Spicery, *sb.* RG. 151

Spill, *sb.* == a splinter of wood; 'not worth a spill.' 850 B. Ital. spillo. AS. speld

Spill, *v. a.* == destroy. 306 B.; part. 'ispild.' O. and N. 1025

—— *v. n.* == miscarry. Wright's L. P. p. 84

Spin, *v. a.* Alys. 6806; part. 'ysponne.' Alys. 7251

Spinnandweb, *sb.* == spider. Ps. lxxxix. 9

Spire, *sb.* == a sprout, twig. O. and N. 18. ON. spira

Spire, *v. a.* == inquire, learn. HD. 2620. Alys. 2569. AS. spirian. Scotch, speer

Spit, *sb.* == kitchen spit. RG. 207. AS. spitu

—— *v. a.* == pierce with a spit, RG. 207

Spit, *v. a.* [spret]. Alys. 979

—— *v. n.* Rel. Ant. ii. 211

Spore, an error for 'swore' == neck? O. and N. 1123

Spouse, *sb.* == husband. RG. 431

—— == matrimonial fidelity. O. and N. 1332

—— *v. a.* RG. 368, 422; part. 'yspoused.' RG. 393

Spousebreach, *sb.* RG. 26

Spousehood, *sb.* RG. 26, 367

Spousing, *sb.* == marriage. RG. 431

—— == matrimonial fidelity. O. and N. 1553

Sprawl, *v. n.* HD. 475

Spray, *sb.* == twig of a tree. RG. 552. AS. spree

Spread, *v. a.* HD. 95.

—— == overspread. Sermon, 30; part. 'ysprad.' RG. 545

Spread, *v. n.* Wright's L. P. p. 70. AS. sprædan

Spret. See Spit

Spring, *v. n.* RG. 15; pret. 'sprong.' RG. 384; part. 'isprung.' O. and N. 300. AS. springan

Spring, *sb.* == fountain. Wright's L. P. p. 70

Springe, *sb.* == snare. O. and N. 1064

Sprit [spreot], *sb.* == bowsprit. Alys. 858. AS. sprit

Sprout, *sb.* HD. 1142. Ps. lxxix. 12. AS. sprote

Spur, *sb.* RG. 544. AS. spor

—— *v. a.* RG. 376

Spurless, *adj.* Pol. S. 71

Spurn, *v. a.* Ps. xc. 12

Sputing, *sb.* == disputing. O. and N. 1572

Spy, *sb.* Body and Soul, 130. Alys. 3530

—— *v. a.* == look out, devise. Alys. 7013

Spyrie ? Alys. 2995. Possibly a mistake for 'squyrie,' i. e. the squires

Squat, *v. a.* == squash, crush. Ps. cix. 6. AS. cwatan, to shake

Squire, *sb.* RG. 536, 380

Stability, *sb.* Ritson's AS. viii. 98

Stable, *adj.* RG. 551, 455

—— *v. a.* == stablish; part. 'ystabled.' Alys. 4690

Stably, *adv.* RG. 551, 123

Staff, *sb.* RG. 126. AS. stæf

Stage, *sb.* == platform. Alys. 5585

Stake, *sb.* RG. 51. AS. stáca

Stake, *sb.* == a blow. Alys. 2835. AS. stician, to stab, fix in

Stake, *v. a.* == hazard; part. 'steke.' Alys. 69

Stale, *sb.* == stealing. M. Ode, st. 128

Stall, *sb.* 'stal ne stode' == neither ox nor horse, i. e. in no capacity. O. and N. 1630

Stall, *sb.* == stable. Wright's L. P. p. 48. AS. steal

Stallion, *sb.* [stalun]. Cok. 165

Stalward, *adj.* RG. 384, 538. AS. stæl-weorð, that which is worth taking

Stalwardhede, *sb.* RG. 213, 274

Stalwardly, *adv.* RG. 394, 399

Stalwardman, *sb.* RG. 400

Stalworthi, *adj.* == stalward. HD. 24

Stammer, *v. n.* Rel. Ant. ii. 211

Stamp, *v. a.* == pound, bruise. Alys. 332

Stamyn, *sb.* == a linsey garment. 2245 B. Fr. estamine

Stand [stonde], RG. 372. 3 s. pres. 'stent.' 1925 B.; 'stont.' RG. 1; pret. 'stood.' RG. 388

Standard, *sb.* RG. 303, 400. Fr. estendart, from tendre. The word originally meant the centre of an army, where a pole was fixed bearing a dragon, whose mouth was turned in the intended direction of march. Hence 'dragon' is sometimes used by RG. for a 'standard'

Standard, == standardbearer. Alys. 1995

Star, *sb.* RG. 416, 548. AS. steorra

Star, *sb.* == sedge. HD. 939. Swed. starr. ON. stör

Stare, *v. a.* HD. 1037

Stare. 'Aȝeyn stare,' Pol. S. 217, is probably 'gain-stayer,' i. e. opponent

Stark, *adj.* == strong. HD. 341. Wright's L. P. p. 87. AS. stearc

Start, *v. n.* == leap suddenly. RG. 460

Startle, *v. n.* == stumble along. Body and Soul, 60

Starve, *v. n.* == die. Alys. 579; die of hunger. Alys. 1234

Starving, *sb.* Ps. cvi. 20

Starwise, *adj.* O. and N. 1316

Stat, *sb.* == place, or ground? Alys. 2268. ON. stadr

State, *sb.* == condition. RG. 380, 433, 491

Stathel, *v. a.* == establish. Ps. xxi. 12. AS. staðolian

Stathelnes, *sb.* == substance. Ps. cxxxviii. 15. AS. staðolnes

―― == firm foundation. Ps. lxviii. 3

Statute, *sb.* Pol. S. 88

Stayelnes, *sb.* == substance. Creed of St Athan. 14

Stead, *sb.* == place. 5 B.; [stide]. F. and P. 17. AS. stede

Steal, *v. a.* RG. 564

―― *v. n.* == come secretly upon one. Alys. 4032

Stealingly, *adv.* [stelendelich] == secretly. Alys. 5080

Steam, *sb.* HD. 591

Stedde, *part.* == fixed. Ps. lxxxvii. 8

Stedfast, *adj.* RG. 529, 533

Stedfastly, *adv.* Ps. xliv. 5

Stedful, *v. a.* == make firm, prosperous. Ps. lxiv. 10

Steed, *sb.* RG. 544

Steel, *sb.* RG. 2

Steelen, *adj.* Alys. 2301

Stefne. See Steven

Steke, *v. a.* See Stick, *v. a.*

―― == shut up, enclose. Ps. xvi. 10; pret. 'stake.' ON. steckr, a fold

Stench, *sb.* RG. 405, 407

Steo, *v. n.* == step, or go. See Stie

Step, *sb.* RG. 338, 459

―― *v. n.* RG. 338

Stepmother, *sb.* RG. 122, 287

Stere, *sb.* == stern of a ship. K. Horn, 1421; the place where the ship is 'steered'

―― == rudder. Cok. 152. AS. steóre

Stere, *adj.* == staunch, true to? K. Horn, 1390. Connected with AS. stearc. Germ. starr

Sterling, *sb.* == a coin of sterling money. RG. 563, 565. Germ. sterling

Stern, *adj.* RG. 377; [steorne]. Alys. 508, 511. AS. styrn

Sterne, *sb.* == star. HD. 1809. Ps. cxxxv. 9. ON. stjarna

Sternhede, *sb.* == sternness. RG. 369

Sternly, *adv.* RG. 369

Sterre, *adj.* == stiff, brittle. Alys. 4437. ON. starr

Stert, *sb.* == tail. HD. 2823. AS. steort

Stet, *vb.* == stops, delays. Alys. 4146

Steven, *sb.* [stefne] == voice. O. and N. 314. AS. stefen

Stevening, *sb.* == appointment, assignation. Wright's L. P. p. 46

Stew, *sb.* Cok. 107. Dan. stuve

Steward, *sb.* HD. 667. SS. steowien. MG. staujan. See Gloss. Rem. to Laʒ. iii. 471

Sthenche. Evidently an error for 'schenche,' to pour out. RG. 118

Sti, *sb.* == path. Wright's L. P. p. 111. HD. 2619. AS. stíg

Stick, *sb.* HD. 914. AS. sticca

Stick, *v. a.* == pierce; part. 'ystyked.' Pol. S. 190

—— == fasten [steke]. 683 B.

—— == place. pret. 'stok.' RG. 367; *part.* 'istekke.' Pol. S. 203. AS. stician

Stie, *v. n.* == go [steo]. Rel. S. i. 38. 3 s. pres. 'stiʒth.' O. and N. 1403; pret. 'stowe.' Alys. 1209. AS. stígan

Stiff, *adj.* RG. 377

Stiffly, *adv.* RG. 251

Still, *adj.* == quiet. RG. 367. HD. 2309

Still, *v. a.* 467 B.

Stilly, *adv.* RG. 548, 564

Sting, *v. a.* == pierce; part. 'ystonge.' Wright's L. P. p. 84; 'isstunge.' O. and N. 515. AS. stingan

Stinging, *sb.* Ps. lix. 5

Stink, *v. n.* 2422 B.

—— *v. a.* == make to stink. Rel. Ant. ii. p. 176

Stint, *v. a.* == stop, or hinder. Ritson's AS. viii. 63; imper. 'stunt.' Wright's L. P. p. 50; pret. 'stunte'? Ibid. p. 31

—— *v. n.* == stop, halt? 1126 B. AS. stintan, which is, however, always neuter

Stir, *v. a.* [sterin]. Body and Soul, 72; pret. 'sturede.' RG. 17, 22

Stirring, *sb.* Ps. lxxxviii. 10; cxx. 3

Stirrup, *sb.* 190 B. AS. stíg-ráp

Stith, *sb.* == anvil. HD. 1877. AS. stýð

Stithe, *adj.* == strong. Wright's L. P. p. 99; [stithye]. Ibid. p. 31

Stithstream, *sb.* == deluge, flood. Ps. xxviii. 10

Stivour, *sb.* == a musical instrument, sort of trumpet. Alys. 2571. Fr. estive

Stock, *sb.* == stem of a tree. O. and N. 25

Stode. See Stud

Stoke, *sb.* == a thrust. Alys. 7096

Stonde, *sb.* == drinking vessel. Rel. S. v. 110. OHG. standa

Stole, *sb.* Alys. 4714

Stone, *sb.* RG. 394, 517

—— *v. a.* RG. 298

Stonedead, *adj.* HD. 1815

Stoop, *v. n.* Alys. 1103. AS. stúpian

Stop, *v. a.* == stop up. Alys. 6228. Ps. lxii. 12. Dut. stopfen

Stopple, *sb.* RG. 223

Stor. See Stour

Store, *sb.* RG. 395, 396

—— *v. a.* part. 'ystored.' RG. 18

Storm, *sb.* Ps. xlix. 3

Story, *sb.* == tale. HD. 1641

Stot, *sb.* == horse. O. and N. 495. AS. stotte

Stound, *sb.* == a space of time. RG. 388, 559. AS. stund

Stoup, *sb.* == cup. RG. 268. AS. stoppa

Stour, *adj.* == strong, great. Wright's L. P. p. 87; [stor]. Ps. xxxvii. 15. AS. stór

Stout, *adj.* 512 B. Dut. stout

Stoute, *v. a.* == disturb, annoy. Manuel d. Pecches, 2951. AS. strútian

Stover, *sb.* == provision, fodder. Alys. 1866. Fr. estouvier

Stow, *sb.* == a place. Wright's L. P. p. 98. AS. stow

Stowe, *sb.* == went, mounted. See Stie

Straile, *sb.* == a couch. Ps. xl. 4. AS. strǽl

Strain, *v. a.* == tighten, stretch; part. 'istrained.' 1479 B.

Strait, *adj.* 260 B.

Straitly, *adj.* == rigorously. RG. 373

207

Strand, *sb.* (of the sea). K. Horn, 39

Strange, *adj.* HD. 640

Strangeman, *sb.* RG. 254

Strangle, *v. a.* HD. 510

Straple, *sb.* == strap. 1479 B. AS. strapol

Straw, *sb.* [stro]. Pol. S. 152; [strie]. HD. 998. AS. streow

Stream, *sb.* HD. 2687

Stream, *v. n.* == flow. Ps. lxi. 11

Street, *sb.* RG. 7

Strench, *sb.* == strain, stretch. Rel. S. i. 14. AS. strec

Strene, *sb.* == progeny. Alys. 511; [strende]. Ps. ix. 27. AS. strýnd

—— *v. a.* == beget. HD. 2983; fornicate. Ps. lxxii. 27. AS. strýnan

Strength, *sb.* RG. 377, 490; [strenge]. RG. 302

—— == violence. Pilate, 101

—— *v. a.* == strengthen. Ps. lxviii. 5

Strenkil, *v. a.* == sprinkle. Ps. l. 9. Cf. Swed. stänka

—— *sb.* == hyssop. Ps. l. 9

Streon, *sb.* == the knot in the yolk of an egg, the point where generation commences. Fr. Sci. 6. AS. streon

Stride, *v. n.* Wright's L. P. p. 111

—— *sb.* Ritson's AS. viii. 32

Strie. See Straw

Strife, *sb.* RG. 408, 567

Strike, *v. n.* == go on, flow. Wright's L. P. p. 44. AS. strican. See Laȝamon, i. 171, 397, and the Legend of St Katherine (Abbotsford Club), vv. 2514, 733, for exx. of this sense in Semi-Saxon

—— *v. a.* == strike sail. K. Horn, 1043

String, *v. a.* == pierce. Cf. our phrase, 'string papers together,' i. e. pierce them, and then unite them by a string. Body and Soul, 207. Another form of 'sting'

—— *sb.* RG. 456; == rope. Ps. civ. 11. AS. streng

—— == direction of going? Ps. cxxxviii. 3

Strip, *v. a.* 2242 B. Pilate, 185

Strive, *v. n.* RG. 26; [struen]. Marg. 25. Fr. estriver. Swed. sträfwa. Germ. streben. ON. strita. AS. stríð

Striving, *sb.* RG. 467

Stroke, *sb.* RG. 536, 401

Strong, *adj.* RG. 544, 546; comp. 'stronger.' RG. 266; sup. 'strongest.' RG. 111

—— == violent. RG. 84

Strongly, *adv.* HD. 135

Strout, *sb.* == contention. HD. 1039. AS. strúdan

—— *v. n.* == make a disturbance. HD. 1779

Stroy, *v. a.* [struye] == destroy. Marg. 52

Struen. See Strive

Strumpet, *sb.* Pol. S. 153. Span. estrupar. Lat. stuprum. The 'm' is inserted, as in 'pamphlet,' from Span. 'papelete'

Strut, *sb.* == display, show. Manuel d. Pecches, 3350

Stubble, *sb.* [stubbe]. O. and N. 506. ON. stubbr

Stud, *sb.* == of horses, &c.; [stode]. Cok. 35. O. and N. 495. AS. stód

Stude, *sb.* == place. RG. 383, 473

Study, *sb.* 1199 B.

Stumble, *v. n.* Rel. Ant. ii. 211

Stump, *v. n.* == stumble. O. and N. 1392. Swed. stapla

Stunt. See Stint

Sturbing, *sb.* == disturbance. Marg. 48

Sturdy, *adj.* RG. 387. ON. styrdr

Sturgeon, *sb.* HD. 753. Fr. estourgeon. ON. starri. Swed. stör

Stuten, == started? HD. 599

Subprior, *sb.* [sousprior]. RG. 494

Subtle, *adj.* == bad. Wright's L. P. p. 23

—— *v. a.* == make bad. Ibid. p. 23

Succour, *sb.* RG. 568

—— *v. a.* RG. 399

Such, *adj.* 10 B.; 'a such.' 1179 B.; [swiche]. O. and N. 1345; 'such' absol. == such thing. RG. 419

Suck, *v. a.* pret. 'soken.' Alys. 6119

—— *v. n.* part. 'sucking' (of children). 1496 B.

Suddenly, *adv.* Ritson's AS. xviii. 42

Sue [sywe], *v. a.* == follow. RG. 396, 502

Suing [sywinge], *sb.* == following. RG. 502

Suere, *sb.* == neck. RG. 389. AS. sweora

Suffer, *v. a.* == permit. Wright's L. P. p. 93. RG. 499; part. 'isuffred.' 1303 B.

————— *v. n.* == endure. 1242 B.

Sufferance, *sb.* Alys. 3192

Sugar, *sb.* Wright's L. P. p. 26

Suit, *sb.* == do suit? [suite]. RG. 539

Suite [sywete], *sb.* == company. RG. 191

Sulle, 'ar sulle' == their selves? Pol. S. 152

Sully, *v. a.* == soil. O. and N. 1238

Sum, *sb.* RG. 563

Summer, *sb.* RG. 514; [sume]. O. and N. 709

Summon, *v. a.* RG. 377, 504

Summoner, *sb.* Pol. S. 157

Sumpter, *sb.* == attendant on the baggage. Alys. 6023

Sun, *sb.* RG. 548, 549

Sunbeam, *sb.* HD. 592

Sunday. RG. 495

Sunder [sondres], *adj.* == sundry, different. Alys. 3303

Sunegi, *v. n.* == sin. O. and N. 926

Sunrising, *sb.* Alys. 2901

Sunspring, *sb.* Ps. xlix. 1

Suoddring, *sb.* == sleep. RG. 264. AS. swodrian

Sup, *v. n.* HD. 1766

Supper, *sb.* HD. 1762

Supple, *adj.* RG. 223. Fr. souple

Surance, *sb.* == assurance. 1910 B.

Suspend, *v. a.* RG. 563

Suspicion, *sb.* Alys. 452

Sustain, *v. a.* RG. 440, 442; part. 'ysusteyned.' RG. 375

Sustenance, *sb.* RG. 378

Sutheth, *vb.* == showeth. RG. 458

Suththe. See Siththe

Swage, *v. a.* == assuage; part. 'swaged.' Pilate, 175

Swain, *sb.* RG. 53. AS. swán

Swallow, *v. a.* 2209 B.; part. 'i-suolʒe.' O. and N. 146. AS. swelgan

Swallow, *sb.* == the bird so called. Alys. 3787. AS. swalewe

Swan, *sb.* HD. 1726. AS. swan

Swart, *adj.* RG. 490

Sway, *sb.* == noise. Alys. 2801. AS. swég

Swear, *v. n.* pret. 'suore.' RG. 445, 446; part. 'swore.' Pol. S. 150; 'isworen.' Rel. S. v. 60

Swearer, *sb.* RG. 429

Sweat, *sb.* [swot]. HD. 2662. AS. swát

—— *v. n.* Fragm. Sci. 202

—— *v. a.* Wright's L. P. p. 70

Sweep [swopen], *v. a.* Rel. S. v. 151

Sweet, *adj.* RG. 435

Sweeting, *sb.* Wright's L. P. p. 52

Sweetly, *adj.* == sweet. Wright's L. P. p. 52

—— *adv.* Rel. Ant. ii. p. 193

Sweetness, *sb.* Wright's L. P. p. 68. St Swithin, 156

Swell, *v. n.* Body and Soul, 23; pret. 'sval.' O. and N. 7

Sweng, *sb.* == trick. O. and N. 795. Lit. 'a blow.' AS. sweng. Cf. our expression, 'a stroke of policy'

Swepe, *v. a.* == strike, exercise. Ps. lxxvi. 7. AS. swip. ON. svipa

Sweping, *sb.* == a blow. Ps. xxxiv. 15; xxxvii. 18

Swere, *v. a.* == oppress. Fragm. in Warton, H. E. P. vol. i. p. 22. OHG. swárjan.

Swice, *v. n.* == cease. O. and N. 336; [iswike]. O. and N. 927

—— == faint, fail. Wright's L. P. p. 48. AS. swícan

Swich, *adv.* == as if. O. and N. 566

Swift, *adj.* Ps. xli. 5

Swiftly, *adv.* Ps. cxlii. 7

Swike, *v. a.* == deceive. RG. 115. AS. swícan, swícol

—— *sb.* == deceiver, traitor RG. 105

Swikedhede, *sb.* RG. 357

Swikedom. RG. 512, 569. AS. swícdom

Swikeldom, *sb.* O. and N. 163

Swikelhede, *sb.* O. and N. 162

Swile, *v. a.* == wash. HD. 919. AS. swilian

Swim, *v. n.* 410 and 164 β. AS. swimman

Swine, *sb.* RG. 376

Swing, *v. a.* == strike, beat. Wright's L. P. p. 84. AS. swingan

Swink, *v. n.* == labour. RG. 41; [iswinc]. Moral Ode, st. 94

—— *sb.* == labour, toil. RG. 40, 234. AS. swincan

Swire, *sb.* == neck. Wright's L. P. p. 35. AS. sweora

Swise. See Swithe

Swithe, *adj.* == vehement. 340 β. AS. swíð

—— *adv.* == quickly. HD. 140, 682

—— == very. HD. 111; [swise], O. and N. 1565. AS. swíðe

Swithe, *v. a.* == burn; pret. 'swath.' Ps. cv. 18; part. 'swithand.' Ps. lxxxii. 15. ON. svíða

Swiving, *sb.* == fornication. Pol. S. 69 Swed. besofva

Swo, *adv.* == so. Wright's L. P. p. 49

—— == as if. O. and N. 76

Swoon, *sb.* RG. 13. AS. a-swunan

—— *v. n.* [swoghen]. Alys. 5857; part. 'yswowe.' RG. 290. Alys. 2262; 'yswawe.' Alys. 2379

Swooning, *sb.* K. Horn, 454

Swop, *sb.* == blow. Marg. 30. ON. svipa

Sword, *sb.* RG. 395

Swore, == sworn? Pol. S. 157

Swored, *sb.* == neck. Alys. 974

Sworre, *sb.* == war. RG. 413

Swost. Rel. S. v. 152. The rhyme requires 'swoȝ,' for which 'swost' is probably an error; 'swoȝ' may mean 'throw.' See Hall. *s. v.* Swot

Swynde, *v. n.* == waste away. Pol. S. 150. AS. swindan

Sygaldry, *sb.* == nonsense, trick. Alys. 7015. Fr. singe, singerie? In the Manuel des Pecches, v. 503, 'sygaldry' occurs as a verb, in the sense of 'sing charms, or spells'

Syke, == sigh, *q. v.*

Synagogue, *sb.* Ps. lxxxi. 1

Sytoling, *sb.* == playing on the citole or guitar. Alys. 1043

Sywe, Sywinge. See Sue

Sywete. See Suite

T.

Tabard, *sb.* == a short cloak worn by military personages. Alys. 5476. Fr. tabar. Ital. tabaro. See Wright's Vocabb. p. 133

Tabernacle, *sb.* RG. 20

Tabor, *sb.* == a musical instrument. RG. 396

Taboring, *sb.* Alys. 925

Tache, *v. a.* == spot or stain. Wright's L. P. p. 70. Fr. tache

Tail, *sb.* (cauda). RG. 416. AS. tægel

—— == retinue of followers. RG. 305

Tail, *sb.* == tax. RG. 524. Fr. taille

—— == figure. RG. 117. Fr. taille

Tail, *v. a.* == cut up. Alys. 2133. Fr. tailler

—— *sb.* == slaughter. Alys. 2217

Tailed, *adj.* RG. 416

Taillage, *sb.* == tax. 343 B.

Take, *v. a.* 3 s. pres. 'tas.' Ps. i. 4; 'thas'? HD. 1129; pret. 'took.' RG. 384

—— *v. n.* to 'take on' about a thing == be annoyed at it. 639 B.

Tale, *sb.* == story. HD. 5; talk. O. and N. 3. RG. 195

—— == number, reckoning. HD. 2025

—— *v. n.* == shout, speak. Alys. 1415

Talent, *sb.* == disposition. Alys. 1280. Fr. talent

Taleuace, *sb.* == a large shield. HD. 2323. Fr. talevas. See Roq.

Tame, *adj.* RG. 1. AS. tám

—— *v. a.* Pol. S. 214

Taper, *sb.* RG. 456, 534. AS. taper

Tapnage, *sb.* == secresy. Alys. 7131. Fr. tapin, tapinage

Tar, *v. a.* == cover with tar. HD. 707. AS. tyro, tare

Targe, *sb.* == a combination of shields, like the Roman testudo. Alys. 2785

Target, *sb.* Alys. 7395. AS. targe. Fr. targe

Tarry, *v. n.* == delay. RG. 109. Fr. tarier

Tarry, *v. a.* == excite, provoke. Ps. cv. 7. AS. teorian. Fr. tarier

Tarrying, *sb.* == delay. RG. 207

Tarryingness, *sb.* == provocation. Ps. xciv. 9

Tarst, == first. HD. 2688. Cf. 'fyrst,' for 'thirst'

Tasting, *sb.* == experience, trial. Alys. 4043

Taughte, *sb.* == gave over to, put in charge of. HD. 2214. See Betake. AS. tacan. SS. i-tæchen

Tavelen, *v. n.* == play at dice. O. and N. 1664. AS. tæflan

Tavern, *sb.* RG. 195

Taw, *v. a.* == dress leather, curry. Rel. Ant. ii. 175. AS. tawian

Tax, *sb.* Pol. S. 151. Fr. taxer. Lat. taxare

Te, == to, with infin. RG. 65

Te, *v. a.* == draw; [teo], St Lucy, 112; draw out, prolong. 'ne te more speche.' K. Horn, 317. 3 s. pres. 'tihth.' O. and N. 1433; == spreads. 1180 B.

—— == educate. part. 'i-toȝen.' O. and N. 1723

—— *v. n.* == pull, drag. Wright's L. P. p. 59

—— == go, betake oneself. RG. 40; [teon]. Alys. 6954. part. 'ytyght' == arrived. Alys. 7164. AS. teon

Teach, *v. a.* == 2074 B.; [i-tache]. O. and N. 1345. pret. 'taȝte.' RG. 73

Teacher, *sb.* Alys. 17

Team, *sb.* O. and N. 774. RG. 261. AS. teám

Tear, *sb.* RG. 405; pl. 'tern.' Wright's L. P. p. 81

Tear, *v. a.* 2199 B.; 3 p. pret. 'taren.' Alys. 6876

Teat, *sb.* [tit]. Wright's L. P. p. 35. AS. tite

Teem, *sb.* == brood. RG. 261. AS. teám

—— *v. a.* == breed. O. and N. 495

Teen, *sb.* == harm, mischief. RG. 80, 395; [tone]. O. and N. 50. AS. teona. See Gl. Rem. to Laȝamon, iii. 440

—— == sorrow. 1567 B.

—— *v. a.* == vex, annoy. part. 'itened.' Pol. S. 149

—— == grieve. Wright's L. P. p. 92

Teenful, *adj.* Ps. lxxvii. 8

Teh, *sb.* == ill-humour. Wright's L. P. p. 111. Gael. 'taoig.' Scotch, 'tig.' Ital. 'ticchio'

Tel, *sb.* == deceit. HD. 190

Teld, *sb.* == tent. Ps. xviii. 6. AS. teld

—— *v. a.* == pitch a tent. Alys. 1975, 3470. part. 'ytielde.' Alys. 3438; 'ytolde.' Alys. 5901

Teldstede, *sb.* == tent-place. Ps. cxix. 5

Tele, *v. a.* == blame. O. and N. 1375. AS. tælan

Tell, *v. a.* == RG. 41; pret. 'told.' RG. 389; part. 'ytold.' RG. 368

—— *v. a.* == reckon, account. O. and N. 791, 340; 3 s. pres. 'tolth.' RG. 366

Teller, *sb.* == relator. Alys. 1577

Teme, *v. n.* == be a witness? Wright's L. P. p. 32

—— *v. a.* == summon as a witness. M. Ode, st. 54. AS. teáma

Temper, *v. a.* == rule, restrain. RG. 72

—— *sb.* RG. 429

Tempest, *sb.* RG. 378

Temple, *sb.* RG. 14

Ten. RG. 430

Tence, *sb.* == cause of quarrel. Alys. 3025. Fr. tence, tenser

Tende, *v. a.* == light, kindle. RG. 407; part. 'tende.' RG. 534. AS. tendan

Tender, *adj.* RG. 315

Tenor, *sb.* Alys. 2977

Tenstringed, *adj.* Ps. cxliii. 9

Tent, *sb.* Alys. 4302

Tenth, *adj.* RG. 416, 473

Teo, *vb.* == draw. See Te

Term, *sb.* == set time. 1536 B.

Terrene, *adj.* Alys. 5685

Teste, *sb.* == head. Alys. 7112

216

Teyte, *adj.* == lively. HD. 1841. ON. teitr

Tha, == they. Ps. cxxiii. 3

—— == them. Ibid. 6

Thah. See Though

Thakke, *v. a.* == thwack. Cok. 140. AS. þacian

Than, *adv.* of comparison. RG. 459. See Then

Thane, *sb.* HD. 2260. pl. 'thavenes'? RG. 202

Thanene. See Thence

Thank [thonc]. *sb.* RG. 485. Wright's L. P. p. 37

—— *v. a.* RG. 452

Thankfully, *adv.* Pol. S. 156

Thanking, *sb.* Alys. 4065

Thar, *v. impers.* == it needs. See Thore, *v. n.*

Tharmide, *adv.* == therewith. O. and N. 1368

Tharne, *v. a.* == lose, be deprived of. HD. 2492, 1912. See Gloss. to Ormulum, *s. v.* þarnenn

—— == endure. HD. 1687. See the Avowyng of Arthur, st. 66, v. 15

Thas, == takes? See Take

Thas, That. See under The

That, == done? See The, *v. a.*

That, *conj.* RG. 377, et passim

Thave, *v. a.* == give. HD. 296; [thau]. Fragm. in Warton H. E. P. vol. i. p. 22. Cf. 'thane' and 'cayn' in Havelok

—— == bear, sustain. HD. 2696. AS. þafian

THE. def. art.

sing. N. 'the.' RG. 115; 'tho.' RG. 12. 'theo.' Alys. 2325

G. 'thare.' O. and N. 28

D. 'than.' O. and N. 125, 133; 'then.' RG. 543; 'thon.' O. and N. 135; fem. 'thare.' O. and N. 1581; 'there.' Wright's L. P. p. 95

A. 'then.' RG. 542; 'thun.' RG. 508

plur. N. 'theo.' Alys. 3411; 'the.' RG. 42

A. 'the.' RG. 42

constr. with subst. and adj., 'the waters.' RG. 374; 'the new forest.' Ib. 375

with compar. adj., 'the bet, the worse.' RG. 374

The, *dem. pron.*

sing. N. 'the.' O. and N. 798. neut. 'that.' RG. 377; 'thet.' RG. 387

D. 'than.' O. and N. 1684

A. 'thut.' 533

The, *rel. pron.* == who

sing. N. 'the.' O. and N. 1384, 1612; 'that.' RG. 387; 'thit.' HD. 2990

A. 'that.' RG. 387

plur. N. 'that.' RG. 387. Alys. 4656

The, *adv.* == there. HD. 863

The, *v. n.* == flourish, prosper. HD. 2606; Alys. 5472; [y-the]. RG. 428; part. pres. 'theonige,' for 'theoninge.' 149 B.; part. pass. 'ithe3.' 151 B.; 'y-then.' RG. 346. AS. þeon

    The, *v. a.* == do. M. Ode, 44. part. 'that.' HD. 1674. Germ. thun

    The, == or, after 'whether.' O. and N. 822, 1358, 1360, 1406

Thede, *sb.* == country, [theode]. O. and N. 1581. HD. 105; territory. Alys. 96; place. HD. 2890. AS. þeód

    Theft, *sb.* RG. 503

    Thei. See Though

    Thelde, *v. a.* == tell, give account of. Creed of St Athan. 93. ON. þylja. AS. þyle. The AS. þylian does not occur in this sense

    Then, *adv.* [thonne]. RG. 115; [thanne]. O. and N. 508

    ——— == when [than]. O. and N. 421

    Thence, *adv.* gen. of 'then.' [thannes], 1141 B.; [thanene]. RG. 377; [thethen]. Ps. cxxxi. 17

    Thene, *v. n.* == reach to. Rel. S. i. 1. AS. þenian

    There, *adv.* == of place. RG. 367; 'thar.' O. and N. 1612; 'thore.' Body and Soul, 98

    ——— with verbs, 'there has.' RG. 367

    Thereafter, *adv.* RG. 401

    Thereafterward, *adv.* Pilate, 110

    Thereagainst, *adv.* 294 B.

    Thereat, *adv.* RG. 464

    Thereby, *adv.* [tharbi]. O. and N. 244

    Therefore, *adv.* RG. 115; [thar forn]. Ps. xxxi. 4

Therefrom, *adv.* RG. 352

Therehence, *adv.* 1145 B.

Therein, *adv.* RG. 387

Thereof, *adv.* 100 B.; [thurof]. O. and N. 190

Thereon, *adv.* 546 B.

Thereout, *adv.* RG. 537

Thereover, *adv.* 516 B.

Therethrough, *adv.* 75 B.

Thereto, *adv.* 37 B.

Thereupon, *adv.* RG. 393

Therewith, *adv.* 272 B.

Therewithout, *adv.* 439 B.

Therne, *sb.* == a girl. HD. 298; O. Sax. therna. In the Avowyng of Arthur, st. 23, the word occurs under the form 'thorne'

Thertekene, == mark thereto. HD. 2878. AS. tacnian

Thestri, *sb.* for 'the estrie' == the apparition, i. e. of the heavenly host. Wright's L. P. p. 96. Fr. estrie

Thethen, == thence, *q. v.*

Thevethorn, *sb.* == dog rose or wild briar Ps. lvii. 10. AS. þefe-þorn

Thew, *adj.* == in servitude. HD. 262, 221 B. AS. þeow

—— *vb.* See Underthewe

Thewes, *sb.* == manners, morals. Wright's L. P. p. 23. AS. þeáw

Theymen, *sb.* == thew men or yeomen. RG. 330

Theyn, *sb.* == teen, hurt? Rel. Ant. i. 113

Thick, *adj.* RG. 412; used of air. Alys. 4079

—— *v. n.* == become thick. Alys. 3855. Fr. Sci. 309

Thief, *sb.* RG. 277, 428

Thiefly, *adv.* [theofliche]. 285 β. Alys. 4002

Thigg, *v. n.* == beg. Ps. cviii. 10. HD. 1373. AS. þicgan, to receive

Thiggand, *sb.* == beggar. Ps. xxxix. 18

Thigh, *sb.* [thy], RG. 244; [theo]. O. and N. 1495; pl. 'thyes.' RG. 417; 'thes.' HD. 1903. AS. þeoh

Thild, *sb.* == endurance. Ps. ix. 19. AS. þyld

Thin, *adj.* Wright's L. P. p. 37; [thunne]. Ibid. p. 47

Thin. See Thou

Thine, *adj.* before a cons. RG. 238

Thing, *sb.* RG. 367, 379. AS. þing

—— == cause, reason; 'for mine thinge' == for my sake. O. and N. 434

Think, *v. n.* RG. 397; [ithenche]. O. and N. 723; pret. 'thoʒte.' RG. 369; part. 'ithoʒt.' 110 B. 1378 B.; AS. þencan

Think, *v. n.* == seem. 3 s. pres. 'thunth.' O. and N. 1590; 'thinʒth.' Fr. Sci. 96; 'me thunch.' O. and N. 1647; 'me thuncth.' O. and N. 1670; pret. 'thoʒte.' 10 B.; 16 B. AS. þincan

Thinking, *sb.* == thought. Ps. xviii. 15

Thinly, *adv.* Alys. 5922

Thinne, *v. a.* == extend. Ps. lix. 10; cvii. 10. AS. þenian

Third, *adj.* [þrydde]. RG. 397

Thire, *adj.* == thy. O. and N. 429

Thirle, *v. a.* == pierce. Wright's L. P. p. 88. AS. þirlian

—— *sb.* == hole, hence a privy chamber. Ps. civ. 30. AS. þirel

Thirst, *sb.* [virst]. Body and Soul, 87

Thirteen. RG. 390

Thirteenth, *adj.* [thretteoth], 330 β

Thirtieth, *adj.* RG. 441

Thirty. RG. 375

This, *dem. pron.*

sing. N. RG. 367

D. 'thisse.' O. and N. 659; 'þusse.' M. Ode, 172

A. 'this.' Wright's L. P. p. 50; 'thas.' O. and N. 1440

plur. N. This == these. Wright's L. P. p. 42; 'thuse.' Fr. Sci. 122

D. and A. 'thenne.' Wright's L. P. p. 23

Thisterness, *sb.* == darkness. HD. 2191. AS. þýsternes. Germ. finsterniss

Thit, == that. HD. 2990

Thither, *adv.* [þuder]. RG. 543, 387

Thitherward. RG. 387

Thixil, *sb.* == an adze. Ps. lxxiii. 6; but the AS. þixl seems only to mean 'the shaft of a waggon.' In Wright's Vocab. p. 275, we find 'acia' (i. e.

ascia), translated 'a tyxhyl'

Tho, *adv.* == then. RG. 384

—— == when. O. and N. 1688

—— == though, *q. v.*

Thole, *v. a.* == endure. RG. 407, 509; part. 'ytholed.' RG. 24. AS. þólian

Tholemod, *adj.* == long-suffering. Alys. 393. Wright's L. P. p. 72. AS. þólmód

Thong, *sb.* RG. 115

Thonk, *sb.* == thought. O. and N. 490

—— == will; 'hire thonkes,' gen. abs. == with her will. O. and N. 70, 292 B. M. Ode, st. 43. AS. þonc, þanc

Thonkyng, *sb.* == thought. 'heore thonkyng.' Alys. 1660

Thore, *v. n.* == dare. 581 β. 2 s. pres. 'therstou.' 585 β; pret. 'therste.' 895 B. ON. þora

—— *v. n.* == need. 120 β. 3 s. pres. 'tharf.' O. and N. 190; 'thar.' Ritson's AS. viii. 57. AS. þearfan. Germ. dürfen

Thore. See There

Thore, 'on thore lay.' Wright's L. P. p. 95; probably, 'on or according to the law.' 'Thore' is the dat. sing. of the def. art. AS. þære

Thorn, *sb.* 389 β

Thornback, *sb.* == a fish. HD. 759

Thorough, *prep.* See Through

Thoroughly, *adv.* == going right through. HD. 680

Thoste, *sb.* == dung. Pol. S. 237; Ps. lxxxii. 11. AS. þost

Thou, *sing.* N. 'thou.' RG. 115; 'thu.' O. and N. 71; 'thow.' Alys. 3371 G. 'thin.' 'maugre thin.' HD. 1128

A. 'the.' 424 B.

plur. N. 'ȝe.' 26 B.

A. 'ȝou.' 583 β; 'eu.' O. and N. 1791; 'ow.' Ibid. 1696

Though, *adv.* [tho]. RG. 371; [thei]. RG. 64; [thah], O. and N. 1272; [thof]. Creed of St Athan. 79; [theȝ]. 156 B.

Thought, *sb.* 38 and 41 B. Ps. cxviii. 97

—— == care, anxiety. RG. 506. Wright's L. P. p. 53

Thoure, perhaps for 'þo were.' RG. 534, sed qu?

Thousand, *adj.* RG. 368, 454

—— *sb.* Ps. cxviii. 72

Thowen, *adj.* == virtuous. Wright's L. P. p. 23. AS. þeáw

Thraldom, *sb.* RG. 12, 480

Thralhede, *sb.* == thraldom. RG. 47

Thrall, *sb.* == a slave. HD. 1097. AS. þræl

—— == subjection, servitude. RG. 143

Thraying, *part.* == chastening. Ps. lxxii. 14; [ʒraihand]. Ps. cxvii. 18. AS. þreagan

Threat, *v. a.* RG. 110; pret. 'thrat.' Wright's L. P. p. 53; part. 'thrat.' Pol. S. 158

—— *v. n.* Wright's L. P. p. 23

Threaten, *v. a.* RG. 457; 501

Threating, *sb.* 2107 B.

Threde, *v. a.* == either 'dread' or 'threaten.' 2107 B. Numerous examples of the interchange of 'th' and 'd' may be found in the Romance of Lybeaus Disconus, in Ritson's Rom. vol. ii.; as 'thoghty' for 'doughty,' 'tho' for 'do,' &c.

Three. RG. 371; [thrinne]. HD. 716

Threpe, *v. a.* == convict, refute. Ps. xciii. 10. AS. þreapian

Threstelcock, *sb.* == thrush. Wright's L. P. pp. 40, 43

Threte, == destroyed, worn out? Wright's L. P. p. 23. From AS. 'þroten,' part. of 'þreotan,' to vex, oppress, wear out

Thrice, *adv.* RG. 490; [thrye]. RG. 191

Thrie, *sb.* == affliction. HD. 730. AS. þryccan, þrycnes

Thriddendele, *sb.* == third part. Alys. 5161

Thrift, *sb.* Wright's L. P. p. 47

Thring, *v. n.* == push, press. O. and N. 794. AS. þringan

—— *v. a.* == dash to pieces. Ps. lxxii. 20; pret. 'thrange.' Ps. lxxvii. 59; part. 'thrungen.' Ps. lxxii. 22; 'ithrunge.' O. and N. 38

Thrinnes, *sb.* == Trinity. Creed of St Athan. 10, 11. AS. þrínes

Thriste, *adj.* == bold. O. and N. 758. AS. þrist

Thrive, *v. n.* RG. 11. ON. þrífaz. Dan. trives

Thrivemon, *sb.* == a thrifty man. Pol. S. 159

Thriven, *adj.* == virtuous, good. Wright's L. P. pp. 23, 26; 'thriven and thro.' Body and Soul, 87; 'thryven in thro.' Wright's L. P. p. 26, and see p. 39

Thro, *adj.* == bold, good. See under Thriven. AS. þreá

Throat, *sb.* Body and Soul, 148. AS. þróte

Throatbolle, *sb.* == windpipe. Rel. S. v. 173. AS. þrótbolla

Throe, *sb.* [thrawe]. Alys. 606. AS. þreág

Throghe, *sb.* == pit, sepulchre. Ps. lxvii. 7; lxxxvii. 5. AS. þruh

Throne, *sb.* 2343 B.; [trone]. Wright's L. P. pp. 26, 47

Throng, *sb.* Alys. 3639. AS. þringan

Through, *prep.* == on account of. [thurf]. 21 B.; [thurs]. O. and N. 821; [thurch]. O. and N. 1396

—— == by means of. [thurth]. O. and N. 1426

—— == throughout (of time). [thur3]. O. and N. 447

—— == throughout (of place). [þoru]. RG. 373

—— == throughout. [þoru]. RG. 367

Throughgo, *v. n.* Ps. c. 2; pret. 'thurghyhode.' Ps. civ. 18

Throughout, *prep.* [þoru out]. RG. 416

—— *adv.* == entirely. O. and N. 877, 878; [thurfout]. 262 B.

Throw, *sb.* == a space of time. RG. 261; hence 'a turn.' O. and N. 260. AS. þrag

Throw, *v. a.* Rel. S. i. 37; pret. 'threw.' K. Horn, 1108; part. 'ithrow.' F. and P. 14

—— == throw from a horse. Alys. 2226; pret. 'threowe.' Alys. 2791

—— *v. n.* == fall from a horse. Alys. 2224

Throwing, *sb.* == unhorsing a knight. Alys. 1614

Thrughe, == a pit. See Throghe

Thrush, *sb.* [thruisse], Cok. 94

Thrust, *v. a.* == push out. HD. 1152

Thrustle, *sb.* == throstle, or thrush. Wright's L. P. p. 26

Thulke, == this. RG. 373, 549; == that. RG. 412. From AS. þylc, i. e. þyllíc, the like. It is not used in AS. for the dem. pron., but occurs in La3amon in this sense

Thuman, *sb.* == yeoman. RG. 470

Thund, *adv.* == yonder. Fragm. in Warton, H. E. P. vol. i. p. 21

Thunder, *sb.* RG. 378

—— *v. n.* Ps. xvii. 14

Thundering, *sb.* RG. 414

Thursday. RG. 419, 532

Thurte, *adv.* == athwart, across, astride. HD. 10. AS. þweor

Thus, *adv.* RG. 443

Thuster, *sb.* == darkness. O. and N. 198. AS. þýstru

Thusterness, *sb.* == darkness. O. and N. 369; [thisterness]. HD. 2191

Thuvele, *sb.* == twigs, underwood. O. and N. 278. AS. þúfe

Thy, *adj.* RG. 238; [thire]. O. and N. 429

Tide, *sb.* == time. 37 β. AS. tíd

—— *v. n.* == happen. RG. 418. 1813 B.; [itid]. O. and N. 1254; 3 s. pres. 'tid.' RG. 134

Tideful, *adj.* == opportune. Ps. xxxi. 6

Tiding, *sb.* == news. RG. 383, 441

Tie, *v. a.* part. 'iteid.' 521 β

Tiger, *sb.* Alys. 5227

Tike, *sb.* == dog. Pol. S. 238. ON. tík

Till, *v. n.* == reach, extend. RG. 8, 151. Fr. Sci. 246. From ON. til == to; cf. AS. 'till,' an end, object

Till, *v. a.* == cultivate. RG. 21, 41. AS. tilian

Tilling, *sb.* Pol. S. 149; [talling]. Alys. 5932

Tilth, *sb.* Ps. civ. 12. AS. tilð

Timber, *sb.* Alys. 2885

Timbre, *sb.* == timbrel. Alys. 191

Time, *sb.* RG. 9, 370. In Ps. cxxxi. 5, 'times' is used for 'brows,' evidently a mistranslation of the Latin 'tempora'

Timeful, *adj.* == suitable. Ps. cxliv. 15

Timely, *adv.* == in good time. RG. 258

Timing, *sb.* == time, season. Frag. in Warton, H. E. P., vol. i. p. 22

Timpan, *sb.* == drum. Ps. lxvii. 26; Ps. cxlix. 3

Tin, *sb.* RG. 1, 6

Tine. See Tende

Tine, *v. a.* == lose. HD. 2023. ON. týna

Tinsel, *sb.* == perdition, destruction. Ps. lxxxvii. 12. ON. týna

Tite, *adv.* == quickly. Ps. cv. 13; xxxvi. 2. AS. tíd, tídlíce

Tithe, *v. n.* == pay tithes; pret. 'tetheȝede.' RG. 261

Tithe, *v. a.* == grant. RG. 114. AS. tiðian

Tithing, *sb.* == a division of the hundred. RG. 267

Tithing, *sb.* == a tenth part [teoþing]. Judas, 135

Tiȝth. See Te

To, *prep.* 'to this land,' 'to Scotlande.' RG. 367

—— == towards. 'to men.' RG. 369

—— sign of dative case. RG. 370

To, *adv.* == till. Alys. 5902. Ps. xvii. 38

To, *adv.* == too, *q. v.*

To, with infin., 'to fle that cas.' RG. 367; [te]. RG. 65

To, == two, *q. v.*

Toad, *sb.* == frog; pl. 'tade.' Ps. lxxvii. 45

—— == toad. Body and Soul, 210

To and fro. Body and Soul, 184

Tobeat, *v. a.* == beat violently. O. and N. 1608

Toberste, *v. n.* == burst; part. 'to-borste.' Body and Soul, 159

—— *v. a.* == break in two; pret. 'tobarst.' Alys. 2154

Tobreak, *v. a.* == break in pieces. RG. 288, 419

—— *v. n.* K. Horn, 1109

Tobrede, *v. a.* == enlarge. Ps. iv. 2. AS. to-brædan

Tobrede, *v. a.* == tear in pieces; part. 'tobrode.' O. and N. 1006. AS. 'tobredan'

Tobrenne, *v. a.* == kindle. Ps. ii. 13

Tobrise, *v. a.* == bruise; part. 'tobrised.' HD. 1950

Tobune, *v. a.* == strike violently. O. and N. 1164. AS. bana, bona

Tobuste, *v. a.* == batter, bang. O. and N. 1608

Tobuy, *v. a.* == buy; pret. 'tobohte.' Wright's L. P. p. 93

Tochine, *v. a.* == split in pieces. O. and N. 1563; part. 'tocoon.' Alys. 573. See 'tochon,' in Gloss. to Laȝ. AS. tocínan

Tocleave, *v. a.* pret. 'toclef.' RG. 17, 401

Tocome, *v. n.* == come to, arrive. RG. 367

Tocrush, *v. a.* HD. 1992

Todash, *v. a.* RG. 540

Today, 295 β

Todele, *v. a.* == divide. RG. 492, 529

Todraw, *v. a.* == tear in pieces, destroy. RG. 422. Wright's L. P. p. 111

―――― == draw or carry. RG. 509

Todrive, *v. a.* == drive away, put to flight. RG. 458. Alys. 6216

Toe, *sb.* RG. 539; pl. 'to.' Marg. 46

Toflatt, *part.* == flattened. Alys. 5833

Toflight, *sb.* == refuge. Ps. xvii. 3

Tofore, *adv.* == before. RG. 377

Toforen, *adv.* == before. Wright's L. P. p. 110

Tofrusshe, *v. a.* == smash. HD. 1993

Tofye, *v. n.* == dissolve in corruption. Wright's L. P. p. 101. ON. fægja, to clean out. See 'Defyyn' and 'Fyin' in the Prompt. Parv., and the notes there

Together, *adv.* RG. 435; [togare]. K. Horn, 876

Tognaw, *v. a.* Alys. 6119

Tognide, *v. a.* == dash, bruise; pret. 'tognodded.' Ps. ci. 11. AS. gnídan

Togo, *v. n.* 3 pl. pret. 'togane.' Ps. ii. 2

Tohene, *v. a.* == vex, scorn. O. and N. 1127. AS. hýnan

Tohew, *v. a.* RG. 540; pret. 'tohewe.' Alys. 5704

Token, *sb.* RG. 291

Tokening, *sb.* == a token, or sign. RG. 396

―――― == making signs. Alys. 6439

Toknit, *v. a.* Ps. cxlvi. 3

Tolene, *part.* == lent. Wright's L. P. p. 49

Toll, *sb.* == tax. Pol. S. 237. Alys. 3795. AS. tól

Toll, *v. a.* == tull, allure. O. and N. 1625. ON. túlka, allicere

Tolonst, *part.* == lanced, pierced. Alys. 1621

Tolyvre, *v. a.* == deliver. Pol. S. 237

226

Tomb, *sb.* RG. 224

Tome, *sb.* == leisure. RG. 557. ON. tóm

—— *adj.* == vain, useless. O. and N. 1670. AS. tom. ON. tómr

Tomehed, *sb.* == vanity. Ps. xxiv. 4; xxxiv. 7

Tomorrow. 898 B.

Tomourn, *v. n.* == mourn. Wright's L. P. p. 86

Toname, *sb.* == surname. RG. 431. The reading 'tuo name' is clearly an error

Tone. See Teen

Tong, *sb.* O. and N. 156. pl. 'tangen,' 475 β. AS. tange

Tongue, *sb.* 645 B.

Toningue ? Creed of St Athan. 18. Possibly a mistake for 'theoning.' AS. þeonung, power

Too, *adv.* [to] 'to fewe.' 174 B.

Tool, *sb.* == sword. Alys. 815

Tooth, *sb.* RG. 407

Toothed, *adj.* Alys. 5408

Top, *sb.* == spinning top. Alys. 1706. Dan. top

Top, *sb.* == a lock or curl of wool. O. and N. 428. AS. top

Top, *sb.* == head. Marg. 47

—— == summit. 339 β ON. toppr

Top, *v. n.* == wrestle, fight together. Pilate, 15. Dut. toppen. Kil.

Topaziune, *sb.* == topaz. Cok. 90. Ps. cxviii. 127

Toqueme, *adv.* == agreeably. Creed of St Athan. 5. See Gloss. to Orm. *s. v.* tocweme

Toraced, *part.* == broken in pieces. RG. 22. ON. rekja, part. rakit, to undo, unweave

Toraunced, *part.* == broken in pieces. RG. 216. This is probably only another form of the preceding word

Toreave, *v. a.* == tear; pret. 'torof.' RG. 29

Torede, *v. a.* HD. 118

Torel, *sb.* == tower. Alys. 3239

Torend, *v. a.* Alys. 6622, 7881

Torforth, == multitudes? Alys. 3205. W. torf

227

Torive, *v. a.* == split. Alys. 6217; part. 'toriven.' HD. 1954

Torment, *sb.* St Andrew, 18. St Kath. 165

Tormenting, *sb.* St Andrew, 57

Tormentor, *sb.* St Andrew, 81

Tort. See Turd

Toshake, *v. a.* O. and N. 1645

Toshene, *v. a.* == destroy. O. and N. 1118. AS. to-scǽnan

Toshiver, *v. n.* Alys. 2728

—— *v. a.* HD. 1993

Toslit, *v. a.* O. and N. 694

Tospill, *v. a.* Ps. xliii. 8

Tospread, *v. a.* RG. 160

Toswolle, *part.* == swollen. Pol. S. 157

Tote, *v. n.* == look, spy. HD. 2104. Swed. titta

Totear, *v. a.* Alys. 6297; pret. 'totare.' Alys. 4658; part. 'totorn.' HD. 1948

Tothriste, *adj.* == very bold. O. and N. 171. AS. þrist

Tothute, *vb.* pret. == thou hast confounded. Ps. xiii. 6. AS. þýwan?

Totill, *v. a.* == cultivate. Fr. Sci. 42

Totorve, *v. a.* == throw missiles at. O. and N. 1164. In v. 1117, 'totorneth' is probably a misprint for 'totorveth.' AS. torfian

Totose, *v. n.* == hurt, injure. O. and N. 70; part. 'totused.' HD. 1948. AS. teosu

Totread, *v. a.* 3 pl. pret. 'totraden.' Alys. 3946

Totwitch, *v. a.* == pluck at. O. and N. 1645. AS. twiccian

Touch, *v. a.* 2229 B.

Touching, *sb.* St Lucy, 33

Tough, *adj.* [tou]. RG. 515; [touȝt]. RG. 510; [toȝte]. O. and N. 703; [tohte]. O. and N. 1444. AS. tóh

Toupe, *sb.* == a tup, ram. Ritson's AS. viii. 107. Sw. tuppa, a cock

Tour, *sb.* == arrangement, business. RG. 468. Fr. tour

Tournament, *sb.* RG. 384, 534

Tourney, *sb.* 213 B.

Tourneying, *sb.* == jousting in tournaments. Alys. 1045

Toute, *sb.* == rump. Cok. 134. Dut. stuit. ON. torta. Cf. Fr. touton.

228

Toward, *prep.* == on the side of; 'toward Normandye.' RG. 2

—— *adv.* == this way; 'toward, fraward.' Ps. cxviii. 8

Tower, *sb.* RG. 402

Towhen, *adv.* == how long? Ps. iv. 3; lxxxviii. 47

Town, *sb.* RG. 378, 512

Townsman, *sb.* Rel. Ant. i. 144

Towrench, *v. a.* == extricate. Body and Soul, 155

Towrest, *v. a.* == force open. Body and Soul, 189

Toyear, == this year. 235 β. Ritson's AS. viii. 183

Tprot, == interjection of contempt. Pol. S. 223

Trace, *sb.* 'took a trace' == retired. Alys. 7771. Fr. traxir

Traitor, *sb.* RG. 519

Traitory, *sb.* == treason. Alys. 3983

Transcript, *sb.* 548 B.

Transmigration, *sb.* RG. 9

Trappe, *sb.* == trappings. Alys. 1606

Travail, *sb.* RG. 379, 395

Trayed, *part.* == annoyed. Alys. 3046. AS. tréga

Treachery, *sb.* RG. 56

Treachour, *sb.* RG. 455

Treacle, *sb.* [tracle]. Cok. 82. See Triacle

Tread, *v. a.* RG. 132

—— == copulate. part. 'itrede.' O. and N. 501

Treason, *sb.* RG. 385, 447

Treasure, *sb.* RG. 375

Treasurer, *sb.* Alys. 826

Treasury, *sb.* RG. 374

Treble, *adj.* == triple. Alys. 6606

Treche, *sb.* == track. RG. 145. Fr. trache

Tree, *sb.* == RG. 408, 536; [trough]. Alys. 6829; [trowe]. Alys. 6762

Treisuses. Rel. Ant. ii. p. 176; probably a corruption of Fr. 'trés usés;' old worn pieces of leather, to the use of which the cobblers were restricted in mending shoes. The alutarii, or cordwainers, on the other hand,

229

were confined to the *making* of shoes with *new* leather

Trenne, *v. a.* == separate. Rel. Ant. ii. 212

Tresche, *sb.* == trench. AG. 552

Trespass, *sb.* RG. 374, 528

—— *v. n.* Pol. S. 198

Tressed, *adj.* Alys. 5409

Tressure, *sb.* == tresses. Wright's L. P. p. 105

Treye, *sb.* == sorrow. Rel. Ant. i. 113. AS. tréga

Triacle, *sb.* == medicine, remedy. Alys. 5071. Wright's L. P. p. 26

Trichard, *sb.* == deceiver. Pol. S. 69

Trick, *v. n.* == deceive [trichen]. Pol. S. 69

Trie, *adj.* == choice. Cok. 19, 73; Rel. Ant. ii. p. 176

Trifle, *sb.* RG. 417. Lit. 'a small piece,' from AS. trifelan, to pound

—— *v. n.* part. 'trifling.' St Dunstan, 74

Trinity, *sb.* RG. 532

Tripe, *sb.* Alys. 1578. Rel. Ant. ii. p. 176. Fr. tripe. Ital. trippa

Trobles. Rel. Ant. ii. p. 176; probably a corruption of Fr. 'troblés,' waste, spoilt leather; from Fr. 'trobler' == corrompre, gâter, Roq. See Treisuses

Trod, *sb.* == tread, or track. Body and Soul, 212. AS. trod

Tromcheri, *sb.* == trumpery? Rel. Ant. ii. p. 176. Fr. troncer, to break into small pieces. Cf. Gawin Douglas's 'trumpis,' fragments, which is probably the origin of the modern form

Trome, *sb.* == a company. HD. 8. AS. truma

Trone. See Throne

Tronn (sic in MS.), *sb.* == a steelyard. Rel. Ant. ii. p. 176

Trotevale, *sb.* == trifling, joke. Body and Soul, 146. Lat. titivillitia

Troth, *sb.* == betrothal. K. Horn, 694

Trouble, *adj.* == troubled, murky. Alys. 4709

Troué, *sb.* == hole. Alys. 7465. Fr. trou

Trough. See Tree

Trow, *v. a.* == believe. RG. 110

Trowe, *sb.* == trust, belief. Wright's L. P. p. 100. AS. treów

Trowe. See Tree

Truage, *sb.* == fealty. RG. 39, 372

Truce, *sb.* RG. 529. AS. trúwa. Fr. tréve, truwe

True, *adj.* RG. 377

Trueness, *sb.* RG. 391

Truly, *adv.* RG. 93

Trump, *sb.* == trumpet. RG. 396

Trumper, *sb.* == trumpeter. Alys. 3426

Trumping, *sb.* Alys. 925

Truncheon [tronchon], *sb.* == part of a broken spear. Alys. 3745

Trundle [trendli], *v. n.* == roll. O. and N. 135. AS. trendel

Truss, *sb.* Wright's L. P. pp. 110, 111. Fr. torser, trusser

—— *v. a.* == pack up. HD. 2017. Alys. 990

—— == fasten. Alys. 5477

—— *v. n.* == prepare oneself. RG. 487. Alys. 7160

Trust, *v. a.* RG. 468, 469

—— *v. n.* [triste]. O. and N. 760; [traiste]. Ps. cxxiv. 1

Trusty, *adj.* Wright's L. P. p. 47

Truth, *sb.* RG. 388, 457; [trauthe]. Creed of St Athan. 4; [trauht]. Ibid.

Try, *v. a.* == refine, as gold; part. 'ytried.' Alys. 828

Trysthor, *sb.* == traitor. RG. 302

Trywede, *sb.* == truth, good faith. RG. 358

Tubrugge, *sb.* == townbridge. RG. 543. Pol. S. 222

Tuenge, *v. n.* == pinch. See Twinge

Tuesday. RG. 552

Tug, *v. n.* Body and Soul, 226; part. 'ytuht.' Pol. S. 220. AS. tcohhian

Tuke, *v. n.* == harass, punish. O. and N. 63. AS. tucian

Tumble, *v. n.* Alys. 2465. AS. tumbian

Tumbrel, *sb.* == a porpoise. HD. 757. Swed. tumlare

Turd, *sb.* == excrement [tort]. O. and N. 1684. AS. tord

Turf, *sb.* HD. 939. O. and N. 1165 AS. turf

Turn, *v. n.* == return; 'turnde again.' RG. 387. 53 B.

—— with 'to' == become; 'turn to ill.' RG. 375

—— == turn against a person. RG. 367

—— *v. a.* == turn one's back on a person. RG. 525; part. 'yturned.'

—— == convert. St Swithin, 10

Turnay, *sb.* == tournament. Alys. 141

Turneying, *sb.* Alys. 1045

Turtle, *sb.* == dove. Ps. lxxxiii. 11. Wright's L. P. p. 26

Tusk, *sb.* Ps. lvii. 7. AS. tux

Twege, *sb.* == doubt. M. Ode, st. 177. AS. tweogan

Twelfth, *adj.* RG. 416, 446

Twelfthnight. Alys. 6403

Twelve. RG. 18, 492

Twelvemonth, *sb.* == year. Pol. S. 71

Twentieth, *adj.* RG. 439

Twenty. RG. 440

Twere, *sb.* == doubt, subject of doubt, O. and N. 989. AS. tweo. S. Goth. twe

Twibil, *sb.* == axe. Wright's L. P. p. 110. AS. twý-bill

Twice, *adv.* [tuye]. RG. 222

Twifald, *v. n.* == hesitate. Ps. lxv. 14; cv. 33

Twinge, *v. a.* [tuenge] == pinch. St Dunst. 81. O. and N. 156

—— == persecute. Ps. xvi. 9. Dan. tvinge.

Twinging, *sb.* == persecution. Ps. xvii. 19

Twinkling, *sb.* == 'in the twinkling of an eye.' Wright's L. P. p. 106. AS. twinclian

—— == twangling, or tinkling (of a harp). Alys. 2572

Twinne, *v. a.* == divide. Ps. liv. 10

—— *v. n.* == separate, stand aloof from. Ps. xvi. 13. AS. twý

Two [tuo]. RG. 368; [to]. RG. 538

n. pl. 'tweie.' O. and N. 793

gen. pl. 'tweire.' O. and N. 886; 'twam.' O. and N. 1475; 'twom.' O. and N. 989

Twom. See Two

Tyffen, *v. a.* == adorn. Alys. 4109. Manuel des Pecches, 3204, 3208. ON. typpa.

Tyfyng, *sb.* == ornament. Manuel des Pecches, 3242

Tyrant, *sb.* RG. 389. pl. 'tyranne.' Alys. 7499

U.

Ughtening, *sb.* == dawn, See Uȝtening, Uȝten

Umben, *prep.* == around. Wright's L. P. p. 35. AS. ymbe

Umbestonde, *adv.* == formerly. HD. 2297. Wright's L. P. p. 46

Umbewhile, *adv.* == at times. Wright's L. P. p. 49

Umbistand, *v. a.* == surround; pret. 'umbistode.' HD. 1875

Umbiyeden, *vb.* == surrounded. HD. 1842

Umgang, *sb.* == circuit. Ps. xi. 9

Umgive, *v. a.* == surround. Ps. vii. 8

Umgo, *v. n.* == go round; imper. 'umga' Ps. lviii. 7

Umgripe, *v. a.* == embrace. Ps. lxxviii. 8

Umklip, *v. a.* == embrace. Ps. xlvii. 13

Umlap, *v. a.* == encircle. Ps. xxxix. 13; lxx. 11. AS. læppa, a hem, border

Umlock, *v. a.* Ps. lxxvii. 62

Umset, *v. a.* == surround. Ps. xxi. 13

Umshadow, *v. a.* == overshadow. Ps. xc. 4

Umstanding, *sb.* == circumstance. Ps. cxl. 3

Umtipped, *part.* == dressed. Ps. cxliii. 12. See Tyffen

Unalike, *adj.* 140 β

Unarmed, *adj.* RG. 543

Unaware, *adj.* [unwar, uniwar]. RG. 88

Unbecomely, *adj.* K. Horn, 1097

Unbegotten, *adj.* [unbeȝet]. Signa ante Jud. 31

Unbind, *v. a.* RG. 74, 318; part. 'unbound.' RG. 161

Unblithe, *adj.* HD. 141. Wright's L. P. p. 30

Unbold, *adj.* Wright's L. P. p. 100

Unborn, *adj.* Manuel des Pecches, 4857

Unbought, *adj.* Rel. Ant. i. 114

—— == unrecompensed. M. Ode, st. 30

Unbrede, *v. a.* == open. Pol. S. 156. AS. on-bredan

Unbroad, *adj.* [unbrad]. Pol. S. 156

Unburied, *adj.* RG. 219, 416

Unbuxom, *adj.* == disobedient. Rel. S. vi. 10

Unbuxomness, *sb.* Manuel des Pecches, 3013

Uncle, *sb.* RG. 446

Unclean, *adj.* RG. 351

Uncleanness, *sb.* RG. 434

Unclothe, *v. a.* HD. 659

Uncomely, *adj.* Body and Soul, 59

Uncouth, *adj.* == unknown. Alys. 5993; == unknowing in an act, sense. Wright's L. P. p. 103? AS. uncúð

Uncunning, *sb.* 1024 B.

Under, *prep.* RG. 480; 'under that' == until. RG. 451

—— *v. a.* == put under. Ps. xvii. 48

Under, *sb.* See Undern

Underandnes, *sb.* == harmlessness. Ps. vii. 9. AS. derian

Underdo, *v. a.* == cheat. K. Horn, 1471

Underfang, *v. a.* == take up. RG. 371; pret. 'underfong'

—— == understand. HD. 115

—— == elect. RG. 447

—— == receive, acknowledge. RG. 461. Wright's L. P. p. 59

Underfind, *v. a.* == discover. Wright's L. P. p. 45

Underfoot. 2031 B.

Underganging, *sb.* == humiliation. Ps. xl. 10

Undergo, *v. a.* == make to go under. Ps. xvi. 13

Underhand, == under one's hand, in one's power. RG. 141

Underlay, *v. a.* == put under. Ps. viii. 8

Underlout, *v. n.* == bow to. Ps. lix. 10; xxxvi. 7. AS. underlútan

Undern, *sb.* == third hour of the day, or 9 A.M. 2482 B.; [under]. Wright's L. P. p. 41. AS. undern. MG. undaurns

Undernime, *v. a.* == take up. Body and Soul, 111

Understand, *v. a.* RG. 386; 'Thu nart understonde' == thou dost not understand. RG. 453

—— *v. n.* RG. 78; 'To understonde hym' == 'suggest to himself or devise.' RG. 431

Understanding, *sb.* Ps. cx. 10; cxviii. 73

Underthewe, *v. a.* == subdue. Alys. 1406. AS. under þeowan

Underwit, *v. a.* == understand; pret. 'underwat.' O. and N. 1089

Underȝete, *v. a.* == understand. RG. 401; perceive, discover. RG. 165. AS. under-gitan

Undeserved, *adj.* RG. 54

Undo, *v. a.* == destroy. RG. 384, 477

—— == open. Wright's L. P. pp. 58, 71

Undreh, == intolerable? Wright's L. P. p. 41. AS. dreogan

Uneasily, *adv.* 2252 B.

Uneasy, *adj.* 1482 B.

Uneaten, *adj.* [un-y-ete]. 296 β

Unelde, *sb.* == extreme old age. Ps. lxx. 18

Unele, *sb.* == sickness. RG. 377. AS. unhǽlu

—— == wickedness. RG. 384

—— *adj.* == evil. RG. 428

—— *v. n.* == become sick. RG. 349

Unfain, *adj.* Rel. Ant. i. 113

Unfast, *adj.* == insecure. Ps. xvii. 27

Unfele, *adj.* == evil. O. and N. 1379. See 'unfæle' in Gloss, to Laȝ.

Unfest, *adj.* == insecure. Ps. xxv. 1; xxvi. 2

Unfestand, *adj.* == insecure. Ps. ix. 4

Unfete, *adj.* == not feat, not good. Wright's L. P. p. 43. Fr. faiteis

Unfiled, *adj.* == undefiled. Ps. xvii. 31

Unfillandlike, *adj.* == insatiable. Ps. c. 5

Unforholde, *adj.* == unrewarded. M. Ode, st. 30. AS. unforgolden

Unfree, *adj.* == niggardly, illiberal. Rel. Ant. ii. p. 191

Unfulmaking, *sb.* == imperfection. Ps. cxxxviii. 16

Ungirt, *part.* RG. 526

Unglad, *adj.* Wright's L. P. p. 29

Ungood, *adj.* O. and N. 129. Ps. i. 1

Ungreithe, Ungreithed, *adj.* == unready. Wright's L. P. p. 99. 2241

B.

Ungrete, *sb.* == smallness. O. and N. 752

Unhallowed, *adj.* RG. 349

Unhealth, *sb.* M. Ode, st. 96, 8

Unhele, *v. a.* == uncover. Ps. xxviii. 9. AS. unhélan

Unhendly, *adv.* RG. 412

Unholde, *adj.* == unpleasant. Wright's L. P. p. 24. AS. unhold

Unhonest, *adj.* == foul, indecent. Alys. 6472

Unhooded, *adj.* Ritson's AS. xvii. 126

—— == lay, a layman. O. and N. 1176

Unhosed, *adj.* RG. 526

Unicorn, *sb.* Alys. 6710. Ps. xxviii. 6

Unisome, *adj.* == disunited. O. and N. 1520

Uniune, *sb.* == pearl. Cok. 87. Lat. unio

Unker, == of us two. See I

Unkevel, *v. a.* == uncover. HD. 601

Unkindly, *adv.* == against nature or kind. HD. 1250

—— == cruelly. 1540 B.

Unkindness, *sb.* RG. 31

Unkunde, *adj.* == not legitimate (of a king). RG. 423

Unkundede, *sb.* == unkindness. RG. 479

Unlast, *v. n.* == not to last. Ps. lxxxix. 6

Unlaw, *v. a.* == outlaw. RG. 473. 602 B.

Unlawfully, *adv.* Wright's L. P. p. 53

Unlede, *adj.* == wicked. O. and N. 974. AS. unlǽd

Unlength, *sb.* == want of length. O. and N. 752

Unliche, *adv.* == only. Alys. 69

Unlike, *adj.* O. and N. 804

Unlovesome, *adj.* Alys. 6423

Unlust, *sb.* == misery, want of pleasure. Body and Soul, 95

Unmade, *adj.* Creed of St Athan. 31

Unmarried, *adj.* RG. 31

Unmeek, *adj.* Ps. iv. 3

Unmeet, *adj.* Wright's L. P. p. 23

Unmerry, *adj.* [unmurie]. O. and N. 346

Unmethe, *sb.* == want of moderation. O. and N. 352. AS. unmæte

Unmight, *sb.* == weakness. 1443 B.

Unmighty, *adj.* Wright's L. P. p. 22

Unmild, *adj.* O. and N. 61; 1497 B.

Unnait, *adj.* == vain, useless. Ps. ii. 1. AS. unnet

Unnaitlike, *adv.* == vainly. Ps. xxxviii. 12

Unnaitnes, *sb.* == vanity. Ps. xl. 7

Unne, *v. a.* == love. Wright's L. P. p. 40. ON. unna

Unne, *v. n.* == grant, allow. M. Ode, 158; 1 s. pres. 'an.' O. and N. 1737. AS. unnan

Unnethe, *adv.* == scarcely. RG. 377, 491

Unnoteful, *adj.* == useless. Ps. lii. 4

Unorn, *adj.* == rude. K. Horn, 328. AS. unórne, unórnlíc

Unornelske, *adv.* == rudely. HD. 1941

Unpared, *adj.* Pilate, 232

Unplye, *v. a.* == unfold. Alys. 3000

Unquert, *sb.* == sorrow. Ps. xxx. 13. See Quert

—— *adj.* == sorrowful. Ps. x. 3

Unred, *sb.* == want of wisdom. O. and N. 161. AS. unrǽd

Unreken, *adj.* == disorderly, bad. Wright's L. P. p. 100. AS. ungerec

Unride, *adj.* == large. HD. 964; unwieldy. HD. 1795; deep, or wide (of a wound). HD. 1981, 2673; numerous. HD. 2947. AS. ungerýdu

Unright, *sb.* RG. 375, 417

—— *adj.* 330 B.

Unrighteous, *adj.* Ps. v. 6

Unrighteousness, *sb.* Ps. xxxvi. 7

Unrightfulness, *sb.* O. and N. 1740

Unripe, *adj.* O. and N. 320

Unroned, *adj.* == desolate. Ps. lxxviii. 7. See Rone

Unroningness, *sb.* == desolation. Ps. lxxii. 18

Unryde, *v. n.* == make incursion, attack. Manuel des Pecches, v. 904. AS. onrídan

Unsaht, *adj.* == unreconciled. Wright's L. P. p. 42. AS. unsæht

Unseemly, *adj.* Wright's L. P. p. 31

Unsele, *adj.* == miserable, bad. O. and N. 1002. AS. unsæl

Unselines, *sb.* == misery. Ps. xiii. 3

Unselthe, *sb.* == misfortune. M. Ode, st. 96. O. and N. 1261

Unsete, *adj.* == not good, or right. Wright's L. P. pp. 23, 31. AS. unsidu

Unsewed, *part.* Pilate, 169

Unshapen, *adj.* == uncreated. Creed of St Athan. 23

Unshent, *adj.* == unpunished. Manuel des Pecches, 2733

Unshrined, *adj.* RG. 518

Unshut, *adj.* Alys. 2767

Unsithe, *sb.* == misfortune. O. and N. 1162. AS. unsið

Unsode, *adj.* == unsodden, unboiled. O. and N. 1005

Unspeedy, *adj.* Ps. lxxxviii. 35

Unspring, *v. n.* == open? Alys. 2902

Unspurn, *v. a.* == kick open. K. Horn, 1106

Unstable, *adj.* RG. 510

Unsteadfast, *adj.* Moral Ode, st. 122

Unstoken, *part.* == unfastened. Alys. 2682

Unstrength, *sb.* == weakness. O. and N. 151

Unstrong, *adj.* O. and N. 561

Unswere, *v. a.* == free from oppression. Fragm. in Warton, H. E. P. vol. i. p. 22

Unthank, *sb.* gen. abs. 'unthank his' == against his will. Body and Soul, 215. Cf. 'his thonkes,' &c. *s. v.* Thonk. AS. unþanc; and see the Gloss. to Laʒamon and the Ormulum, *s. v.* Unthanc

Untheand, *adj.* == disobedient. Rel. S. vi. 9. AS. þewian

Unthenfol, *adj.* == unthankful. Pol. S. 159

Unthewe, *sb.* == bad manners, vice. Wright's L. P. p. 73. O. and N. 194. AS. unþeáw

Untholandlik, *adj.* == unendurable. Ps. cxxiii. 5. AS. þólian

238

Untid, *sb.* == unfitness, that which is unseasonable, or wrong. Body and Soul, 43. AS. untíd

Untie, *v. n.* == become untied [untuen]. Wright's L. P. p. 101

Untilled, *adj.* RG. 372

Untime, *sb.* == wrong time. Manuel des Pecches, 2965

Untiȝth, *sb.* == lit. want of discipline; hence wrong, wickedness. Body and Soul, 107. AS. tyht

Untoun, *adj.* == lit. 'not suited to the town;' hence, rude, uncivil. Wright's L. P. p. 32

Untrue, *adj.* Wright's L. P. p. 32

Untrueness, *sb.* == wickedness. M. Ode, 135

Unused, *adj.* RG. 214

Unwarned, *adj.* == undefended. RG. 51

Unwate, *sb.* == misfortune. O. and N. 1265, 1196. AS. hwatu, auguries; hence, unhwatu, bad auguries, misfortune

Unwater, *v. a.* == give out water. Ps. lxxvii. 20

Unwatery, *adj.* Ps. lxii. 3

Unwelde, *sb.* == weakness. Ps. lxx. 9

Unwemmed, *adj.* == unspotted, undefiled. Ps. xviii. 8

Unwight, *sb.* == wretch. O. and N. 33, 218

Unwill, *adj.* == desirable. O. and N. 347. AS. onwill

Unwill, *adj.* == unpleasant. O. and N. 422. AS. unwilla

Unwisdom, *sb.* Ps. xxi. 3; lxviii. 6

Unwise, *adj.* Wright's L. P. p. 101. Pol. S. 153

Unwitandnes, *sb.* == ignorance. Ps. xxiv. 7

Unworshiply, *adv.* Manuel des Pecches, 980

Unworth, *sb.* 654 B.

—— *adj.* 653 B.

Unworthy, *adj.* RG. 412. O. and N. 339

Unwraste, *adj.* == weak, wicked. Wright's L. P. p. 37. Alys. 878; [unwerste]. O. and N. 178. AS. unwrest. ON. hres, spirited; óhres, languid, weak. See the Gloss. to Laȝamon and the Ormulum, *s. v.*

Unwre, *v. a.* == discover. RG. 508. See Unwreon

Unwrench, *sb.* == trick, evil design. O. and N. 169. Rel. S. v. 94. AS. unwrenc

Unwreon, *v. a.* == unfold. Alys. 336; part. 'unwreʒe.' O. and N. 846

Unwrought [unwroʒten], *adj.* == undone, destroyed. O. and N. 162

Unwunne, *sb.* == sorrow. Wright's L. P. p. 47

Up, == upon; prep. RG. 321, 437

—— *adv.* RG. 143

Upbear, *v. a.* Alys. 5163; part. 'upborn.' Ps. cxxx. 1

Upbraid, *v. a.* 1784 B.

Upbraiding, *sb.* Ps. xxxviii. 9

Updraw, *v. a.* Alys. 2633

Upe. See Upon

Upfeng, *v. a.* == take up; pret. 'upfang.' Ps. cxvii. 13

Upheave, *v. a.* == lift up. Ps. iii. 4; part. 'uphoven.' Ps. lxxiv. 11

—— *v. n.* == rise. Ps. vii. 7

Upland, *sb.* Manuel des Pecches, 1318

Uplift, *v. a.* Ps. lxxxvii. 16

Upon, *prep.* Wright's L. P. p. 26; [upe]. RG. 505, 506

Upperest, *adj.* Alys. 7068

Uprear, *v. a.* Ps. cxliv. 14

Uprise, *v. n.* Ps. vii. 7; pret. 'upras.' Ps. cxxxviii. 18; part. 'uprisynde.' Alys. 2270

Uprising, *sb.* RG. 379. F. and P. 6

Upstand, *v. n.* == stand up. Ps. ii. 2

Upsteghing, *sb.* Ps. ciii. 3

Upstie, *v. n.* == go up. pret. 'upstegh.' Creed of St Athan. 75

Uptake, *v. a.* RG. 387; pret. 'uptoke.' Ps. xxvi. 10

Upward, *adv.* RG. 321

Urling, *sb.* == edge. Ps. cxxxii. 2. Fr. orle. Ital. orlo

Urne, *v. n.* == run. O. and N. 638; pret. 'ourne.' RG. 405; 'orn.' Wright's L. P. p. 58; part. 'urmynde,' a mistake for 'urnynge.' RG. 402; 'y-eornd.' Alys. 4357. AS. yrnan

Usage, *sb.* == custom. Alys. 4211. RG. 191

Use, *v. a.* Alys. 5256; part. 'y-used.' 476 B.

Usurer, *sb.* Manuel des Pecches, 2453

Ute, *adv.* == let us; used with verbs. M. Ode, st. 168. AS. ute

Utenlad, *sb.* == a foreigner. HD. 2153. AS. utlænd

240

Uthalve, *adv.* == on the outer part. O. and N. 110

Uthest, *sb.* == outcry. O. and N. 1696

Utschute, *sb.* == outbreak, excess. O. and N. 1466. AS. útscyte

Utterest, *adj.* == uttermost. Ps. cxxxiv. 7

Uvel. See Evil

Uȝten, *sb.* == morning, the dawn. K. Horn, 1424. AS. uhta

Uȝtening, *sb.* == the dawn. Ps. c. 8; lxxii. 14

V

Vacant, *adj.* RG. 472

Vad, *adj.* == dirty, faded. Fragm. Sci. 273

Valley, *sb.* RG. 55

Vault, *sb.* == cellar. Alys. 7210. Fr. volte, from Lat. volutus, volvere

Vauntward, *sb.* RG. 457

Vavassor, *sb.* == a subtenant of a fief, or tenant paravail, who held of a mesne lord. Alys. 3827. Ducange derives it from vassus vassorum

Vawe, == fain, *q. v.*

Vaȝt, 'vor vaȝt;' probably a mistake for 'vor naȝt,' or 'vor noȝt.' RG. 253

Vein, *sb.* RG. 28. Alys. 2414

Veir, *adv.* == truly. Alys. 1001, 5676; 'in veire.' Alys. 5679

Velasour, *sb.* A corruption of 'valvassor,' another form of 'vavassor.' Alys. 3305

Vengeance, *sb.* RG. 333, 429

Venison, *sb.* RG. 243. Alys. 6353

Venom, *sb.* RG. 43, 106. Fr. venin. Lat. venenum

—— *adj.* == envenomed. Alys. 2860

Venomed, *part.* [i-wenemyd], Legend of St Patrick, in Warton, H. E. P. vol. i. p. 17

Venomous, *adj.* 440 B.

Veolthe, == filth, *q. v.*

Verade, *sb.* == a multitude. K. Horn, 172. AS. werod

Verament, *adv.* == truly. Alys. 1346

Verdict, *sb.* RG. 141

Verger, *sb.* == orchard. Alys. 1938. Fr. vergier, from 'vert'

Vermin, *sb.* Alys. 6128

Verse, *sb.* 219 β

Verss, == fresh, *q. v.*

Vert, *v. n.* == go to harbour among fern, said of a buck. Ritson's AS. iii. 8. Fr. vert?

Vestment, *sb.* 954 B.

Vetuse, *adj.* == old. Alys. 7948. Lat. vetus

Vice, *sb.* RG. 195

Victual, *sb.* [vitaile]. Alys. 5817

Vie, *sb.* == life. Marg. 1

Vie, *v. n.* == succeed, do well. Fr. Sci. 319; 658 B. Fr. voie, avoier, to excite, irritate; hence, challenge; and lastly, to succeed in a contest. See Burguy, *s. v.* Voie

Vigorous, *adj.* Alys. 6923

Vigour, *sb.* == strength. Alys. 1431. Lat. vigor

Vigour, *sb.* == idol. See Figure

Vile, *adj.* RG. 435, 506; comp. 'vylloker' == viler. 2500 B.

—— *v. a.* == make vile. part. 'yviled.' RG. 435

Vilely, *adv.* RG. 435, 519

Villany, *sb.* RG. 536, 547

Vilte, *sb.* == vileness. RG. 519

Vine, *sb.* Manuel des Pecches, 884

Vintner, *sb.* RG. 542

Vintry, *sb.* RG. 542

Violence, *sb.* 924 B.

Virgin, *sb.* 2342 B.

Virgin, *adj.* == pure. Alys. 334

Virst. See Thirst

Virtue, *sb.* RG. 86

Virtuous, *adj.* == valorous. Alys. 2408; great, powerful. Ibid. 5244

Vis, *sb.* == visage. Alys. 267, 5954

Visage, *sb.* Alys. 6425

242

Vision, *sb.* RG. 363, 428

Visitation, *sb.* Manuel des Pecches, 2103

Voice, *sb.* RG. 283

Void, *v. a.* == empty. Alys. 373

Vorsuolwe, == swallow. See Forswallow

Vouchsafe, *v. a.* == vouch a person safe. Pol. S. 199

Vow, *v. n.* Manuel des Pecches, 2806

Vow, *sb.* RG. 477

Vowel, *sb.* Rel. Ant. ii. 174

Vowson. See Advowson

Voyage, *sb.* RG. 392

Vyen, *part.* == fixed. Fragm. apud Warton, H. E. P. vol. i. p. 21. AS.
fégan

Vygour. See Figure

Vyssare, == fisher, *q. v.*

Vysseth, *sb.* == fishing. RG. 264

W.

Wade, *v. n.* == go. RG. 99. HD. 2654; [wede]. HD. 2641. AS. wádan

Wag, *v. a.* == move. HD. 89. AS. wágian

—— *v. n.* [wawen]. Alys. 1164. Fr. Sci. 342

Wager, *sb.* Pol. S. 218

Wagh, *sb.* == a wall. Ps. lxi. 4. AS. wáh

Wail, *v. n.* pret. 'waile.' Alys. 4653

Wailing, *sb.* Alys. 7883, 2365

Wain, *sb.* RG. 416. AS. wǽgen

Wait, *sb.* == musician. Alys. 4312, 7769

—— == sentinel. Ritson's AS. viii. 143

Wait, *v. a.* == watch. Wright's L. P. p. 91

Waiten, *v. n.* == keep watch. HD. 1754

Wake, *v. a.* == awaken, pret, 'weiȝte.' 446 β; 'wight.' Alys. 2925

—— *v. n.* == be awake. 681 B. AS. wacan

Wake, *v. a.* == watch. 2215 B. AS. wæccan

Waken, *v. n.* == awake. HD. 2164

Waker, *sb.* == a person apt to wake. Fr. Sci. 286

Wale, *v. a.* == choose. Wright's L. P. p. 33. Germ. wahlen

Walk, *v. n.* K. Horn, 981; pret. 'welk.' Wright's L. P. p. 100. AS. weallian. Germ. wallen, to go

—— == travel; part. 'iwalken.' Marg 49

Walken, == welkin, *q. v.*

Walker, *sb.* == a fuller, or whitener of cloth. 1135 B. AS. wealcere. Ital. gualcare, to full

Wall, *sb.* RG. 549, 555

—— *v. a.* Alys. 2658

Walled, *adj.* Alys. 6068

Wallyng, == boiling. See Well, *vb.*

Wan, *adj.* == pale. Wright's L. P. p. 93; [won]. Ibid. p. 28. AS. wonn, wan

Wand, *sb.* RG. 290. ON. vöndr

Wander, *v. n.* Pol. S. 240

Wandreth, *sb.* [wondred] == sorrow. Pol. S. 150. ON. vandrædi

Wane, *v. n.* Ps. ix. 7. AS. wanian

Wane, *sb.* == want. M. Ode, 179; [wone]. Wright's L. P. p. 30. AS. wana

Wanene. See When and Whence

Wanhope, *sb.* == despair, want of hope. RG. 323

Want, *v. n.* == wish? RG. 468

Want, *v. n.* == be wanting. pret. 'wondede.' Ps. xxii. 1

Want, *v. a.* == be without, lack. Wright's L. P. p. 44. AS. wana, a deficiency

War, *sb.* RG. 374

—— *v. n.* == [worry], make war. RG. 370; pret. 'werrede.' RG. 77

—— *v. a.* == war against a person or thing. pret. 'worrede.' RG. 371, 70; part. 'ywerred.' RG. 3; 'iworred.' Ibid.

Ward, *sb.* == guard. RG. 461

—— == division of an army. Alys. 1996

—— *v. a.* RG. 41, 491

Warden, *sb.* RG. 314, 436

Ware, *sb.* == wares. HD. 52; reward. Pol. S. 192. AS. wáru

Ware, *sb.* == thing, affair. Moral Ode, st. 32 (Hickes); but the Egerton MS. st. 34, reads 'gare,' i. e. gear

Ware, a collective term, 'watres ware.' Ps. xvii. 16; 'windes ware.' Ibid. v. 11; probably the AS. ware

Ware, *sb.* == spring. Ps. lxxiii. 17. Lat. ver. O. Engl. veer

Ware, *adj.* Wright's L. P. pp. 30, 103; [yware]. RG. 388; [iwarte]. O. and N. 1219. AS. wǽr

Warentment, *sb.* == military apparel. Alys. 7943. Fr. garnement

Wariness, *sb.* [iwarness]. O. and N. 1226

Waring, *sb.* == price. Ps. xliii. 13

Warison, *sb.* == reward. Alys. 2512. Fr. guérison

Warn, *v. a.* == advise a person. HD. 2834. AS. warnian

Warn, *v. a.* == refuse a thing to a person. RG. 367, 550

—— == hinder. 1274 B.

Warned, *adj.* == defended, said of a city. Ps. xxx. 22; fortified. Ps. cvii. 11

Warnesture, *sb.* == garrison. RG. 94

Warrant, *v. a.* == insure safety to a person, keep harmless. Alys. 2132

Warp, *v. a.* == throw. HD. 1061; 3 s. pres. 'werth.' HD. 1176; place [worp]. O. and N. 596; pret. 'warp.' O. and N. 45

—— == strike. part. 'iworpe.' O. and N. 1119. AS. weorpan

Warring, *sb.* == fighting. Alys. 6095

Warring, *sb.* == cursing. Manuel des Pecches, 1289

Warrior, *sb.* Alys. 1461

Warye, *v. a.* == curse. See Werien

Warȝtreo, *sb.* == cursed tree, gibbet. 2233 B. AS. werg, accursed

Was. See Be

Was, == whose. See Who

Wash, *v. a.* RG. 435; [whosshe]. Wright's L. P. p. 70; pret. 'wosh.' 273 β; 'wesche.' Ps. lxxii. 13

Wassail, *sb.* RG. 117

—— *v. n.* HD. 2098

Waste, *sb.* == reckless spending. RG. 376

—— == wilderness. Alys. 7121

—— *v. a.* RG. 136

Wastel, *sb.* == cake of fine flour. HD. 779

Wasteyn, *sb.* == wilderness. Manuel des Pecches, 1767

Wate, *sb.* == luck, hap, that which is foretold. RG. 31, 411. AS. hwatu, divination

Water, *sb.* RG. 371, 402

—— *v. a.* Ps. lxxvii. 15

Watercress, *sb.* Alys. 5767

Waterdog, *sb.* Alys. 5771

Waterless, *adj.* Ps. cvi. 25

Wathe, *sb.* == torment. Ps. cxiv. 3. AS. wíte

Watloker, == much rather. See Whatloker.

Wave, *sb.* 525 β; [wawe]. Alys. 5018. AS. wǽg, wáðuma

Wawe, *v. a.* == move. RG. 207. Alys. 2634. AS. wegan, wágian

Wawe, *v. n.* == wag, *q. v.*

Wawing, *sb.* == motion. Fr. Sci. 385

Wax, *sb.* Pol. S. 151. AS. weax

Wax, *v. n.* RG. 9, 442; part. 'ywox.' RG. 412. AS. weaxan

Waxing, *sb.* Fr. Sci. 335

Way, *sb.* == road. RG. 7, 391; 'to fly his way.' O. and N. 308. 'Do way,' an expression like our 'Get along with you.' Alys. 7646; pl. 'weyre.' Body and Soul, 63

Way, *sb.* == mass? Ritson's AS. viii. 31. AS. wæcg

Wayle, *sb.* == a girl. Wright's L. P. p. 38. AS. wylen

Waynoun, a proper name? Wright's L. P. p. 47

Wayte, *sb.* See Wait

Wayteglede, == watch-the-fire, i. e. one who sits in the chimney corner, poking over the fire? Wright's L. P. p. 47. Cf. the Norse phrase Kólbitr; and see the Introduction to Dasent's Popular Tales from the Norse, pp. lxxx-lxxxii. 1st Edit.

We. See Woe

We. See I

We. See With

Weak, *adj.* HD. 1012

Weal, *sb.* 1277 B.

Wealth, *sb.* Ps. lxxii. 12

Weapon, *sb.* HD. 1436. O. and N. 1367

Wear, *v. a.* RG. 390; pret. 'werede.' RG. 434

Weariness, *sb.* RG. 240

Weary, *adj.* RG. 19

Weather, *sb.* RG. 560

Web, *sb.* Fr. Sci. 315

Webbe, *sb.* == weaver. Pol. S. 188

Wed, *sb.* == pledge. Pol. S. 151. Wright's L. P. p. 110. RG. 393. AS. wed

Wed, *v. a.* == marry. RG. 295, 439; said of the priest who marries two persons. Pol. S. 159. AS. weddian, wed

Wedbreak, *sb.* == adulterer. Ps. xlix. 18

Wedding, *sb.* St Lucy, 88. Manuel des Pecches, 1712

Wede, *vb.* == wade, go. See Wade

Wedlock, *sb.* Marg. 11

Wednesday. RG. 509

Wee. See Woe

Weed, *sb.* == garment. RG. 560. AS. wǽd

Weed, *sb.* == herb. Alys. 796. AS. weód

Week, *sb.* RG. 113; pl. 'wouke.' RG. 387. AS. weoc

Weeles. See Well, *sb.*

Ween, *v. n.* == think. RG. 369. O. and N. 237. 2 s. pres. 'wanst.' O. and N. 1642. AS. wénan

—— *v. a.* == impute. Ps. xxxi. 2

Weep, *v. n.* RG. 420; [wyppen]. O. and N. 1064

Weeping, *sb.* RG. 405. Wright's L. P. p. 30; [wyping]. Ibid. p. 85

Wef, *sb.* == whiff or scent. Body and Soul, 56. AS. wiffan

Weight, *sb.* == a measure, weight. Ps. lxi. 10. AS. wæg

Weir, *sb.* Ps. cxiii. 8; [wore]. Wright's L. P. p. 28. AS. wǽr

Welaway, *interj.* 1179 B.

Welcome, *adj.* RG. 508

—— *v. a.* 473 B.

Welde. See Wield

Welk, *v. n.* == fade, become pale. Ps. lxxxix. 6. See Weolewe

Welkin, *sb.* == the sky. Wright's L. P. p. 114; [walken]. Alys. 5799. Ps. cl. 1; dat. s. 'weoluce.' O. and N. 1680. AS. welcn, wolcen

Well, *adj.* == good. 89 B.

—— *adv.* RG. 375. O. and N. 31

—— == rightly. Rel. S. i. 20

Well, *sb.* (of water). RG. 1. Wright's L. P. p. 94; pl. 'weeles.' Ps. xvii. 5. AS. well, wyl

Well, *v. n.* == boil, well up. Wright's L. P. p. 40; [walle]. RG. 28; pret. 'wal.' Body and Soul, 218; part. 'wallyng.' Alys. 1622. AS. weallan

—— *v. a.* == boil. Marg. 60

Wellnigh, *adv.* == almost. O. and N. 44

Wellquemand, *part.* == pleasing. Ps. xci. 15

Wellqueme, *sb.* == pleasure. Ps. lxxxviii. 18; cv. 4

Wellquemeness, *sb.* == pleasingness. Ps. cxl. 5

Wellset, *v. a.* Ps. civ. 9; cxi. 5

Wellsetting, *sb.* Ps. cxviii. 91

Welly, *adv.* == kindly. Ps. l. 20

Wem, *sb.* == a spot or scar. RG. 336. St Kath. 151. AS. wem, womm

Wem, *v. a.* == to defile, corrupt. Ps. lxxxviii. 35; [wemmy]. RG. 206; part. 'wemmed.' Ps. xv. 10. AS. wemman

Wemed, *adj.* 'prout wemod' == with a proud stomach. Fr. Sci. 285. 'Wem' is still used for 'womb' in the North of England. AS. wamb

Wemless, *adj.* == spotless. Creed of St Athan. 6. Ps. xiv. 2

Wemmand, *sb.* == sinner. Ps. cxviii. 158

Wemmedness, *sb.* Ps. c. 3

Wemming, *sb.* RG. 336

Wemmy, *v. a.* == defile. See Wem, *vb.*

Wench, *sb.* Cok. 139. Ps. lxvii. 26. AS. wencle. See Gloss. to Orm. *s. v.* wenchell

Wend, *v. n.* == go. RG. 8. AS. wendan

—— == turn (as in bed). Wright's L. P. p. 28

—— *v. a.* == turn. HD. 2138; change. Wright's L. P. p. 91

Wending, *sb.* == departure. Alys. 920

Wene, *adj.* == frequent, rife? Pol. S. 150. AS. wune, custom. Dut. wennen

Weole, *sb.* == wealth. Pol. S. 156. AS. weola

—— == happiness? Wright's L. P. p. 44

Weolewe, *v. n.* == fade, become pale. Wright's L. P. p. 50. AS. wealwian

Wepmon, *sb.* == man. Pol. S. 153. O. and N. 1377. AS. wæpman

Were. See Be

Were, *v. a.* == defend. HD. 2298. Alys. 5836; [werye]. Alys. 3533. AS. werian. Germ. wehren

Were, *sb.* == man, husband. O. and N. 1339. AS. wer

Werewed, *part.* == worried, killed? HD. 1915

Werien, *v. a.* == curse. O. and N. 1172; [werre]. Manuel des Pecches, 1291; [warye]. Id. 1292. AS. werigan

Werth, == throweth. See Warp

Weryying, *sb.* == protection. Wright's L. P. p. 75. Ps. xxi. 20; [weryng]. Alys. 2798. AS. werian

West. RG. 544

West, *vb.* == shows? Alys. 238. AS. wísian

Westerness, *sb.* == the West country. K. Horn, 949

Westward, *adv.* RG. 20

Wet, *sb.* Fr. Sci. 136. AS. wæt

—— *v. a.* Wright's L. P. p. 31; pret. 'watte.' RG. 322; part. 'wet.' Wright's L. P. p. 30

—— *v. n.* == become wet. Wright's L. P. p. 36

—— *adj.* [wete]. Wright's L. P. p. 85

Wete, *v. n.* == weep. Wright's L. P. p. 84

Wether, *sb.* Ps. lxiv. 14. RG. 52. AS. weðer

Weve, *v. a.* == make to go, cut off; part. 'weved,' 'yweved.' Alys. 3839, 3807

Weve, *v. n.* == go, move. RG. 64. Another form of 'wawe,' 'wave,' 'wag'

Weved, *sb.* == altar. RG. 369, 419, 433. AS. weofod

Weye, *sb.* == woe, *q. v.*

Weȝe, *v. a.* == carry, O. and N. 1020. AS. wegan

Whale, *sb.* [hwal]. HD. 755; [qual]. HD. 753. AS. hwæl

Whalebone, *sb.* [whalles bone]. Wright's L. P. p. 38

What, *interr. pron.* O. and N. 1438

—— *rel. pron.* O. and N. 1439

—— *interj.* O. and N. 1296

What—what, == some—some. RG. 402

Whate, *adv.* == quickly. Alys. 2639. AS. hwæt

Whatkin, *adj.* == what kind of. Ps. lv. 10

Whatloker, *adj.* == much rather. RG. 429, 357. 1249 B. (?) AS. hwætlíc, comp. hwætlicor

Wheat, *sb.* Alys. 5193. AS. hwǽte

Wheel, *sb.* RG. 408. AS. hweol

Whelp, *sb.* Ps. ciii. 21. AS. hwelp

When, *adv.* [wanne]. RG. 367, 378; [hwenne]. Rel. S. iv. 1; [hwanne]. O. and N. 1416; [hwan]. O. and N. 1468; [whan]. 290 β; [wane]. O. and N. 521; [wone]. O. and N. 324

Whence, *adv.* gen. of 'when;' [whonene]. O. and N. 138; [wanene]. O. and N. 1298; [whannes]. 288 β; [whethen]. Ps. cxx. 1

Where, *adv.* [war]. RG. 40. O. and N. 526; [whar]. 1078 B.

Whereby, *adv.* [warbi]. RG. 101

Wherefore, *adv.* 126 B.

Whereof, *adv.* RG. 405

Wheresoever, *adv.* 1389 B.

Wherethrough, *adv.* [war þoru]. RG. 432

Whereto, *adv.* 447 B. O. and N. 464

Whet, *v. a.* == sharpen; part. 'y-whet.' Alys. 6607. AS. hwettan

Whethen, == whence, *q. v.*

Whether, *adv.* RG. 16; [whar]. 67 B; 'whether—the' == whether—or. O. and N. 1358, 1360

—— *adj.* RG. 408

Whey, *sb.* [wei]. O. and N. 1007. AS. wæg

Which, *rel. pron.* RG. 472; [hwucche]. O. and N. 934; [wuch]. O. and N. 1376

—— == what. 974 B. RG. 454

While, *sb.* == time. O. and N. 1589

—— with the def. art. == whilst [þe wule]. RG. 377

Whilom, *adv.* == formerly (dat. pl. of while). Wright's L. P. p. 87

Whine, *v. n.* [wonie]. O. and N. 973. AS. wánian. Dut. weynen

Whining, *sb.* [wonyng]. O. and N. 311

Whistle, *v. n.* Alys. 5348, 5263. AS. hwistlian

White, *adj.* RG. 2, 228; [with]. HD. 48

—— *sb.* == white of an egg. HD. 240

Whiten, *v. a.* Ps. l. 9

Whither, *adv.* 693 B.

Whitherward, *adv.* 59 B.

Who, *rel. pron.* [hoo]. RG. 40; [hwo]. O. and N. 1193

gen. 'was.' RG. 475

dat. and acc. 'whom.' RG. 10; 'wham.' 116 B.; 'hwam.' Rel. S. ii. 2; 'hwan.' O. and N. 1508

Who, == one, 'as who seith' == as one saith. RG. 328; 'alle ho' == every one. O. and N. 66

Whole, *adj.* == sound. RG. 377. 676 β

Whore, *sb.* RG. 279

Whoredom, *sb.* RG. 241, 479

Whoreling, *sb.* Rel. S. vii. 29

Whoreson, *sb.* Alys. 880

Whoso, *pron.* Wright's L. P. p. 26; [whose]. Ibid. p. 114

Why, *interr.* [wu]. RG. 307; [hwi]. O. and N. 1256; [wi]. O. and N. 1232

—— *rel. adv.* O. and N. 474; [whi]. 1573 B.

Wick, *adj.* == wicked. RG. 208. From AS. wǽc, weak

—— == bad, wretched; 'wikke clothes.' HD. 2458

Wicke, *adj.* 'wicke tune,' O. and N. 730, means probably 'establishments.' From the AS. wíc-tunas

Wicked, *adj.* Wright's L. P. pp. 24, 30; 'a wicked weed' == a wretched garment. Serm. 40

Wickedness, *sb.* Pol. S. 230

Wickehede, *sb.* == wickedness. Body and Soul, 43

Wicket, *sb.* K. Horn, 1106. Fr. guichet

Wiclik, *adv.* == wickedly. Ps. xliii. 18

Wide, *adj.* RG. 410.

Widow, *sb.* HD. 79. AS. wuduwe

Wield, *v. a.* == govern, rule. 816 B.; [wolde]. RG. 147

Wife, *sb.* RG. 26, 380

Wigeling, *sb.* == an out-of-the-way place? Ps. cvi. 40. AS. wicelian, to stagger, to go out of the direct road

Wight, *sb.* == a man. RG. 533. 470 β. AS. wiht

Wight, *adj.* == active. HD. 9; [with]. HD. 1756; comp. 'wyghtyore.' Alys. 2396. Swed. vig

—— *adv.* == immediately, quickly. Wright's L. P. p. 44

Wighth, *sb.* == a space of time. Alys. 5362; a space. Ps. viii. 6. AS. wuht, wiht

Wightness, *sb.* == valour, activity. Alys. 5001

Wike, *sb.* == dwelling. O. and N. 604. AS. wic

Wike, *sb.* == office, duty. O. and N. 603; station. Alys. 4608. See Gl. to Orm. *s. v.* Wikenn

Wike, *v. n.* == be weary. Wright's L. P. p. 87. AS. wícan

Wikness, *sb.* == wickedness. Ps. v. 5

Wil, *adj.* == wild, uncertain. HD. 1042

Wild, *adj.* == fierce. RG. 374, 510; 'wild beasts.' RG. 375

Wilderness, *sb.* == a desolate place. RG. 15

Wildfire, *sb.* RG. 410

Wile, *sb.* == trick, deceit. Ritson's AS. viii. 180. AS. wile

Wilful, *adj.* RG. 359; [willesful]. RG. 77

—— == voluntary. Ps. lxvii. 10

Wilfully, *adv.* == without a cause. Ps. xxxiv. 7; lxviii. 5

Will, *sb.* RG. 367

—— *v. n.* == wish. RG. 384; pret. 'wolde.' RG. 550

Will, *v. aux.* pres. 1 s. 'wole.' 39 B.; 2 s. 'wolt.' 40 B.; 'wlt.' O. and N. 499; 3 s. 'wule.' O. and N. 1360; 'wile.' O. and N. 1358; pret. 3 s. 'wolde.' 17 β; 2 s. 'woldest.' 35 B. 'Will' is constantly used with the infin. of the verb to form an imperative, as 'nil þou niþe' == strive not. Ps. xxxvi. 8, and cf. Ps. lxxiv. 5, 6

Willesful, == wilful, *q. v.*

Willing, *sb.* Rel. Ant. ii. 212

Wilne, *v. n.* == wish. RG. 217. AS. wilnian

—— *v. a.* == covet, desire. RG. 46; part. 'y-wilned.' RG. 309

Wimple, *sb.* Marg. 47. AS. winpel

Win, *v. a.* == subdue, get possession of [i-winne]. RG. 519; recover, obtain. RG. 523, 549; pret. 'wonne.' RG. 384; 'wonde.' RG. 258; 'wan.' Alys. 5561. AS. winnan

Wind, *sb.* RG. 367

Wind, *v. a.* == twist. pret. 'wond.' Pilate, 126. AS. windan

Windmill, *sb.* RG. 547

Window, *sb.* Wright's L. P. p. 91

Wine, *sb.* RG. 6, 542. AS. wín

Wine, *sb.* == a friend. M. Ode, 111. AS. wine

Wineyard, *sb.* == vineyard. Wright's L. P. p. 41. AS. wín-geard

Wing, *sb.* RG. 28

Winli, *adj.* == winsome. Ps. xxiii. 3. AS. wynlíc

Winne, *sb.* == joy. Pol. S. 195. AS. wyn

Winne, *sb.* == labour. O. and N. 670. AS. win

Winsome, *adj.* == lovely, delightful. Ps. lxxviii. 9. AS. wynsum

—— *v. n.* == be propitious. Ps. cii. 3

Winter, *sb.* RG. 371, 539

Wipe, *v. a.* RG. 435. AS. wípian

Wippen, *v. n.* == weep? O. and N. 1064

Wire, *sb.* [wyred]. Alys. 208. AS. wír

Wirwed, *part.* == strangled. HD. 1921. Dut. wurghen

Wisdom, *sb.* RG. 384

Wise, *sb.* == manner, 'in no wise.' 1212 B.; [wes]. O. and N. 748

Wise, *adj.* RG. 468, 506; sup. 'wisest.' RG. 266

Wisely, *adv.* RG. 550

Wisse, *v. a.* == direct. HD. 104. 1057 B. O. and N. 971. AS. wísian

Wissing, *sb.* == advice. HD. 2902. AS. wissung

Wit, *sb.* == knowledge, sense. RG. 457, 526; [i-wit]. O. and N. 772

Witch, *sb.* Wright's L. P. p. 38. AS. wicca, a wizard

—— *v. n.* == sing charms. Ps. lvii. 6

Witchcraft, *sb.* Body and Soul, 27

Witching, *sb.* == witchcraft. St Lucy, 122

Wite, *v. a.* == know. RG. 374; [y-wyte]. RG. 10; [iwite]. RG. 487; [wot]. 1625 B.; [wat]. O. and N. 1200; [wod]. Ib. 1188; 2 s. pres. 'wost.' O. and N. 717; pret. 'wuste.' RG. 374; 'wiste.' 208 B.; 'west.' Alys. 5834; part. 'iwiste.' 137 B.

Wite, *v. n.* == think, or expect. 2 s. pres. 'west.' O. and N. 47; pret. 'wiste.' RG. 93

Wite, *v. a.* == defend. RG. 487; pret. 'wuste.' RG. 549; S. S. witen. See Gloss. to La3.

Wite, *v. n.* == go forth. Ps. lxxxix. 6; part. 'wited.' Ps. ix. 22; 'witand.'

Ps. cxviii. 118. AS. wítan

Wite, *v. a.* == blame. O. and N. 1354; accuse. Wright's L. P. p. 39. AS. witian

Witerlike, *adv.* == certainly. HD. 671. Ps. ii. 6

Witermon, *sb.* == a wise man. Wright's L. P. p. 28

With, *prep.* == together with. 279 B.; [we]. RG. 457

—— == by means of. RG. 41

—— == against. O. and N. 62

—— == from. O. and N. 610. AS. wíð

With, *adj.* == white, *q. v.*

With, *adj.* for 'wight,' *q. v.*

With, *adj.* == pleasant? Wright's L. P. p. 45. AS. wéðe

Withal, *adv.* RG. 28

Withclepe, *v. a.* == oppose. Alys. 1301

Withdraw, *v. a.* RG. 447

—— *v. n.* Ps. cxviii. 115; 'withdraw of' == withdraw from. RG. 497

Wither, *adj.* == hostile. Rel. S. i. 12; S. S. wiðer. See Gloss. to Laȝ.

Withering, *sb.* == adversary. K. Horn, 154

Witherthreat, *v. a.* Ps. xxxiv. 19; lxxiii. 10

Witherwendand, *part.* == opposing. Ps. iii. 8

Witherwine, *sb.* == adversary. RG. 325. AS. wiðer-winna, from winnan, to strive

Witherword, *sb.* == a hostile word. Ps. xc. 3

Withhold, *v. a.* == to hold with, or make to accompany. HD. 2356, 2362

—— == restrain. Alys. 2302

Within, *adv.* RG. 375, 549

Without, *adv.* RG. 549. 267 B.; [widh wute]. O. and N. 1593

—— *prep.* RG. 369; [witute]. O. and N. 183; [withouten]. 33 B.

Withsay, *v. a.* RG. 369, 374

Withseek, *v. a.* == seek out. part. 'wuthsoht.' Rel. S. v. 54

Withsitten, *v. a.* == oppose. HD. 1683

Withstand, *v. n.* == oppose. 725 B.

Withy, *sb.* == halter of withy. Alys. 4714. AS. wíðie

Witless, *adj.* == mad. RG. 216; at a loss. Pilate, 242

255

Witness, *sb.* RG. 29

Witterli, *adv.* == certainly. Ps. cxix. 1. ON. víturlega

Witty, *adj.* == clever. RG. 189; full of knowledge. O. and N. 1187. F. and P. 31

Witword, *sb.* == testimony. Ps. xxiv. 10. AS. wit-word

Wive, *v. n.* == marry. RG. 35

—— *v. a.* part. 'iwived.' RG. 529

Wiving, *sb.* == marriage. RG. 294

Wlak, *adj.* == lukewarm. Fr. Sci. 290 AS. wlæc

Wlate, *v. a.* == loathe. Ps. v. 7. AS. wlættian

—— *v. n.* == feel disgust for. O. and N. 354

—— *sb.* == disgust. O. and N. 1504. AS. wlætte

Wlatful, *adj.* == loathsome, abominable. Ps. lii. 2

Wlating, *sb.* == loathing, disgust. Ps lxxxvii. 9. AS. wlætung

Wlite, *v. n.* == look. Wright's L. P. p. 43. AS. wlítan

—— *sb.* == countenance. O. and N. 439; Ps. xliv. 5. AS. wlíte

Wlonk, *adj.* == fair, proud. Pol. S. 156. AS. wlanc

Wluine, *sb.* == she wolf? HD. 573. Probably a metathesis of the ON. ulfinna,

  thus ulvin } vluin

Wo, *sb.* RG. 172, 485; [wai]. O. and N. 120; [wee]. Pol. S. 152; [weye]. Alys. 3449; [wa]. Ritson's AS. viii. 152. AS. wá

Wo worth, i. e. woe be to, &c. Body and Soul, 7

Wobegone, *adj.* Body and Soul, 220

Wode, == went. See Go

Woderove, *sb.* == the woodruff; the asterula odorata of botanists. Wright's L. P. p. 43. In Wright's Vocab. p. 140, 'wuderove' is given as the transl. of 'hastula regia' or 'muge de bois'

Wodewale, *sb.* == woodpecker. Wright's L. P. p. 26

—— == wild thyme? Alys. 6793. AS. wudufille. Palsgrave has 'wodewale, a herbe'

Woht, *sb.* == sin. See Woʒ

Wolc, *sb.* == some bird. Wright's L. P. p. 26

Wold, *sb.* == power, governance. Alys. 6716

Woldeneyed, == wall-eyed. Alys. 5274. Probably from the ON. vagl i augum == festuca, pterygion. 'En hinde, som trækker sig over öiet.' B. Haldorson.

Wole, *adj.* == evil. O. and N. 8; [wle]. O. and N. 35. AS. wól

Wolf, *sb.* RG. 369

Wolfling, *sb.* Alys. 6272

Wollen, *sb.* == wollen garment. Fr. on Seven Sins, 16

Woman, *sb.* RG. 380; [wimman]. RG. 535. pl. 'wymmen.' Wright's L. P. p. 33

Womanly, *adj.* RG. 457

Womb, *sb.* RG. 369. AS. wamb

Wombed, *adj.* RG. 377; [wemod]. Fr. Sci. 286

Wombeling, *sb.* == womb. Alys. 5674

Won, *sb.* == hope. RG. 419; [iwon]. 1022, 1712, B.; [wunne]. Pol. S. 153

—— == opinion. HD. 1972. AS. wén. ON. von

Won, *sb.* == plenty. RG. 2, 265; [iwon]. Rel. S. v. 76

—— == riches. Wright's L. P. p. 24. Alys. 5658; [wane]. Ritson's AS. viii. 50; SS. winne, wunnen

Won, *sb.* == dwelling. Wright's L. P. pp. 46, 51. AS. wunian

Won. See Wan

Wonde, *v. n.* == fear, hesitate. K. Horn, 345. AS. wandian

Wonde, *v. n.* == cease. Wright's L. P. p. 29. AS. wendan

Wonde, *v. n.* == wound? Alys. 6525

Wonde, *adj.* == wicked. Rel. S. v. 112. ON. vondr. AS. wonn

Wonder, *sb.* RG. 376

—— == a wonderful thing. RG. 7, 417

—— *v. n.* O. and N. 228

—— *adj.* == wonderful. RG. 416

Wonderful, *adj.* RG. 414

Wondering, *sb.* Wright's L. P. p. 40

Wonderliche, *adv.* == wonderfully. RG. 489

Wondred, == sorrow. See Wandreth

Wone. See When

Wone, *sb.* == want. See Wane, *sb.*

Wone, *sb.* == opinion. HD. 1711. AS. wénan

257

Wone, *adj.* == wont. HD. 2297; [i-wune]. O. and N. 1318; [y-woned]. RG. 377

—— *sb.* == custom. RG. 392. AS. wune

Wong, *sb.* == cheek. Wright's L. P. pp. 28, 30, 31. AS. wang

Wong, *sb.* == field, plain. HD. 397, 1444. AS. wang

Wonie, == whine, *q. v.*

Woning, *sb.* == a dwelling. RG. 275; [wonyghing]. Alys. 5930

Woningstede, *sb.* Ps. lxxxvi. 7. Ritson's AS. viii. 53, 200

Wonne, *v. n.* == dwell. RG. 41. AS. wunian

Wonying, == whining, *q. v.*

Woo, *v. a.* [woȝe]. K. Horn, 558; [wowe]. Wright's L. P. p. 44. AS. wógan

Wood, *sb.* RG. 374, 565. AS. wudu

Wood, *adj.* == mad. RG. 496. AS. wód

Woodward, *sb.* == the keeper of the wood. Pol. S. 149

Wooing, *sb.* Wright's L. P. p. 28

Wool, *sb.* RG. 2

Woolmonger, *sb.* RG. 539

Woolpack, *sb.* RG. 539

Wop, *sb.* == weeping. RG. 476

Word, *sb.* RG. 377, 501

—— == tidings. RG. 153

Woren, *v. a.* == trouble, disturb. Wright's L. P. p. 24. AS. worian

Worewed, *part.* == worried. See Worry

Wori, *adj.* == troubled (of water). 255, 274 β

Work, *sb.* RG. 448

—— *v. a.* == cause. Wright's L. P. p. 42, make, fashion; part 'ywroȝte.' RG. 447, 'ywort.' RG. 174

—— *v. n.* == do work. 186 B. Wright's L. P. p. 60; pret. 'wraht.' Ibid. p. 42, 'wroȝte.' RG. 287

Workman, *sb.* St Swithin, 55

World, *sb.* KG. 367

Worldly, *adj.* Fragm. on Seven Sins, 16

Worly, *adj.* == excellent, beautiful. Wright's L. P. pp. 39, 45;

[wurhliche]. Ibid. p. 51. AS. wurðlic

Worm, *sb.* RG. 490

Worry, *v. a.* 1598 B.; part. 'worewed.' HD. 1915. AS. wérian

Worse, *adj.* RG. 374, 501

Worship, *sb.* [wurthsipe]. O. and N. 1097, 1342

Worshipful, *adj.* Ps. lxxi. 14

Worst, *adj.* Wright's L. P. p. 99

Worst. See Worthe

Wort, *sb.* == a root. RG. 341. AS. wyrt

Worth, *sb.* == value. RG. 373

—— *adj.* == worthy of, 'what hii were wurth.' RG. 374

Worth, *adv.* = forth. RG. 457

Worthe, *v. n.* == be, become. [iworthe]. 947 B. 2 s. pres. 'worst.' 1812; 3 s. pres. 'worth.' RG. 512; 1 pl. 'wortheth.' RG. 454; 3 s. imper. (in the phrase 'wo worth.') Body and Soul, 7; part. 'iworthe.' O. and N. 660. AS. weorðan

Worthful, *adj.* O. and N. 1479

Worthing, *sb.* == glory, honour. Fragm. in Warton, H. E. P. vol. i. p. 22. AS. weorðung

Worthship, *sb.* == worship, *q. v.*

Worthy, *adj.* == excellent. 412 B.

—— == powerful. Ps. xlix. 3

Wot, == know. See Wite

Wote ? RG. 361

Wou, See Woȝ

Would, *sb.* See Will

Wound, *sb.* RG. 49. Wright's L. P. pp. 85, 84

—— *v. a.* part, 'ywonded.' RG. 49

Wow, See Woȝ

Wowe, *sb.* == wall. HD. 1963. K. Horn, 1000. AS. wáh

Wowe, *v. n.* == to woo, *q. v.*

Woȝ, *sb.* == wrong. O. and N. 164. RG. 39; [wou]. RG. 375, 550; [wow]. RG. 379; [woht]. Rel. S. ii. 16. AS. wóh

Wrake, *sb.* == evil, destruction. O. and N. 1192. AS. wræc

Wrakeful, *adj.* == wicked. Wright's L. P. p. 23. AS. wræcfull

Wrath, *sb.* 451 B. AS. wráð

—— *v. n.* == be angry. Ps. iv. 5

—— *v. a.* == make angry. RG. 376, 253

Wrathless, *adj.* Wright's L. P. p. 42

Wray, *v. a.* == betray. 1226 B; [wrye]. Alys. 442. AS. wreian

Wrayli, *v. n.* == chatter, rail, abuse. St Swithin, 70. Dut. rallen. Swed. ralla

Wreche, *sb.* == vengeance. RG. 380, 419. AS. wræc

Wreche, == misery. RG. 252. But we should probably read 'wrechede'

Wreier, *sb.* == betrayer, spoiler. HD. 39

Wreke, *v. a.* == avenge. HD. 1363. AS. wræccan

Wreker, *sb.* == avenger. Ps. viii. 3

Wren, *sb.* O. and N. 564. AS. wrenna

Wrench, *sb.* == trick. RG. 570, 535. AS. wrence

Wreon, *v. a.* == cover. Alys. 1606; 3 s. pres. 'wrieth.' Alys. 1992; part. 'ywrye.' RG. 56, 92. AS. wreon, wríhan

Wrestle, *v. n.* RG. 22, 361. Alys. 1046. AS. wræstlian

Wrestling, *sb.* O. and N. 793. Alys. 1046

Wretch, *sb.* 524 β AS. wræcca

—— *adj.* == wretched. 449 B.

Wretched, *adj.* comp. 'wretcheder.' 2432 B.

Wretchede, *sb.* == wretchedness. RG. 386, 511

Wretchedly, *adv.* RG. 446

Wrethen—writhen, *part.* == twisted. Alys. 5723

Wrey, *v. a.* == accuse. Pol. S. 198, 199; part. 'wreynt.' Pol. S. 157. AS. wrégan

Wrie, *v. n.* == move away. Wright's L. P. p. 48. AS. wrigan, whence our 'wriggle'

Wrieth, == covereth. See Wreon

Wrikke, *v. n.* == wriggle. St Dunstan, 82; 'wrikkend' == walking, going. Rel. Ant. ii. p. 216. AS. wrigan

Wring, *v. a.* (one's hands). Body and Soul, 174; (clothes). HD. 1233

—— == keep tight hold of. Sermon, 20

—— == twist; part. 'wrong.' Alys. 6447

—— == press down, overcome; pret. 'wrong.' Marg. 47. AS. wringan

Wringer, *sb.* Sermon, 21

Writ, *sb.* HD. 136

—— == Scripture. Wright's L. P. p. 101

—— == letter. Alys. 4502

Write, *v. a.* pret. 'wrot.' 164 B.; part. 'iwrite.' 1425 B.

Writeling, *sb.* == trills in a song? O. and N. 48, 912. From AS. wriðan == to writhe or twist

Writhe, *v. n.* == bend easily. Body and Soul, 116. AS. wríðan

Wro, *sb.* == hole or corner. HD. 68. Su. Goth. wra. Dan. vraa

Wronehede. Probably a mistake for 'wronghede' == wickedness. O. and N. 1398

Wrong, *adj.* == mistaken. Wright's L. P. p. 31. ON. rángr. AS. wringan

Wrong, *sb.* == injustice, oppression. Wright's L. P. p. 68. 1616 B.

—— *adv.* == badly. O. and N. 196

Wrong, *part.* == twisted. See Wring

Wrongwis, *adj.* == wicked. Ritson's AS. viii. 177; [wrancwise]. Moral Ode, 129

Wrot, *sb.* == snout. Rel. Ant. ii. 211. AS. wrót

Wroten, *v. n.* == to root. Earth, st. 3. AS. wrót

Wroth, *adj.* == angry. RG. 31; timid. Alys. 544. AS. wráð

—— == poor, base. Wright's L. P. p. 38

—— *sb.* == evil, unkindness. RG. 31

Wrotherhele, *sb.* [wrothe hele] == injury, destruction. RG. 143, 164. Body and Soul, 225. See Gloss. Rem. to Laȝamon, iii. 444

Wrought. See Work, *vb.*

Wrying, *sb.* == treachery. Alys. 3514

Wune, *sb.* == custom. O. and N. 272. AS. wune

Wunne, *adj.* == accustomed? Wright's L. P. p. 46

Wunne, *sb.* == joy. Wright's L. P. p. 47. AS. wyn

—— == hope. See Won

Wyred, == wire, *q. v.*

Wyt, *sb.* == calamity, blame. Body and Soul, 62. AS. wíte

Y.

Y, == in. Pol. S. 151

Yard, *sb.* == rod. RG. 22; [ʒurd]. 2385 B.

—— == staff or sceptre. Ps. xliv. 7. AS. gyrd

Yard, *sb.* == courtyard. HD. 702. AS. geard

Yare, *adj.* == ready. RG. 396; [ʒarte]. O. and N. 1220. AS. gearo

—— *v. a.* == make ready. HD. 1350

Yare, *adv.* == of yore. 1512 B. AS. geara

Yate, *v. a.* == tell. Ritson's AS. viii. 80. ON. géta

Yawn, *v. n.* [ʒonie]. O. and N. 292; [yene]. Body and Soul, 202. Alys. 485. AS. ganian

Ybrad. See Braid

Ycholle, == I shall. RG. 405

Ycoled, *part.* == helmeted, armed. Alys. 2686. AS. col, a helmet

Ydle. See Isle

Ydought. See Dow

Yea. 36 B.; [ya]. Alys. 3571

Year, *sb.* RG. 373. AS. gear

Yearn, *v. a.* Wright's L. P. p. 43; [eorne]. O. and N. 1202

—— *v. n.* Wright's L. P. p. 63. AS. geornian

Yearning, *sb.* Wright's L. P. p. 72

Yell, *v. n.* [ʒulle]. 498 β; 2 s. pres. 'ʒollest.' O. and N. 223; pret. 'ʒal.' 502 β. AS. geallian

Yelling, *sb.* [ʒullinge]. 487 β. O. and N. 1641

Yellowman, *sb.* [ʒeolumon], Pol. S. 158

Yelp, *v. n.* == speak. Alys. 1065. AS. gilpan

—— == boast [ʒulpe], O. and N. 1650; part. 'y-yolpe.' Alys. 3368

Yelping [ʒulping], *sb.* == boasting. RG. 209, 210

Yeme, Yheme, Yheming. See ʒeme

Yene, *sb.* == yawn, *q. v.*

Yepe, *adj.* == ready. Alys. 1193. See ȝep

Yering, *sb.* == yearning, desire. Ritson's AS. viii. 79

Yesterday. Ps. lxxxix. 4

Yet, *adv.* [ȝut]. RG. 372; [ȝot]. O. and N. 1695

Yfere, *sb.* == companions. Alys. 6906. AS. ge-fera

Yhaht. See Hatch

Yhatered, *part.* == clothed. Alys. 5922. See Hattren

Yhete, *v. a.* == cast, pour out. Ps. lxviii. 25; pret. 'yhet.' Ps. xli. 5; pl. 'yhotten.' Ps. lxxviii. 3; part. 'yotten.' Ps. lxxiii. 21. AS. geotan. See 'ȝete'

Yhoten, *sb.* == giant, Ps. xviii. 7. AS. eóten

Yield, *v. a.* == give up. Alys. 3176; pret. 'yolde.' RG. 387; part. 'y-yolde.' RG. 449; 'iȝulde.' 612 B. AS. geldan

—— == repay. Alys. 132

—— *v. n.* == turn out. K. Horn, 495

Ylef, *vb.* == believe thou. RG. 265

Ylome, == frequently. See Ilome

Ylong, *adv.* == belonging to, proper to. Wright's L. P. pp. 61, 74. AS. gelang

Ymette, *adj.* == moderate? Wright's L. P. p. 35. AS. gemet

Ymone, *adv.* == together, in concert. 380 β AS. gemana

Ympne. See Hymn

Ynele, == I ne will—I will not. RG. 314

Ynote, *part.* == noted, known. Alys. 59

Yoke, *sb.* RG. 453. AS. geoc

—— *v. a.* part. 'y-yoked.' Rel. Ant. ii. 211

Yolk, *sb.* Fr. Sci. 240. AS. geolca

Yond, *adv.* [ȝund] == yonder. 1 β. AS. geond

Yond, *adj.* == farther, as the 'yond half,' or farther side. Ritson's AS. viii. 200. 713 β

Yornandlike, *adj.* == desirable. Ps. xviii. 11

Young, *adj.* RG. 377; comp. 'younger.' RG. 423; sup. 'youngest.' RG. 381. AS. geong

Younghede, *sb.* [ȝonghede] == youth. Legend of St Cuthbert, in

Warton, H. E. P. vol. i. p. 15, *n.*

Younglike, *adj.* Ps. cxviii. 141

Youngling, *sb.* Alys. 2366

Your, *adj.* RG. 455; [ower]. RG. 500; [or]. Wright's L. P. p. 32

Youth, *sb.* Body and Soul, 111; [ʒeuʒede]. Moral Ode, st. 178. AS. geogoð

Youthhede, *sb.* Ps. xlii. 4

Yox, *v. n.* == sob. 1570 B. AS. geocsa

Yoxing, *sb.* == hiccuping. RG. 34

Ypotanos. See Hippopotamus

Yraʒte, *vb.* == procreated? O. and N. 106

Yse, *sb.* == iron. Alys. 5149. AS. ísen. Germ. eisen

Ysome, *adv.* == together. RG. 3, 83. AS. gesome

Ysteot, *part.* == fastened. Alys. 2768

Yswerred, *adj.* == having necks. Alys. 6264. AS. sweora

Yswowe, *part.* == in a swoon. Alys. 2262. See Swoon

Ythe, *adv.* == easily. K. Horn, 61. AS. eáðe

Ythen, *part.* == flourishing, prosperous. See The, *vb.*

Ytolde, *part.* == pitched (of a tent). Alys. 5901. See Teld

Yvortrou, *adj.* == mistrustful. RG. 342

Ywrye. See Wreon

ʒ.

ʒarewe, *adj.* == ready. O. and N. 378. AS. gearo

ʒark, *v. a.* == make ready. RG. 391, 399. Alys. 1411. AS. gearcian

ʒarte. See Yare

ʒavre, == ever, or perhaps 'of yore.' O. and N. 1178

ʒef. See If

ʒeines. Rel. S. i. 16. Probably instead of 'tharto ʒeines' we should read 'thar toʒeines' == there against, i.e. against death. AS. to-geánes

ʒeme, *sb.* == care. RG. 135. AS. gýman

—— *v. a.* == care for, take care of. HD. 131

Ʒeming, *sb.* == care. Ps. cxl. 3

Ʒende, *sb.* == end. RG. 169

Ʒene ? O. and N. 843

Ʒeode, *vb.* == went. See Go

Ʒep, *adj.* == active. Wright's L. P. p. 39; bold. O. and N. 465. AS. gæp

Ʒephede, *sb.* == boldness. O. and N. 683

Ʒerne, *adv.* == earnestly. RG. 487. AS. georne

Ʒete, *v. a.* == cast. Body and Soul, 189. See yhete

Ʒeuʒede, *sb.* == youth, *q. v.*

Ʒeve, == give, *q. v.*

Ʒeynchar, *sb.* == repentance. Wright's L. P. p. 46. See App. to Mapes's Poems, p. 343. AS. cerran with 'gen'

Ʒeʒe, *v. n.* == jog along, go. Wright's L. P. p. 111

—— *v. a.* == jog. Pol. S. 158

Ʒif. See If

Ʒiverness, *sb.* == avarice. Rel. S. vii. 11. AS. gífer

Ʒoe, == she. See under He

Ʒoe, == joy, *q. v.*

Ʒokkyn, *sb.* == joking? Wright's L. P. p. 50

Ʒomere, *adj.* == sorrowful. O. and N. 415. AS. geomor

Ʒonie, == yawn, *q. v.*

Ʒoʒelinge, *sb.* == chattering, gabbling. O. and N. 40. Probably the same as the later 'gaggle,' which is used of a confused noise of people talking, in the Poem on the Deposition of Richard II. p. 18, and of geese, in Churchyard's Pleasant Conceit penned in Verse (1593), cited in the pref. to Nash's Pierce Penniless. (Shaksp. Soc.'s ed.), p. xviii.

Ʒraihand. See Thraying

Ʒuling. See Yelling

Ʒulle. See Yell

Ʒulpe. See Yelp

Ʒulping. See Yelping

ADDENDA.

Baru, add AS. bearh

Bert, *v. n.* == crepitum ventris edere. Rel. Ant. ii. p. 211

Bidde, *v. n.* == need, ought. HD. 1733. Another form of 'bud.' Dan. bör. Compare Chaucer's 'bode.' Rom. Rose, 790

Birde, *sb.* For HD. 2760, read Wright's L. P. pp. 25, 30

Birde, *vb. pret.* == it behoved. HD. 2760. ON. byrjar. Dan. bör

Brol ? Rel. Ant. ii. 192

By, *v. a.* == to defame. Manuel des Pecches, 1355. ON. bía, maculare

Ferblet. Possibly 'suffused with blood,' 'sanguine.' Cf. 'forbled,' in the Anturs of Arthur at Tarne Wathelan, st. 51

Graueth. Probably for 'graveth,' or 'geraveth,' from AS. reáf, clothing

JOHN CHILDS AND SON, PRINTERS.

www.ingramcontent.com/pod-product-compliance
Lightning Source LLC
Chambersburg PA
CBHW062132280526
45788CB00001B/139